THE ILLUSTRATED ENCYCLOPEDIA OF

WELL BEING

THE ILLUSTRATED ENCYCLOPEDIA OF

WELL BEING

FOR MIND, BODY, AND SPIRIT

GENERAL EDITOR

DR. JULIAN JESSEL-KENYON M.D., M.B., Ch.B.

CONSULTANT EDITOR

C. NORMAN SHEALY M.D., Ph.D.

GODSFIELD PRESS

Library of Congress Cataloging-in-Publication Data Available

First paperback edition published in 1999 by Sterling Publishing Company, Inc.
387 Park Avenue South, New York, N.Y. 10016

© 1999 Godsfield Press

Designed for Godsfield press by
THE BRIDGEWATER BOOK COMPANY

Editorial contributors:
Richard Craze, Dr. Michael Dixon, Dr. Tim Harlow,
Margaret Crowther, Dr. Melissa Styles,
Marcus Webb, Maria Webb

Distributed in Canada by Sterling Publishing
c/o Canadian Manda Group, One Atlantic Avenue, Suite 105
Toronto, Ontario, Canada M6K 3E7
Distributed in Australia by Capricorn Link (Australia) Pty Ltd
P O. Box 6651, Baulkham Hills, Business Centre, NSW 2153, Australia

Printed in Singapore

ISBN 0-8069-2061-0 (trade)
ISBN 0-8069-1977-9 (paper)

THE ILLUSTRATED ENCYCLOPEDIA OF

WELL BEING

contents

What is Well-Being?

Well-being is optimal physical, emotional, and spiritual health. This is something of a new concept in medicine but the idea is now gaining ground and is workable thanks to the breadth of knowledge we have in each of these areas. Taking a dynamic, three-dimensional approach to health, The Encyclopedia of Well-Being presents a comprehensive range of physical, spiritual, and emotional problems in a way that can be easily understood by the lay person. Well-being is simply a question of balance, rather like the constantly fluctuating Yin / Yang balance underpinning traditional Chinese medicine. This dynamic view of well-being appears to conflict with the fixed views of the body that conventional medicine has come to rely on. Blood tests, for example have apparently fixed values; in fact all physical measures have a natural variation, often coupled with natural 24 hour cycles (so-called circadian rhythms). Therefore, a practitioner who takes a holistic approach will prescribe for any situation will vary from time to time. This is most clearly seen in traditional Chinese medicine and homeopathy. By way of contrast, in conventional medicine it is usual to take the same medication for long periods of time if your problem is chronic.

It is often said that we are what we eat and deciding to follow a healthy diet is an important step on the road to achieving all-round well-being.

The book balances conventional and complementary approaches to the most common problems we will have to face. It reflects the current health-care trend where patients take a more active part in the management of their illnesses. This is evidenced by the mushrooming charities set up and run by patients suffering from particular illnesses such as multiple sclerosis and chronic fatigue syndrome. The days of the paternalistic doctor are over. Today's aware person wants to know the facts about any illness and what they can do to help themselves and that is what this book is about. At this point it is worth looking at the phenomenal growth of complementary medicine over the past 20 years. Complementary therapies form the bulk of effective self-help measures and are also very safe. What makes this book unique is that it fully endorses the use of these measures in a single self-help volume on total well-being.

COMPLEMENTARY MEDICINE

Complementary medicine is an umbrella term used to describe many different and often unrelated therapies. These approaches have often been called unconventional, alternative, holistic, and fringe. What unites them is that they are forms of treatment still not widely used in conventional medicine and at the time of writing are not taught as part of the orthodox undergraduate curriculum.

The World Health Organization considers that many complementary treatments are the traditional medicine upon which two-thirds of the world relies as the main source of primary care.

Recent surveys in the US and Australia indicate that enormous sums are currently being spent out of pocket on complementary medicine, and that this is increasing. The provision of complementary medicine in the industrialized world is largely within the private sector, but there is more and more interest from various national health services in Europe, and from medical insurance companies and health maintenance organizations in the United States, who see complementary medicine as popular, effective and safe. They also see it as being less technologically based than many medical specialties, so offering a lot of cost advantages for them.

Well-being is not only about a healthy body, it also encompasses mental and emotional well-being. Taking up yoga or setting time aside for meditation helps to encourage inner calm.

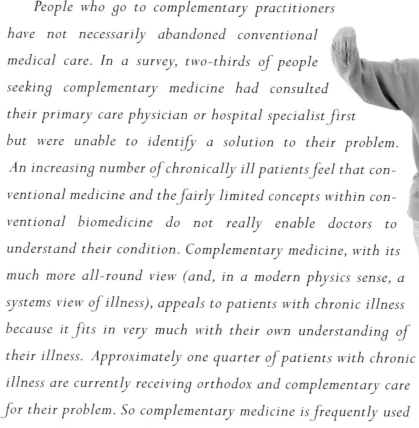

People who go to complementary practitioners have not necessarily abandoned conventional medical care. In a survey, two-thirds of people seeking complementary medicine had consulted their primary care physician or hospital specialist first but were unable to identify a solution to their problem. An increasing number of chronically ill patients feel that conventional medicine and the fairly limited concepts within conventional biomedicine do not really enable doctors to understand their condition. Complementary medicine, with its much more all-round view (and, in a modern physics sense, a systems view of illness), appeals to patients with chronic illness because it fits in very much with their own understanding of their illness. Approximately one quarter of patients with chronic illness are currently receiving orthodox and complementary care for their problem. So complementary medicine is frequently used to complement orthodox medicine instead of as an exclusive alternative. The most recent term for this form of medicine is "integrated" medicine.

Patients seeing complementary medical practitioners appear to have a greater knowledge about their own health than most other people and this book will help you achieve the same. For instance, patients attending a homeopath are more likely to believe that a good diet, cutting down on smoking, having time to relax and meditate and sleeping properly, are positive health measures. They also have more "internal" beliefs about their ability to control their health and use complementary practitioners to facilitate consultations about the management of their medical problems. Patients going to complementary medical practitioners are more positive about their consultation style—it would seem that conventional physicians have a lot to learn from the complementary medical profession in this

T'ai Chi is increasingly popular in the West. The slow, controlled, and graceful movements calm the mind, countering stress and tension.

Conventional medicine continues to play a major role in healthcare. Many people feel, however, that it does not offer the holistic approach typical of complementary remedies.

area, particularly in allowing the patient to play an active part in the management of his or her own health. This could wrest some degree of control from the conventional doctors, who still in many instances take a paternalistic and controlling approach.

The increasing popularity of complementary medicine is a complex issue, almost certainly involving a variety of factors, and there is a great need for further research in this area. Because of its increase in popularity, complementary medicine is now recognized by many conventional physicians. Patient demand has quite rightly triggered an increase in the demand for information about complementary therapies. This had led to the development of many journals and books and the beginnings of discussions for undergraduate and postgraduate courses designed to teach doctors of the future something about the subject.

Plants have been used for medicinal purposes for thousands of years. Herbal remedies can help to treat certain ailments and improve well-being without the harmful effects of synthetic drugs.

FINDING THE RIGHT TREATMENT

This book recommends that, in some cases, it is necessary to consult a health professional. When this is your own doctor this is no problem, but what if you need to consult a complementary practitioner? It is more likely than not that your own family doctor will know little or nothing about complementary medicine and will not be able to advise; in fact a significant number of family doctors have a prejudiced view of complementary medicine based on very scant knowledge. Thankfully the dissemination of information on complementary medicine is growing apace to correct this situation but if your family doctor does not know the local complementary practitioners or know how competent they are, how do you find the right therapy and the right practitioner? This book will help you choose the right therapy, although in chronic illness often a particular combination of complementary therapies needs to be used to obtain maximum benefit. Where the way forward is unclear, try consulting a practitioner trained in several complementary disciplines.

Fresh, unadulterated foods bring enormous health benefits

The use of herbs to treat illness and to maintain well-being has an ancient history.

Although there aren't many, they are becoming more numerous and a single consultation with such a practitioner could be enough to guide you to the right complementary therapy for you and your condition.

CONSULTING THE BEST PRACTITIONER

Find out who practices the particular therapy that you want in your area from the local telephone book, then check their qualifications. Help from the national body dealing with that particular therapy can be useful and the address of the appropriate umbrella body can be obtained either from the practitioner or through the Internet. Try to obtain some feedback on the practitioner you wish to use: there is nothing better than a personal recommendation. It is worth checking that the practitioner is registered with an appropriate professional body. This generally means that the practitioner will operate under a code of ethics of practice and has access to further education in the field through journals and conferences, as well as supervision from more experienced practitioners in the organization.

It also ensures that in the case of a complaint which cannot be settled with the practitioner alone, the patient can resort to a formal complaints procedure via the professional body.

Your body's internal health will reflect the foods you eat. Live yogurt, for instance, counteracts harmful bacteria.

When trying to find out how experienced a practitioner is the following factors should be borne in mind: does he or she work full- or part-time and how many patients a day do they see? There is a lot of difference in experience between a new practitioner and one who has been seeing 20 patients a day for 20 years. And lastly, you must be happy with the practitioner you are seeing and be confident that he or she knows their limits and is prepared to refer you to somebody else for further advice if necessary.

KEEPING YOUR PERSPECTIVE

To maintain your well-being you will have to be vigilant and prepared to change. Listen to yourself and your body and don't rely on a health regime that's inflexible. Go with what you find day by day and listen to the observations of your condition that are given by those with you, especially those who love you and know you well. It is also important to be aware of your own limits, however comprehensive your observations and the information in this encyclopedia. In the worst case scenario you could treat yourself entirely through reading books on complementary therapies and fail to recognize that what you need is a proper diagnosis and conventional medical attention. Some people can feel so empowered by their knowledge that they feel they know better than their doctors! This is resulting in the emergence of patients who now manage their own illnesses totally, which can be difficult to cope with both from a complementary and a conventional point of view. The situation has been fueled by a small number of arrogant doctors who dismiss complementary medicine as quackery, much to the anger of many of their patients.

To conclude, use this book wisely and with judgment, and in so doing it will find a real place in your own quest for well-being.

Julian Jessel-Kenyon

Southampton, April 1998

Being massaged is a sensuous and relaxing experience. It stimulates the body systems and encourages a sense of emotional well-being.

SECTION ONE

whole body

WELL-BEING

contents

Introduction

Conventional health-care methods tend to focus on an individual aspect of health and often neglect the body as a whole. The term "holistic" has become widely used to describe any system of healthcare that encompasses all areas of well-being: the body, mind, and spirit. Holistic medicine revolves around our ability to keep fit and well, provided that facets of our lifestyle are correctly balanced. It would be unreasonable, for example, to expect your body to function at its best if you get very little exercise, despite eating a balanced diet. In adopting a holistic lifestyle, you must pay close attention to all aspects of life and balance the physical (exercise, sports) with the biochemical (food and nutrition) and emotional (relaxation and meditation).

BODY BOOSTERS

Simply by getting more exercise, the heart and lungs are stimulated, circulation is boosted, and the brain receives more oxygen and nutrition. The hormonal changes that occur during exercise make us feel better—we release "happy" hormones during physical exertion. The knock-on effects can benefit the chemistry of the blood, reducing fat levels and increasing our metabolic rate, which helps us maintain a stable body weight. Combine exercise with the correct dietary balance and some time for relaxation, and see how your body, as a whole, could benefit.

Jogging is one exercise you can do anywhere—on a beach, in a park, or along the street. Running with a friend is fun and helps to set a comfortable pace.

This section of the encyclopedia concentrates on the preventive aspects of caring for health, and covers many things you can do to improve your chances of good health. For example, the largest organ of the body, the skin, needs special care and protection if you are to avoid the ravages of the elements. The wind can crack your skin and make it appear older than it actually is, and the sun can cause serious problems such as solar keratoses (precancerous skin changes). The organs of elimination (kidneys, lungs, bowels, and liver) are fully described. You may think there is not much you can do to improve their performance, but we show you simple methods of supporting their health and vitality, without the need for specialized knowledge or dietary supplements.

Physical mobility is valuable and needs safeguarding. Yoga exercises, such as this tree posture, keep joints supple, encourage good balance, and help breathing.

CARING FOR BODY SYSTEMS

The immune and circulatory systems lie at the center of any preventive program. If these vital systems are not functioning well, the body cannot distribute life-giving oxygen to the cells and brain, nor can it adequately mobilize defense systems against invading organisms. Easy-to-follow guidelines will help you to maximize the potential of these interrelated body systems, and so enable you to make the best use of the preventive scheme described in this section.

IN FULL WORKING ORDER

In order to enjoy your health, physical mobility is essential. We tend to take this aspect of life for granted until an ache or pain is felt in a joint or muscle. This section describes a complete musculoskeletal health package, with useful tips and suggestions to help you avoid trouble and prevent chronic problems developing in this highly integrated body system. In completion, the special sense organs of the eyes, ears, and brain are included in the preventive section of the encyclopedia. Research shows that these organs too can greatly benefit from the holistic approach to healthcare.

HEART

*T*he heart is the legendary center of the emotions. It is also simply an efficient pump, which sends blood around the body and the lungs. The muscle of the heart receives blood from a number of small blood vessels, which can become "furred up" with cholesterol deposits, causing angina and possibly a heart attack. It is, therefore, vital to do everything possible to stop the arteries getting furred up in the first place.

The heart constantly pumps blood around the body through a network of arteries and veins. It has its own blood supply, fed by the coronary arteries.

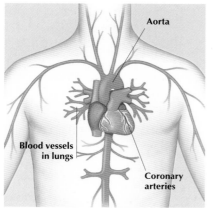

Aorta

Blood vessels in lungs

Coronary arteries

To avoid heart disease aim for at least half an hour of sustained vigorous exercise, twice a week —but check with your doctor beforehand.

Try to set aside time for exercise at least twice a week. A session should last for a minimum of half an hour. As the heart contracts, blood is forcibly expelled from the left ventricle to supply the body, while the right ventricle sends blood to the lungs where it receives oxygen. At the same time, the left atrium is filling with oxygenated blood from the lungs and the right atrium is receiving deoxygenated blood returning from the body. In order to keep the two chambers from mixing, one-way valves prevent backflow.

The muscular fibers of the heart run in a spiral direction so that at each contraction, blood is literally wrung out of the organ, making the heart a very efficient pump.

Clogging of the arteries that feed the heart muscle often causes a pain known as angina. When a vessel becomes completely blocked, the muscle it supplies dies, resulting in a heart attack (myocardial infarction).

High blood pressure can cause enlargement of the left ventricle of the heart, a condition which causes shortness of breath on exercise, and, left untreated, can cause heart failure.

THE CONVENTIONAL APPROACH

Drugs to treat angina open up the coronary arteries to provide relief from pain. However there are a number of medications that can be used to prevent angina, and angioplasty (a nonsurgical procedure to clean out blood vessels) may also be indicated. Bypass surgery is often recommended if medication fails to help. After a heart attack, drugs are used to regulate the heart and lower blood pressure, helping to prevent further attacks.

High blood pressure (see p.118) is normally controlled with drugs that relax the arteries and heart. Diuretics, which reduce water retention, may be prescribed to reduce strain on the heart.

Fatty deposits, known as atheroma, can clog up the coronary arteries, cutting off oxygen supply to the heart, leading to angina or a heart attack.

1

2

3

1 Normal artery

2 Formation of atheroma

3 Formation of blood clot

COMPLEMENTARY THERAPIES

HERBAL MEDICINE

The traditional herbal remedy for heart problems is the hawthorn berry (*Crataegus oxyacantha*). Taken as an extract, it stimulates and regulates heartbeat, reducing blood pressure and easing the stressed heart.

OSTEOPATHY

Manipulating the thoracic spine between the levels of the first and fourth vertebrae can reduce high blood pressure. Relief from muscular tensions may ease the physical stresses that often maintain hypertension, if hypertension is stress-related.

HOMEOPATHY

For treatment of heart pains, Aconite may help with acute pain that follows activity. Nux vomica is indicated in cases of high blood pressure, especially in people who are outwardly calm and find it difficult to express feelings of stress.

NUTRITIONAL THERAPY

The key nutrient for heart health is coenzyme Q10 (Ubiquinone). This nutrient feeds the cardiac muscle and supports its metabolic processes, protecting it from damage by poor circulation. A daily 30mg dose is normally recommended.

PREVENTION

Preventing heart disease starts with changing your lifestyle. Look at your diet, eating habits, and the amount of exercise you get. Cutting down salt, sugar, and fat in your diet can help to reduce coronary heart disease and lessen the threat of angina. Exercise stimulates circulation and can lower the risk of hypertension and heart attack. See also p.158–p.161.

AVOIDING HEART DISEASE

EXERCISE FOR HALF AN HOUR AT LEAST TWICE A WEEK

•

HAVE YOUR BLOOD PRESSURE CHECKED REGULARLY

•

STOP SMOKING

•

WATCH YOUR WEIGHT

Including garlic, onions, oily fish, and olive oil in your diet can help to counteract the risks of heart disease.

DIETARY ADVICE FOR PREVENTING HEART DISEASE

- Eat more vegetables and fruit of all kinds.
- Avoid butter, hard margarines, lard, and suet. Margarines containing olive oil are better.
- Avoid cream and ice cream. Use lowfat or nonfat milk, and lowfat natural sour cream or yogurt instead of cream.
- Reduce cheese consumption. Use lowfat cottage cheese.
- Keep meat intake down, choose lean cuts and remove visible fat. Chicken and turkey are good.
- Try to eat fish, particularly oily fish, twice a week (mackerel, sardines, tuna, and salmon).
- Don't eat too many eggs—three or less a week is ideal.
- Use monounsaturated oils for cooking. Olive and canola oil are especially good.
- Steam, boil, or grill rather than fry.
- Restrict intake of sugar, cakes, pastries, and cookies (unless made at home with polyunsaturated fats).
- Eat plenty of garlic and onions.
- A good intake of vitamin C may be helpful and possibly small quantities of chocolate.

LUNGS

*T*he body contains two lungs, the right a little larger than the left. Each is composed of a dense network of tiny air tubes, branching ever smaller and surrounded by a rich blood supply. The main function of the lungs is to exchange carbon dioxide in the blood for oxygen in the air. The system can be vulnerable to infection and you can do much to look after your lungs.

Swimming is an excellent "aerobic" exercise, meaning it's an exercise that needs a lot of air or oxygen. Vigorous swimming, which demands breathing deeply, improves lung capacity.

Your lungs are suspended inside the rigid box of ribs that forms the chest. As the thin sheet of muscle, the diaphragm, tightens and the ribs move up, air is drawn into the lungs. Once the muscles relax, the natural elasticity of the lungs pushes the air out again. This is an important lesson for promoting well-being. The effort involved in breathing is when breathing in; on breathing out, the chest, neck, and abdominal muscles need only relax. Many people react to stress by working too hard at breathing; they forget to relax the shoulders and so increase tension. Trust your lungs: they will work better if you consciously relax—they know how to breathe!

Many pollens and dusts can inflame the lungs and produce phlegm. The worst problem facing your lungs is tobacco smoke. Even breathing in someone else's smoke increases the risk of lung damage and cancer (see p.172).

Cold, emotion, smoke, pollution, exercise, and viruses can all trigger an asthma attack. Bronchodilator drugs, applied in a puffer or inhaler, provide quick, effective relief.

Asthma occurs when the smaller airways in the lungs (bronchioles) become sensitive and narrow down or get inflamed (see also p.121). This causes wheezing and shortness of breath in adults; children often just have a persistent cough. See your physician if you have breathing problems since untreated infections or asthma can eventually damage the lungs.

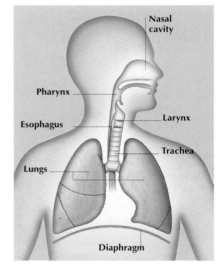

When we inhale, air is filtered by the nose, then passes through the trachea (windpipe) which is divided into two bronchial tubes leading to the lungs. These two bronchi then branch into smaller bronchi, then bronchioles. At the end of the bronchioles are the air sacs (alveoli), where oxygen is absorbed into the bloodstream. The air we breathe is often heavily polluted.

THE CONVENTIONAL APPROACH

For asthma there are preventive and relieving treatments, many in the form of inhalers. These can deliver small doses of medication directly to the lungs and so reduce side effects. There have been real advances in these drugs, helping to stop people from being limited by their asthma. There are also reliable techniques for assessing how well the lungs are working, for use both in the hospital and at home, which aim to put asthmatics in charge of their asthma.

Infections can be treated by identifying the bacterium responsible and using the correct antibiotic. There are effective vaccinations to prevent certain respiratory infections.

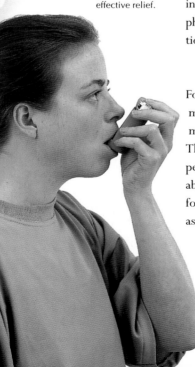

PREVENTIVE MEASURES

SMOKING IS THE SCOURGE OF LUNGS SO KEEP YOUR LUNGS SMOKE-FREE

•

WEAR A MASK IF WORKING OR CYCLING IN POLLUTED AIR

•

RELAX AND LET YOUR LUNGS DO THE BREATHING

COMPLEMENTARY THERAPIES

HOMEOPATHY

A practitioner will take a detailed history to see what may be causing your asthma. Then homeopathic remedies will be prescribed to counteract the cause. Some homeopaths feel able to treat lung infections also (see p.226).

HYPNOTHERAPY

Very useful for relaxation and panic attacks, which can cause breathing trouble. It can also be effective for asthma, especially if it is emotionally triggered. It may help with giving up smoking too (see p.238).

MEDITATION

This is suggested for a wide range of illnesses and problems, but seems very appropriate for lung conditions. Breath control, relaxation, and the boost given to the immune system as a result of meditation, are all helpful (see p.190–p.191).

NATUROPATHY

There is no doubt that some children's phlegm and asthma are triggered by diet, especially wheat, dairy products, citrus fruits, and eggs. Naturopaths will try to eliminate these problems by diet manipulation (see p.223). Good diet may help reduce risk of infections.

ACUPUNCTURE

An acupuncturist can help asthmatics. Products are also available which allow you to treat yourself, using a hand-held probe that applies an electrical stimulus to the acupuncture points. These are obtainable from selected pharmacies.

NUTRITIONAL THERAPY

Most asthmatics are deficient in magnesium so this therapy is useful.

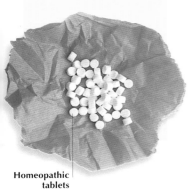

Homeopathic tablets

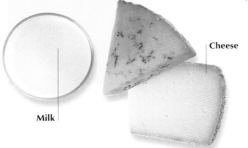

Milk

Cheese

THE BELLOWS BREATH TECHNIQUE

The overall effect of bellows breathing is to achieve a balanced and harmonized exchange of air, along with a calming effect on the whole body.

1 After drawing in a deep breath, contract the abdominal muscles to sharply force the breath out.

2 Without using any abdominal movements, immediately pull a breath in again using the chest.

3 Repeat these steps 12 times. While breathing, try to develop an awareness of energy flow throughout the entire body.

Contract abdominal muscles when breathing out.

Breathe in using chest.

KIDNEYS AND BLADDER

T*he kidneys are vital for well-being because they are responsible for getting rid of waste and maintaining a balance of chemicals in the body. There are things that you can do to prevent them from becoming infected or forming stones. Cancers picked up at an early stage can frequently be cured.*

Women are particularly vulnerable to kidney and bladder infections. A good preventive measure is to get into the habit of drinking plenty of water every day.

Most infections start at the lower end of the body and work up through the bladder to the kidneys. Bladder infections are uncomfortable in themselves, but you should get treatment for them at an early stage to prevent infection spreading toward the kidneys. Cystitis (a bladder infection) is particularly common in women, and there are things you can do to prevent it (see also p.62).

Stones in the kidney, as elsewhere, can be particularly painful. If you have had them, make sure you are properly investigated, as further episodes may be preventable, depending on the sort of stones that you produce. If you are prone to stones, you should aim to drink 7 pints (4 liters) of fluid a day to stop the urine becoming concentrated.

Cancers of the kidney are rare, but check for this if you are getting frequent urine infections or blood in the urine.

Some people are particularly at risk of kidney disease—those with diabetes, high blood pressure, or a strong family history of kidney disease. If this applies to you, discuss prevention with your doctor. Avoid large quantities of painkillers.

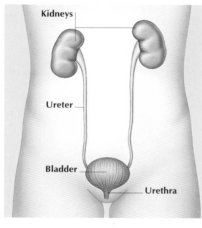

In complementary medicine, kidneys are often seen as the key to health. They filter waste products, which pass through the ureters to the bladder to be expelled as urine.

Kidneys

Ureter

Bladder

Urethra

PREVENTING CYSTITIS

- Drink 3 to 4 pints (1.7–2.3 liters) of fluid a day and empty the bladder at least every three hours.
- Wear cotton underclothes and stockings, not panty hose.
- Wash from the front backward and avoid strong soaps, deodorants, and antiseptics.
- Wash before intercourse (your partner too). Urinate within 15 minutes after intercourse .
- Drink cranberry juice regularly as a bladder antiseptic.

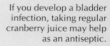

If you develop a bladder infection, taking regular cranberry juice may help as an antiseptic.

COMPLEMENTARY THERAPIES

NUTRIENT SUPPLEMENTS

The most common kidney stones, calcium opalate, are largely prevented by taking 100mg of vitamin B_6 plus 500mg of magnesium oxide per day.

ACUPUNCTURE

Those suffering from bladder spasms and kidney stones are thought to possess an imbalance of yin and yang energy. Needles are inserted at certain points to help relieve the problem.

LIVER

*Y*our liver is a large and complicated organ, responsible for regulating and processing glucose, carbohydrates, fats, proteins, and vitamins as well as removing toxins and producing bile. Someone who has bad liver damage develops yellow jaundice. The skin then becomes yellowish because bile builds up and the liver is unable to release it into the gut. Infections, toxins (including drugs), and gallstones pose the greatest threat to the well-being of your liver.

Hepatitis A and B are the most common forms of infection and can now be prevented by inoculation. Hepatitis B and other forms are spread by blood, semen, vaginal secretions, and saliva. Hepatitis C is a more recently recognized form of hepatitis and is spread by sexual contact and sharing needles for intravenous drug use. There is no vaccination available for it, and at the present time there is no effective treatment. Other infections are known to cause hepatitis—the infection is mild in the case of infectious mononucleosis, (the "kissing disease"), but it is serious if you catch leptospirosis. The latter can be prevented by avoiding any possible contact with rat's urine (a hazard of bathing in contaminated water).

Some chemicals and several medical drugs can cause liver damage in susceptible people. Seek help if your urine becomes brown and frothy or your skin yellowish, especially if you are experiencing abdominal pain, nausea, and extreme fatigue. The most common toxin causing liver damage is alcohol (see p.170). Gallstones—usually solid lumps of cholesterol—form when the chemical composition of bile is upset. They occur more frequently in women.

COMPLEMENTARY THERAPIES

NATUROPATHY
High-fiber diets with good fluid intake may help increase the removal of toxins and bile acids from the liver.

NUTRIENT SUPPLEMENTS
Large doses of vitamin C, administered intravenously, are often recommended.

HERBAL MEDICINE
Milk thistle decoction or seeds are useful to prevent gallstones. This helps to fortify the liver and eliminate toxins.

WHO SHOULD RECEIVE A HEPATITIS B VACCINATION?

- Drug addicts
- Individuals who change sexual partners frequently
- Close family contacts of a case or carrier
- Babies of mothers who carry hepatitis B and families adopting children from countries with high prevalence of hepatitis B
- Hemophiliacs
- Patients with kidney disease
- People coming into contact with blood or bloodstained fluid
- Some occupations (e.g. morticians, health-care providers, embalmers, surgeons, police, ambulance workers, firefighters, and jail staff.
- Those traveling to areas where hepatitis B is common

WHO SHOULD RECEIVE A HEPATITIS A VACCINATION?

- Travelers to areas where it is endemic
- Patients with chronic liver disease because they are more vulnerable
- Hemophiliacs
- Sexually active homosexuals
- Everyone, if there is a local outbreak of Hepatitis A

Alcohol is a major cause of liver damage and women are more vulnerable than men. Long-term drinking can lead to chronic hepatitis, needing professional treatment. Complementary therapies for liver disorders include naturopathy and herbal medicine.

CIRCULATION

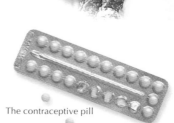

*G*ood circulation is essential. The arteries carry oxygen and food as well as many different sorts of cells, including those used to fight infection or repair damage. The veins take blood and waste products from the rest of the body back to the heart.

Fresh air is invigorating, but in cold weather it is advisable to wrap up warmly to maintain a healthy body temperature.

The main problem with arteries is that they can get furred up with cholesterol, so steps taken to prevent heart disease (see p.16–p.17) will also prevent the clogging up of arteries. The arteries are also involved in temperature control and in cold weather will protect the heart, brain, and vital organs by reducing the supply of blood to the extremities such as hands and feet. Some people find that their hands and feet get cold very easily. Such people are said to have a bad circulation: in fact their circulation is normal, but overreacting.

The veins return the blood to the heart under low pressure, using one-way valves. If the valves stop working, the leg veins balloon out (varicose veins), possibly leading to inflammation (phlebitis). You are more likely to get varicose veins if they are common in your family, or if you have had children, but there are ways of preventing them from getting too bad. Much more serious is a clot in the veins (thrombosis). A clot from the veins in the legs may break off and travel to the lungs, where it can threaten your life. Be vigilant for symptoms in the leg such as pain, swelling, and discoloration. If you are on the oral contraceptive pill, particularly if you smoke, consult a doctor immediately.

The contraceptive pill

Hormonal contraceptives have been linked to cardiovascular disorders, particularly in women over the age of 35 who smoke.

Blood travels from the tissues to the heart through veins at low pressure. Valves in the veins prevent blood from flowing backwards down the legs. Varicose veins occur when valves in the veins become weak, preventing efficient blood flow.

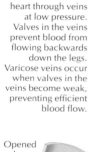

Opened valve

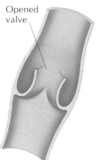

Closed valve

AVOIDING COLD HANDS AND FEET

WEAR WARM GLOVES AND SOCKS

•

KEEP WARM GENERALLY

•

A GLASS OF WINE MAY PROVIDE SHORT-TERM HELP TO STIMULATE THE CIRCULATION

•

MEDICAL INVESTIGATION MAY BE NECESSARY

AVOIDING VARICOSE VEINS

AVOID PROLONGED STANDING

•

WEAR SUPPORT PANTY HOSE OR STOCKINGS IF NECESSARY

•

AVOID BECOMING OVERWEIGHT

•

AVOID CONSTIPATION BY EATING A HIGH-FIBRE DIET (SEE P.158–P.159)

Constipation can be a contributory factor to varicose veins and is prevented by eating a high-fiber diet.

SIGNS OF A CLOT IN A VEIN

SWELLING OF THE LEG AND FOOT

•

PAIN, PARTICULARLY IN THE BACK OF THE CALF

•

FOOT AND LEG DISCOLORED AND WARM

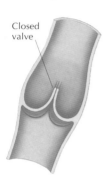

BRAIN AND MIND

*T*he brain is the control center of the body, sending out and receiving instructions via the nerves, hormones, and neuropeptides, which are neuroactive proteins. It is also the seat of consciousness and is responsible for the sensation of well-being. Brain damage occurs most commonly with trauma, infections, and strokes. Disturbances of the mind, most commonly anxiety or depression, depend on what situations, stresses, and influences the mind has been exposed to.

Treatment of injured brains is difficult. It is very important to try and prevent such injuries in the first place, For example, by wearing seat belts in vehicles, and appropriate headgear when necessary.

Infection of the brain by meningitis is very serious. It can be prevented by inoculation or medication if you have been in contact an infected person, or are likely to be. Symptoms of meningitis include a temperature, stiff neck, headache, a rash, and an aversion to light. Medical advice should be sought urgently.

Strokes can be prevented in the same way as heart disease (see p.16–p.17), because these can be caused either by clots traveling up the arteries or by bleeding in the arteries. Medication for blood pressure, and drugs to prevent bleeding will be helpful for some people. Aspirin may be used to prevent clots.

PREVENTING STRESS

Preventing stress means attempting to eliminate or reduce its cause (see p.178–p.185). It is important to be aware if you are under stress—friends and relatives may be better judges of this. Early help from your health advisor will prevent further deterioration and a long-term threat to your well-being. See also Emotional Health p.196–p.197.

PROTECTING YOUR BRAIN AND MIND

FOLLOW A BALANCED DIET WITH ADEQUATE INTAKE OF VITAMIN B

•

AVOID TOXINS SUCH AS HALLUCINOGENIC DRUGS AND TOO MUCH ALCOHOL

•

GET REGULAR EXERCISE (SEE P.155)

•

MAKE TIME TO RELAX

•

UNDERSTAND YOUR OWN LII.

•

TELL YOUR FAMILY AND/ OR WORｔ COLLEAGUES IF YOU FEEL UNDER MENTAL STRAIN

•

AVOID TOO MUCH WORK AND NO PLAY

•

GET ENOUGH SLEEP

For a healthy brain, mind, and nervous system, make sure your diet contains foods rich in vitamin B such as bananas, mushrooms, milk, nuts, and oily fish.

Maintaining a healthy mind means achieving a balanced approach to life. Include plenty of enjoyment, exercise, and relaxation in your daily life to prevent the harmful effects of stress.

COMPLEMENTARY THERAPIES

ACUPUNCTURE
Regular session can help to relieve anxiety and stress and aid relaxation (see p.230).

RELAXATION AND VISUALIZATION
Deep relaxation for at least 15 minutes, twice a day can be of great benefit (see p.239).

HERBAL MEDICINE
Ginkgo biloba in infusion, tincture, or tablet form can help to improve memory and mental alertness.

23

MOUTH

The mouth is a complex organ—it has to be to fulfil its many different roles. You express yourself, eat, kiss, cough, and sometimes breathe with your mouth. A large area of the brain controls the functions of your mouth and deals with the information it gathers. The mouth is part of the front line of defense against many toxins and infections. Dentists spend a lifetime learning about and treating this small but hardworking area.

Sugar is the traditional enemy of teeth, but acidic foods and drinks can be equally damaging to tooth enamel. Try and avoid an excess of either in your diet.

KEY POINTERS FOR A HEALTHY MOUTH

REGULAR DENTAL CARE

•

NO SMOKING

•

GOOD NUTRITION

Cranial osteopathy involves delicate manipulation of the cranium which can ease tensions elsewhere in the body causing digestive problems.

Teeth are vital for eating, but their shape and appearance is also important to us. You need to look after your children's teeth while they are young, to give their mouths a good start. Self-care habits formed during childhood will last for life. Twice-daily brushing and daily flossing is an excellent preventive routine. Regular dental checkups are necessary. Nutrition is fundamental to overall health, but especially that of the mouth. Try and reduce your intake of refined sugars and watch what you eat—it will help promote your general well-being as well as your oral health (see p.173).

Public enemy number one for the mouth is smoking, increasing the chance of cancers of the mouth and throat. Another danger is acid reflux from the stomach, which damages tooth enamel as well as causing unpleasant indigestion and bad breath (halitosis). Being overweight, or eating a lot of fatty food and drinking too much alcohol, worsens acid reflux.

Carrot juice, which is rich in beta-carotene, can help to treat gingivitis or diseased gums, frequently a cause of bad breath.

COMPLEMENTARY THERAPIES

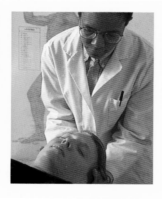

OSTEOPATHY

A problem in the mouth may reflect an imbalance lower in the body, particularly in the digestive system. Osteopathy can be used to restore balance. Cranial osteopaths can have particular skills here (see p.233).

ACUPUNCTURE

There are specific acupuncture sites that help treat oral problems. Points on the invisible meridian channels in the body are recognized to have special significance for the mouth (see p.230).

NATUROPATHY

This can help with gum disease and halitosis. Many people find that foods rich in beta-carotene, such as carrot juice, help. High-fiber diets can be useful for the whole digestive system, and thereby help the mouth (see p.223).

EYES

We all know how vital the eyes are, yet it is easy to forget how remarkable and finely tuned they are. Eyes can see in the gloom of night, and yet also cope with the brightness of a sunny day. They can judge distances accurately and distinguish a colossal number of colors. Despite their complexity, there is a lot you can do to promote the health of your eyes.

The eyes are part of a visual system integrated with the brain. This system is sensitive during the growing years, so care of children's eyes is vital. If a squint is neglected in childhood, the correct visual pathways will not develop, and permanent damage will be caused. More subtle is the need to ensure that children receive enough varied visual stimulation, with visual correction if needed, to maximize their potential for enjoying the world.

This sensitive mechanism also needs care when we are adults. Excessive ultraviolet light, especially with today's damaged ozone layer, can cause early clouding of the lens (cataract). Ensure you have a decent pair of sunglasses that protect against ultraviolet rays. Glaucoma (a rise in pressure inside the eye) can be an insidious threat. It is more common as people age, and can run in families (see p.145). Fortunately it can be treated if detected in time. Diabetes can affect the eyes too. Habits developed for general well-being will often help your eyes (see p.138). People are often better at going for dental checks than eye examinations, but which matters more?

KEY POINTS TO REMEMBER

LOSS OF VISION/FLASHING LIGHTS MUST BE CHECKED BY A DOCTOR URGENTLY

•

EYE PROTECTION IS NOT A LUXURY

•

EYES ARE INVOLVED IN MANY CONDITIONS THAT AFFECT THE WHOLE BODY

DID YOU KNOW?

The eyes have two different light-sensitive receptors. There are around six million cones, which give detailed color vision, and 120 million rods, which respond better in low light. The cones are mainly in the center of the eye, and so at night we see better by looking just to one side of the object we wish to see.

Eyes are our window on to the world and they are worth protecting. Care of children's eyes is essential but even as adults we should protect the eyes from harsh sunlight, dust and grit.

It is advisable to go for regular eye checks so that any possible visual defects, such as short sight, or any health problems can be detected early.

COMPLEMENTARY THERAPIES

CRANIAL OSTEOPATHY

This may be a useful aid in glaucoma but is not a substitute for conventional treatments. It may be best used in a preventive role in someone known to be at risk (see p.233).

HOMEOPATHY

As in much of homeopathy, the remedy is best tailored to the individual. Allium Cepa is a widely used homeopathic remedy for hay fever, which can affect the eyes (see p.226).

NUTRITIONAL THERAPY

Patients who take large doses of antioxidants, such as vitamins E and C, beta-carotene, coenzyme Q-10, rarely have cataracts. Zinc helps to prevent and treat macular degeneration.

EARS

Ears not only enable us to hear, but are also vital organs of balance. The brain receives so much information from the ears that it takes us nearly two years, from birth, to learn to balance well enough to be able to stand reliably. Even in the womb, a baby's ears are picking up speech and sounds from the environment. Parents sometimes discover their baby has an affinity with music played frequently during the mother's pregnancy.

An organ as sensitive as the ear must be protected. Excessive loud noise is a real problem. Sudden noise, such as gunfire, is the most dangerous as muscles bracing the tiny hearing bones (ossicles) do not have time to brace themselves. Ear defenders are vital. Pressure changes can cause ear problems, so be careful when flying if suffering from a cold or congestion. Children are particularly sensitive, as they are less good at "clearing" their ears.

Tinnitus is defined as hearing continuous noise that is not actually there. It can be helped but not cured. Masking the sound with another quiet noise is helpful. Its cause is related to the brain trying too hard to hear, especially in cases where there is loss of hearing of the high tones.

The semicircular canals are the balance organs of the inner ear. They can be temporarily upset by viruses causing vertigo. Motion sickness is caused by the inner ear sending different messages to the brain compared to those coming from the eyes and other senses. Treatments for this are more effective if started before they are really needed.

Ear problems are an area where complementary therapies and conventional medicine can work well together. For example, an otolaryingologist may use a magnetic resonance imaging scan to be sure that there is no tumor, then a complementary practitioner may help with the control of, for instance, dizziness or tinnitus.

The ear consists of three main parts: the outer, middle, and inner ear. Sound waves enter the ear canal and strike the eardrum, triggering movements in the ossicles, creating nerve signals to the brain.

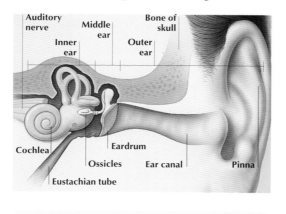

Auditory nerve
Middle ear
Bone of skull
Inner ear
Outer ear
Cochlea
Eardrum
Ossicles
Ear canal
Pinna
Eustachian tube

COMPLEMENTARY THERAPIES

ACUPRESSURE
The devices that stimulate an acupuncture point on the inside of the wrist have been proved to work in motion sickness. Acupuncture can help tinnitus, but needs a skilled acupuncturist. Dizziness can be treated with acupuncture (see p.230).

HERBAL MEDICINE
Ginger and Gingko have been used to treat vertigo. It is important to ensure there is no serious underlying cause for the vertigo, so always consult your GP (see p.224).

Ginger root

HOMEOPATHY
Remedies are useful for relieving earache and dealing with phlegm, which can be a cause of ear problems (see p. 226). *Cocculus indicus* is a good remedy for vertigo.

NATUROPATHY
In children, ear infections are commonly signs of a milk allergy.

PREVENTING EAR PROBLEMS

PROTECT YOUR EARS WHEN USING POWER TOOLS OR MACHINERY
•
DIZZINESS IS A SYMPTOM, SO LOOK FOR A CAUSE
•
TINNITUS CAN BE HELPED AND DOESN'T ALWAYS GET WORSE
•
AVOID FLYING IF YOU HAVE A COLD

Bracelet stimulates acupuncture point on wrist.

NOSE AND THROAT

The throat is more than a simple pipe joining the mouth to the stomach. It is closely connected to the trachea (allowing breathing) and to the larynx (producing speech). Most people take this extraordinary apparatus for granted. It is only when some food goes down the "wrong way," or when someone is unconscious, that the remarkable tightrope of coordination humans walk every day becomes obvious.

The area behind the nose (nasopharynx) is vital for the senses of smell and taste. Dust or pollen can thicken the lining of the nasopharynx, sometimes causing nasal polyps that may block the nose and cause trouble with sinuses and the sense of smell. The nose has a plentiful blood supply that warms the incoming air before it enters the delicate lung tissue. It also filters the air and traps particles that could cause damage or irritate the lung.

A runny nose (rhinorrhea) can indicate a mild infection or allergic rhinitis. Repeatedly blowing and clearing the nose can damage the membranes. Frequent nosebleeds (epistaxis) can signify high blood pressure or simply weakened blood vessels.

CHECKLIST FOR A HEALTHY THROAT

STOP SMOKING TO AVOID THROAT CANCER

•

PERSISTENT VOICE CHANGES MUST BE TAKEN SERIOUSLY

•

DIFFICULTY SWALLOWING MUST BE CHECKED MEDICALLY

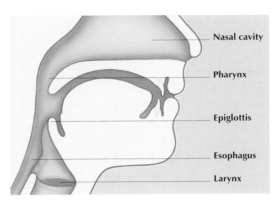

Nasal cavity

Pharynx

Epiglottis

Esophagus

Larynx

The area behind the mouth (oropharynx) and the larynx produce the vibrations of speech and shape the sounds into words. A change in voice may be an important sign of disease of the larynx. The oropharynx also forms food into a parcel to allow it to be swallowed. The dual functions of this area make it vulnerable to coordination problems, especially those from neurological diseases.

The esophagus (gullet) carries food down into the stomach. It is a muscular tube, actively squeezing down food and liquid, so it's actually possible to swallow while standing on your head!

The nose is concerned with the sense of smell, and also filters and warms air before it enters the body. The nasal cavity links to the upper part of the throat (pharynx).

This acupressure point (Tianzhu or Bladder 10), is located at the base of the skull. It can help relieve symptoms relating to nose and throat problems, such as allergic rhinitis, sore throat, headache, and congestion. Apply a constant pressure to both points for about 10 seconds, while slowly breathing in.

COMPLEMENTARY THERAPIES

ACUPUNCTURE

There are specific meridians which can be worked on to help with acid reflux into the gullet (see p.230).

NATUROPATHY

Some people are intolerant of certain foods. A carefully designed exclusion diet can be very helpful in relieving excess acid (see p.223).

AROMATHERAPY

A steam inhalation with eucalyptus can ease congestion of the nose (see p.228).

Cloves

Apples

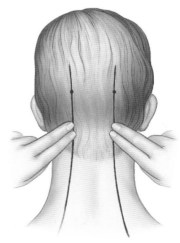

STOMACH AND BOWELS

T*he bowels can be divided into the upper bowel (esophagus, stomach, and small intestine) and the lower bowel (colon or large intestine). The health of your bowels depends upon what you put into your system, so their well-being is in many ways a matter of eating the right food, in the right amounts. Bowel health is also highly dependent on your general state of mind, and stress can upset stomach and bowel function.*

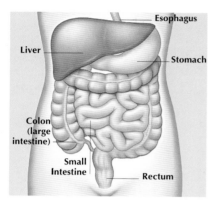

Chewed food passes down the esophagus into the stomach, where it is broken down by acids and enzymes before passing into the intestines.

The food you eat will affect the well-being of your stomach and bowels. Fresh foods rich in fiber, such as apples, dates, or artichokes, make the digestive system work harder, preventing constipation and other disorders.

Overeating can cause food to leak from the stomach back into the gullet, and lead to symptoms of heartburn or acid reflux. A hiatus hernia is where the join of the esophagus to the stomach is faulty, and acid can slosh up from the stomach, causing heartburn. Modern drugs help, but prevention is better. Gastritis and "ulcers" can be triggered by stress and are also frequently caused by a stomach infection (Heliobacter). These can be treated with antibiotics.

Diarrhea is a frequent problem of the lower bowel, and is often caused by infection. Where food hygiene is poor, you should eat only well-cooked food and avoid food washed in contaminated water.

Constipation is prevented by an adequate fluid intake, physical activity and increased fiber in the diet. The bowel was designed

to deal with more fiber than is included in most present-day Western diets. An increase in fiber reduces the likelihood of varicose veins, hemorrhoids, diverticulitis, and cancer, as well as improving well-being (see p.156–p.157).

If cancer of the bowel runs in your family, then screening may be helpful. It is also more common in smokers. Investigate any bleeding from the rectum, as early action can prevent development of a cancer or its progression to a less treatable stage.

Prevent heartburn by cutting back on fatty foods, eating more slowly, and by avoiding or diluting alcohol.

PREVENTING HEARTBURN

AVOID LARGE MEALS

•

AVOID BEING OVERWEIGHT

•

AVOID OR DILUTE ALCOHOL

•

AVOID SMOKING

•

AVOID STOOPING OR LYING FLAT

COMPLEMENTARY THERAPIES

NUTRITIONAL THERAPY

Buttermilk and plain yogurt contain *acidophilus,* a helpful live bacteria that can aid digestion in the bowel. Eating plenty of leafy green vegetables helps prevent bowel cancer.

HERBAL MEDICINE

Ginger aids the digestive process and can help treat diarrhea and flatulence.

HIPS

A nyone who has seen a hurdler in full flight, or a gymnast on the beam, will know how astonishing the hip joint is. When you realize that hips can generally function for the best part of a century, then their versatility is all the more remarkable. But this joint does wear out in time and one of the great advances of conventional medicine has been the development of the artificial hip joint replacement.

The hip is a ball-and-socket joint, with the ball at the end of the thighbone (femur) fitting into the socket in the pelvis. This socket is not fully formed at birth; usually the joint develops during the first year of life. Sometimes the ball-and-socket are not in position at birth, and the hip joint does not develop properly. The resulting poor-quality joint can wear out quickly, causing pain and disability. All babies need to be screened for this: spotted early, the problem can be treated. As children grow there are other hip problems, caused by damage from falls, which should be watched for.

The commonest type of hip damage (osteoarthritis) is often thought of as "wear and tear," and it certainly seems worse in those who put high-impact stress on their hips. There is much more to it than this though, since exercise generally seems to help keep joints mobile and strong. If you keep active, especially with low-impact exercise (such as cycling and swimming) then even sufferers from osteoarthritis of the hip will be able to keep more mobile.

Any kind of exercise that emphasizes flexibility, such as yoga, can help the hips. Be wary of excessive high-impact exercise (see p.154–p.155), which puts extra stress on the joints.

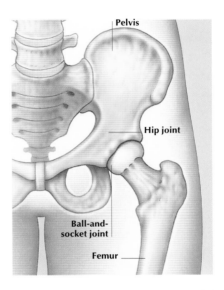

Pelvis

Hip joint

Ball-and-socket joint

Femur

The hip joint is strong and flexible. It supports the body's weight, takes the strain of running and jumping, and gives us an enormous range of movement.

COMPLEMENTARY THERAPIES

ACUPUNCTURE

This can be helpful for relieving the pain from damaged or arthritic joints, enabling them to be kept mobile (see p.230).

CHIROPRACTIC AND OSTEOPATHY

Useful for acute injuries or flare-ups of older damage, this treatment involves achieving the balance of the whole spine and can reduce uneven strain on hips (see p.232 –p.233).

Osteopathy, too, can be helpful; the two therapies are often interchangeable.

KEY POINTS TO REMEMBER

BABIES' HIPS MUST BE CHECKED

•

PAIN FROM THE HIP MAY BE FELT IN THE KNEE

•

ACTIVITIES THAT EMPHASIZE FLEXIBILITY AND AVOID HIGH-IMPACT STRESS ARE BEST FOR THE HIPS

At birth and during infancy, a young child's hips are extraordinarily flexible. Exercise such as yoga helps us to maintain flexibility even into old age.

29

JOINTS

There are two main types of joint. Mobile, or synovial, joints such as knees allow a wide range of movement. These are complex joints with a smooth coating of cartilage on the end of the bones and the joint, lined with lubricating synovium. Fibrous joints are used where less movement is needed, as in the skull or the base of the back.

Joints are located wherever one bone comes into contact with another. Like most joints in the body, the hand is made up of synovial joints where the cartilage at the end of each bone is lubricated with synovial fluid.

The study of joints and their problems is an entire medical specialty (rheumatology). Osteoarthritis is the most common joint disorder, affecting over three-quarters of people over 50. The causes for this are still being researched, but previous injury to, or excessive use of, a joint can make it more likely. Osteoarthritis is also more common as we get older (see p.146–p.147).

Joints can be affected by other disorders such as infections and, of course, by trauma. The joint disease that most people have heard about is rheumatoid arthritis. This is a curious problem, where the body produces a reaction to its own joints, as if they were a foreign body such as an invading virus. Often the joints are only mildly affected, but occasionally there are problems that need powerful treatments.

Osteoarthritis can affect all ages but is most common in the elderly. Regular exercise regime and proper nutrition may help to prevent and relieve the symptoms.

The range and reliability of surgical joint replacements is large, and more is being learned. There is much we can do to promote well-being of joints.

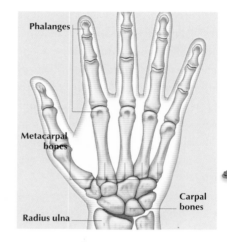

Prevention of excessive wear, and attention to nutrition, can help joints last as long as you do!

DIET

Different diets seem to help joint problems where there are specific food sensitivities. As yet, no single diet can be recommended, but a calcium-rich diet, or calcium supplements seem to be beneficial (see p.163) as does extra vitamin D and predigested collagen.

Osteoarthritis is the most common joint disorder. Gentle stretching exercises, swimming and yoga help to strengthen muscles and improve joint flexibility.

COMPLEMENTARY THERAPIES

HOMEOPATHY, ACUPUNCTURE, AND NATUROPATHY

These may be helpful in rheumatoid arthritis (see p.223, p.226, and p.230).

MASSAGE AND AROMATHERAPY

These can relieve pain and improve mobility (see p.228 and p.231).

OSTEOPATHY AND CHIROPRACTIC

These have been used to align bones and joints correctly, as well as freeing damaged joints (see p.232–p.233).

Wearing a copper bracelet has been found to help osteoarthritis.

MUSCLES

There are three main types of muscle in the human body. Most people immediately think of the skeletal (voluntary) muscle which moves the body, because it is so obvious in sports. Second is the smooth (involuntary) muscle which governs internal organs such as the bowel, bladder, and blood vessels. The last type is found in only one place and is the muscle never allowed to tire: the cardiac muscle of the heart.

Around a quarter of the body's weight is skeletal muscle. Sports demand a higher proportion of fast skeletal muscle: it tires easily but is excellent for sprinting or sudden movement, compared with slow skeletal muscle, which is better for endurance. General well-being is helped by maintaining good muscle tone and fitness, and in this respect the old adage of "healthy body, healthy mind" is true.

It is important to treat the skeletal muscles well. Warming up before exercise will reduce the danger of pulled muscles. Stretching is vital. Muscles have a built-in reflex to prevent damage to the joints by overstretching, and to help in movement. This reflex tightening can be overcome by gentle, constant stretching held for at least 20 seconds. This will overcome the reflex, which lasts around 15 seconds. Warming down after exercise helps too, by maintaining blood flow to remove waste products such as lactic acid.

The heart is the most important muscle to train. Exercise regimes built around your pulse rate should take into account your age and fitness. Just 20 minutes of exercise, three times a week, can be astonishingly useful in preventing heart disease. Care should be taken by those over the age of 40, particularly men, when considering taking up an intensive form of exercise such as jogging. It's better to begin with gentle exercise and gradually build up to more physically stressful sports. Beginners should also avoid excessive bouts of exercising. To improve the condition of smooth muscle, less direct means will be of benefit, for example general relaxation will assist the functioning of the bowels.

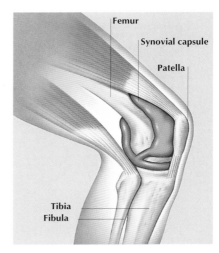

Femur

Synovial capsule

Patella

Tibia
Fibula

The knee joint lies between the femur and tibia. It is partly surrounded by a fibrous capsule lined with a synovial membrane that secretes fluid, allowing the joint to move freely. The membrane can become inflamed through injury, arthritis, or infection.

Massage is often used to treat muscle pain: it stimulates the circulation and can help to relax trigger points or other areas of stiffness.

COMPLEMENTARY THERAPIES

MASSAGE
This is helpful for injury and muscle strains
(see p.231).

CHIROPRACTIC
For relaxing and stretching the muscle (see p.232).

YOGA
Excellent for relaxation of muscles. Yoga works on the links between the muscles and the mind as well (see p.244).

The lotus position

FIBROMYALGIA (FIBROSITIS)

Trigger points can develop in muscles, which then act as painful centers. These may trap nerves and cause a variety of pains and tensions which do not respond well to conventional painkillers. This often affects the neck and back. Exercise, regular amounts of sleep, magnesium supplements, and various complementary therapies, especially acupuncture (see p.230), can help this problem.

BACK AND NECK

The back and neck are part of the same spinal column. The spine is made of small bones (vertebrae) stacked above one another, separated by fibrous disks. These disks act as shock absorbers and allow flexibility. The neck has seven vertebrae (cervical), the chest has 12 (thoracic or dorsal), and the small of the back has five vertebrae (lumbar). A vital part of the spine's function is protection of the spinal cord.

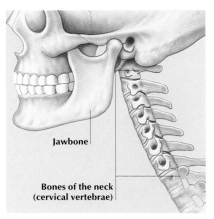

Jawbone

Bones of the neck (cervical vertebrae)

Thirty-three vertebrae make up the spinal column, which runs from the base of the skull down to the back of the pelvis. The spine protects the spinal cord and supports the body and head.

An Alexander Technique practitioner supports the head and spine, encouraging the patient to keep them free from strain.

The spinal column originally evolved to enable movement on all fours. But as humans walk on two feet, sit down, and lift things, the spine has to cope with very different stresses. This means that there is huge scope for promoting the well-being of your spine. As so often, it makes sense to begin in childhood. Children benefit from learning good walking and sitting posture at an early age: good habits that will prevent much ill-health in adult life.

An early appreciation of the importance of seating design is also useful. We should pay much more attention to seating at work, home, and especially in the car. Back disorders cause a colossal amount of ill-health and days off work. Therapists can do a great deal but in the end it is your back, and only you can look after it. Spinal pain is often linked with emotional problems and stress.

Necks can suffer in the same way, but they are also vulnerable to whiplash injuries, which usually occurs in car accidents. This common problem arises as a result of rear-end collisions. A vital routine for both drivers and passengers is to make sure that the head rest on a car is always correctly adjusted for different users. Comfortable seat design is also important, especially for regular or long journeys. See also p.130–p.131.

SLIPPED DISK

A damaged (slipped) disk presses on the nerves coming out from the spine. Painkillers, physiotherapy, or even surgery may be suggested. Loss of bladder or bowel control needs emergency medical assessment.

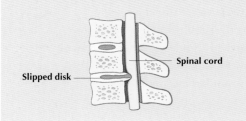

Spinal cord

Slipped disk

COMPLEMENTARY THERAPIES

ALEXANDER TECHNIQUE

This is used as a long-term way of tackling (or better still, preventing) spinal trouble, but brings other health benefits (see p.234).

ACUPUNCTURE

This plays a role in both relieving acute pain and treating long-term pain (see p.230).

AUTOGENIC TRAINING

This is useful for pain relief and relaxation (see p.242).

CHIROPRACTIC AND OSTEOPATHY

This can be very helpful for both acute and long-term spinal problems. Much of the well-being of the spine depends upon the balance of the spine, and these therapies can be useful (see p.232–p.233).

YOGA

Yoga is strongly recommended to increase back flexibility and reduce stress. A qualified Yoga teacher will be able to formulate an exercise program suited to your specific needs, keeping in mind that some movements may aggravate certain back problems. (see p.244)

SKIN

Healthy skin is vital for your well-being. It is a first-line defense against infection, and is visible to the world. Unhealthy skin, blemished with acne, soreness, and itching, can destroy both self-esteem and well-being.

Preventing skin disease means protecting the skin from harmful effects. Skin that dries out can become cracked, infected, and eczematous. This particularly affects people whose hands are constantly immersed in water and detergents, especially in cold weather. Many problems can be prevented by using simple moisturizers.

Greasy skin can lead to blocked pores (blackheads and whiteheads) and acne, especially for those working in very hot conditions. To some extent this can be prevented with appropriate soaps and creams (see p.126–p.127).

Sun damage is an increasing problem, particularly for those with fair skins, since people travel more and live longer. Not only can the sun cause acute sunburn, but also premature aging of the skin, with loss of elasticity, pigmentation, and even cancer (see p.128). Most skin cancers can be fairly easily treated. Some develop from small crusted areas (called solar keratoses), which should be treated before they become cancerous. The most serious skin cancers arise from changes to moles. Keep an eye out for any of the symptoms listed.

MOLE CHANGES TO WATCH FOR

CHANGE OF COLOR
•
CHANGE OF SIZE
•
CHANGE IN SHAPE
•
ITCHING
•
BLEEDING OR CRUSTING

Sun can damage skin badly. People with fair skins should stay no more than half an hour in direct sunlight.

If you have moles, check them regularly. Seek medical attention if you notice any changes, including changes in color, bleeding, or crusting.

INFECTIONS

Fungal infections, particularly between the toes, in the groin, and beneath the breasts, can be prevented by regular washing and careful drying of the area concerned. Careful cleaning of small cuts and possibly an antiseptic (e.g. tea tree oil added to the bath) may prevent bacterial skin infections. Infestations such as lice and scabies can be prevented by avoiding prolonged body contact with an infected person. Regular combing of the hair (particularly with a fine metal comb) will discourage head lice.

AVOIDING SUN DAMAGE

- Wear a hat, particularly if bald.
- Don't exceed the recommended time for sunbathing (e.g. half an hour in direct sunlight is the maximum, but less in strong sun).
- Use sunblocks, especially if you have fair skin or have not been recently exposed to the sun. Sunblocks with a sun protection factor (SPF) of at least 25 are suggested.
- Apply moisturiser to any sunburn.
- Large doses of antioxidants are indicated for the prevention of sun damage.

To keep skin free from fungal infections, wash your feet, groin, and the area below the breasts regularly, and make sure the skin is carefully dried.

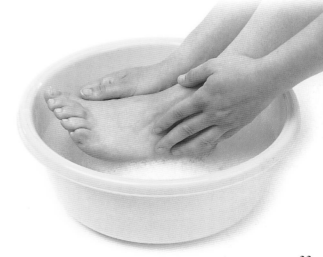

IMMUNE SYSTEM

*T*he *immune system is a vital part of well-being. It defends your body against bacteria and viruses, but also helps to stop cancers from developing or spreading. Sometimes the immune system may overreact, and this overreaction can itself cause diseases such as asthma and eczema. Autoimmune diseases occur when the immune system attacks the body, but fortunately these are rare.*

A strong body tends to have a stronger immune system than a weak one, and to be better able to fight disease. A healthy diet rich in protein, vegetables, fruit, and especially vitamin C will boost your immune system. Evidence shows, curiously enough, that a young child's immune system needs to be exposed to bacteria and viruses. Children who are brought up in a spotless environment are at least three times more likely to develop asthma. A little dirt and some infections, therefore, do no harm; the immune system needs these experiences in order to develop fully. Exercise, too, appears to be important in building up resistance to disease.

The science of psychoneuro-immunology is beginning to explain also how the mind, the nerves, and the immune system all interact. Stress and grief can make you less resistant to infections

and cancer, but research suggests that this is not so if you are able to take control of the situation causing stress. A feeling of being physically or mentally low also has the same effect—witness the way in which we seem to get cold sores, yeast infections, or colds when we are run down. Research has shown that counseling (see p.243) can have a beneficial effect on the immune system for patients suffering from cancer, and therefore suggests that if you cannot remove the source of your stress, then you must change your attitude to it.

If the body is out of balance (e.g. if you are anemic) or if you have a long-term problem with some other part of the body, such as kidney or liver disease, this will tend to make your immune system more sluggish and illness more likely. Take measures to improve your general health.

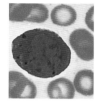

The immune system produces specialized white blood cells, including lymphocytes, which either engulf invading viruses and bacteria or produce antibodies to neutralize them.

You can boost the well-being of your immune system by eating a good diet rich in protein, fresh fruit and vegetables, and especially vitamin C.

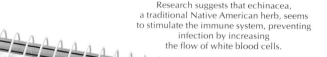

Research suggests that echinacea, a traditional Native American herb, seems to stimulate the immune system, preventing infection by increasing the flow of white blood cells.

HOW TO IMPROVE YOUR IMMUNE SYSTEM

• Eat a balanced diet containing plenty of protein, vegetables, and fruit.
• Ensure you have an adequate daily intake of vitamins B, C, and E, as well as iron. Antioxidants are also powerful immune system strengtheners.
• Avoid antibiotics if your health professional tells you that you will recover from an illness without them.
• Do not smoke, and avoid too much alcohol
• Get regular exercise (see p.154–p.155).
• Avoid stress (see p.183).
• Creative visualization may give your immune system a boost.
• Herbs such as echinacea and ginseng are said to be helpful.

SEXUAL ORGANS

For many people, a healthy sex life is an important part of well-being. Diseases of the sexual organs, particularly infections and cancer, can have a major impact on self-esteem, causing depression and inhibiting sexual feelings. Sexual diseases may be serious in themselves, but some have more serious consequences. Chlamydia and HIV can affect your fertility and life expectancy.

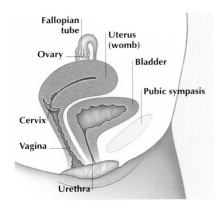

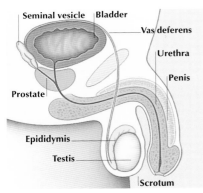

The most common problem affecting sexual organs is infection. The number of patients attending STD (sexually transmitted disease) clinics more than doubles every five years. If you are not in a long-term relationship, you should fully understand and practice "safe sex." If you get symptoms of an STD—pain, discharge or ulcers—seek advice at an early stage.

For females, cancer of the cervix (which was previously the most common cancer of the sexual organs) can be almost entirely prevented by having regular smears (see p.60). Cancer of the uterus is less easy to prevent, but much easier to treat when it occurs. See your doctor if you are over 40 and are experiencing bleeding between periods, or a persistent watery blood-stained discharge. Because the ovaries are relatively hidden, cancer can be difficult to detect, but if you come from a family where cancer of the ovary (or breast) is common, then tell your doctor.

For men, early detection of cancer of the testes is very important. At one time, few men were cured of this cancer, but nowadays most will recover. Examine both testes regularly and if you feel a lump (painful or not) consult your doctor (see p.43).

Women's sexual or reproductive organs consist of the ovaries, Fallopian tubes, uterus (womb), and the vagina.

Male sexual or reproductive organs consist of penis, testes (which are suspended in the scrotum), epididymis, vas deferens and the urethra.

Relationship difficulties can cause tension, conflict, and ultimately loss of libido or other sexual problems.

REDUCE RISKS OF STD

AVOID MULTIPLE PARTNERS, PROSTITUTES, AND OTHER PEOPLE WITH MULTIPLE SEX PARTNERS.

•

AVOID SEXUAL CONTACT WITH PEOPLE WHO HAVE SYMPTOMS OR LESIONS (E.G. URETHRAL DISCHARGE, WARTS, ULCERS).

•

AVOID GENITAL CONTACT WITH ORAL "COLD SORES."

•

USE CONDOMS OR A DIAPHRAGM.

•

HAVE REGULAR CHECKUPS IF AT HIGH RISK OF STDS.

men's health

AND WELL-BEING

contents

Introduction

*S*ome of the health worries men are commonly concerned with are related to sexual disorders, fatherhood, aging, hair loss, and relationships. Improving men's health awareness is an important task in any program of well-being and in the past this has often been overlooked. This section provides key practical information that may not have been available to you until now.*

LIFE EXPECTANCY

Men's life expectancy in the West is around 72 years (as opposed to women's, which is around 78). Statistics indicate that twice as many men commit suicide as women. This seems to indicate that their emotional well-being is as much in need of attention as their physical health. Women are four times more likely than men to survive beyond the age of 85. Men are twice as likely as women to die before the age of 65, even though the causes of their death are usually preventable— e.g. stroke, heart disease, and certain types of cancer.

SURVEY

Recently, the American magazine, Men's Health, *carried out a survey of around 5,000 men in the UK. It revealed interesting facts bout how men view their health, how much information they want, and how much they feel is*

Changing social patterns are encouraging men to rethink their traditional priorities and take a more active part in the rewarding process of parenting.

available. For instance, around 91% of men said that they only visited a doctor when they were actually ill, and didn't discuss other health worries that were bothering them. Some 20% said that they didn't share their health concerns with anyone—including their partner.

UNIQUE TO MEN

Most of the men (88%) believed that more emphasis was placed on women's health than their own. But in the UK there are some 1,000 new cases of testicular cancer each year (and more than half of these are in men under 35). One in three men will encounter some form of prostate disease before the age of 50, yet only 32% of men know anything about their prostate gland. In the next section we will look at some of the disorders and conditions that are unique to men, such as testicular cancer and prostate problems. Here you will find advice on self-examination, and early-warning signs to watch for.

Plenty of fresh air, and engaging in active outdoor sports such as wind surfing, contribute to physical and mental health.

HEALTH AWARENESS

Some men are extremely fortunate and will sail through life with little or no illness. But it is essential for men to know what the symptoms of various disorders are, both to safeguard themselves, and in order to pass the information on to their sons and other male relatives and friends. It is only when men actively start to take an interest in their health, and learn to discuss their health concerns with others, that men's well-being is eventually likely to improve.

The men questioned in the survey were very specific about what they wanted to know. They felt that there was more than enough information on the dangers of smoking and excessive alcohol consumption, but insufficient details about stress-related disorders, diet and nutrition, depression, and relationship management. Women have always been able to absorb health information from women's magazines, while men's magazines have shown little interest in the subject. In the next section, we aim to remedy this lack of information.

Heart disease and obesity are major threats to male health. An additive-free diet, rich in fruit, helps to counteract both.

39

HEALTHY RELATIONSHIPS

*S**tatistics indicate that single men don't live as long as men in long-term stable relationships with a committed partner, so checking the state of your relationship regularly may be more important than you realize. Being involved in a relationship means being prepared to put some time and effort into making sure it stays fresh and vibrant.*

A relationship is not a static thing—it will change and grow over the years, just as you and your partner do. The things that once brought the two of you together may fade, or you may find you grow closer as time goes on.

RELATIONSHIP FIRST-AID

Talk to your partner—the most common failure in any relationship is poor communication. Honesty is vital: don't be afraid to voice your true feelings, even if you think they will upset your partner. If you bottle up your emotions, they have a tendency to come bursting out in the middle of an argument, doing untold damage to the relationship. Take time to discuss things. Don't try to patch up your problems when you are in a rush to get to work. Sit down and talk in a calm environment with few distractions. Each partner should look back over the relationship for the point where things seemed to go wrong, for there is often a root cause of relationship rifts. Try to be brave: healing a damaged relationship may need compromises, or other action that requires a commitment to change. Working hard to mend burned bridges pays off in the end.

Couples who are experiencing serious relationship difficulties often find it helpful to discuss their situation with a professional counselor, who may be able to uncover hidden problems.

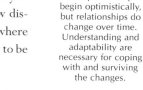

Most partnerships begin optimistically, but relationships do change over time. Understanding and adaptability are necessary for coping with and surviving the changes.

IS THIS RELATIONSHIP WORKING?

Ask yourself these questions from time to time:

- Does this relationship nurture me and provide me with what I want and need?
- Am I giving enough to the relationship?

If the answer to any of these questions is "no," you will then have to then ask yourself why, and what you are prepared to do about it. This may take the form of living with it, changing it, or leaving it. Only you know which is the most sensible option.

SIGNS OF TROUBLE

If you want to know whether your relationship is on track, there are some problem signs you should watch out for and repair before they get any worse.

- Feeling trapped or "held back" by your partner.
- A lack of support and nurturing from your partner.
- Intense jealousy about your partner's work or friends.
- Difficulty in talking to your partner about any problems you may have.
- Recurring arguments about trivia.
- Frequent loss of temper.
- Feeling that you are giving more to the relationship than your partner.
- An unsatisfactory sex life.
- Looking elsewhere for sex, companionship, or emotional support.
- Reluctance to go home.
- Dreading spending time with your partner.
- Boredom or apathy.
- Neglecting your partner.
- Feeling neglected yourself.

Vacations can put a particular strain on relationships, perhaps because couples spend more time in each other's company than at other times.

DUAL-CAREER FAMILIES

Shifting trends in working attitudes, together with financial pressures, have caused a rise in the number of families where both parents work. The resulting stresses can challenge a happy relationship and have been cited as part of the reason for the increased divorce rates. Taking time to understand each other's work-related responsibilities and anxieties, combined with planning quality time together as a family, is vital for the long-term well-being of the relationship.

CHILDREN

Often, both husband and wife have an intense need to achieve. But a husband may expect his wife to give up her job when they have children. This concept of the traditional family, with the husband as breadwinner, can be a flash point for disputes, with the child exposed to the brunt of the resentful atmosphere. It is vital to agree about parental responsibilities and accept that help may be needed at home with childcare duties. At all times, do not forget that the child is the innocent party in the relationship.

VACATION STRESS

A recent survey of 2,000 people on vacation revealed that bitter arguments between spouses erupted on nearly half of all family vacations. Other problems included finding travel very stressful, feeling ill, and wanting to return home. In the UK, the relationship counseling organization Relate reported a rise in clients after vacations, which was attributed to families spending more time cooped up together than they were accustomed to.

FATHERHOOD

*B*ecoming a father for the first time is an exhilarating but scary process. We have so much to learn and so little time to learn it in. We are expected to become immediate experts on all aspects of childcare from changing diapers to sleepless nights, bottle-feeding to childhood illnesses, and tantrums. There is a whole mass of information to take in all at once and the father's emotional well-being can sometimes get lost in it all.

Parenting can be difficult in the early days. Most attention is usually given to the mother but fathers too can suffer tension and anxiety as they adapt to the new experience of fatherhood.

During the transition into fatherhood it is important to be yourself. Do not try to emulate what you think a father should be like: this will tend to end in disaster. Be yourself and allow the natural father in you to grow and develop as your child changes. There will always be aspects of childrearing that you will be good at and others that are best left to your partner. However, only time will tell your true strengths and weaknesses.

Fatherhood is a truly rewarding time of life. The opportunity to pass on the information you have amassed over your life will never be received by such interested ears again. Enjoy it while it lasts because children grow up very quickly!

Becoming a father is a joyful and rewarding experience.

COMPLEMENTARY THERAPIES

YOGA
This ancient art encourages deep relaxation and gives the mind the opportunity to focus better and concentrate on difficulties or empty itself of problems. Many conditions ranging from back and neck pain through to fatigue and insomnia can be helped by yoga.

AROMATHERAPY
There can be no better way to unwind than to allow the physical symptoms of stress and anxiety to be massaged away. Try the following combination of selected oils for a profound sense of relaxation:
4 drops lavender
2 drops sandalwood
2 drops bergamot
3 drops ylang-ylang
mix in 2oz carrier oil (almond oil).

HERBAL MEDICINE
Fathers can become just as stressed as mothers when a new life enters the household. Over this time of adjustment adaptogenic herbs such as Ginseng can offer valuable support to an overstressed system. It is not wise, however, to take Ginseng for more than 3 months without a break.

TESTICULAR PROBLEMS

T*he likelihood of an adult male getting testicular cancer are around one in 500, which is why so much emphasis is placed on testicular self-examination for abnormalities or warning signs. Cases of testicular cancer have doubled in the past 20 years and are showing signs of doubling again in the next 20 years. This cancer can be successfully treated if caught in the early stages.*

Just why the numbers of testicular cancers have so dramatically increased over the past twenty years is somewhat of a medical mystery. Many theories exist, one of which describes compelling evidence that environmental toxins play a key part in the development of cellular mutations that can lead on to the formation of cancer cells. This theory also suggests that the effect of environmental pollution primes the developing cells of the fetus, a time when they are at their most susceptible.

EXAMINING YOUR TESTICLES

FEEL YOUR TESTICLES AND LOOK TO SEE IF THERE ARE ANY LUMPS OR IRREGULARITIES OR CHANGES IN SIZE, TEXTURE, OR SHAPE.

•

FOLLOW THIS PROCEDURE WEEKLY AFTER A WARM BATH, YOU WILL GET TO KNOW WHAT IS NORMAL FOR YOUR TESTICLES.

•

REFER ANY ABNORMALITIES TO YOUR DOCTOR IMMEDIATELY. SOME 90% OF TESTICULAR CANCER IS TREATED SUCCESSFULLY.

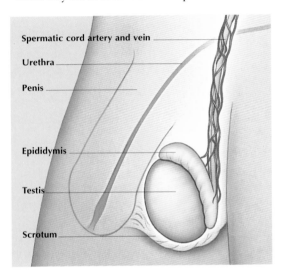

Spermatic cord artery and vein

Urethra

Penis

Epididymis

Testis

Scrotum

The testicles, or testes, are two rounded glands situated in a sac called the scrotum, which lies outside the body. The testes produce sperm, which is stored in the epididymis.

LESS SERIOUS PROBLEMS

There are other problems of a less serious nature that can affect adult males, which you should be aware of:

HYDROCELE Fluid collects in the scrotum, causing a painless swelling. This often occurs after injury. If it doesn't clear up of its own accord (which it probably will), the excess fluid can be drained off in a relatively simple procedure using a syringe and needle.

VARICOCELE The vein above the testicle, which drains the blood from it, becomes swollen due to a damaged valve. It's usually the left testicle that's affected.

Wearing underwear with support usually relieves the condition but if not, or if the condition is considered to be affecting sperm production, a simple surgical operation can be carried out.

ORCHITIS An inflammation of the testicle with accompanying fever, caused by the mumps virus. It can be successfully treated with painkillers and rarely interferes with fertility, though it can cause the testicle to shrink slightly.

EPIDIDYMAL CYSTS A painless swollen cyst in the epididymis, which leads from the back of the testes and where sperm are stored. It is surgically removed if it becomes enlarged or painful.

TORSION OF THE TESTICLE A very painful condition where the testicle twists around in the scrotum, cutting off the blood supply. Emergency surgery is carried out to untwist the testicle.

SEXUAL DISORDERS

Invariably, the problem with sexual disorders is that the longer they persist, the more difficult they are to treat. It is essential to refer any problems to your doctor as soon as they occur. The build-up of depression and anxiety that results from not talking about sexual problems may only make things worse (see p.108–p.109).

LOSS OF LIBIDO

This affects all men at some time during their life and may be caused by stress, worry, tiredness, too much alcohol or smoking, recovery from an illness or major surgery, medication such as sleeping pills, diet, and even boredom. The underlying causes must be dealt with first.

PAINFUL INTERCOURSE

Although this is widely known to affect women, it also affects some men. Possible causes include an allergy or reaction to spermicides or condoms, an infection of the glands of the penis, a too-tight foreskin, or inflammation of the prostate gland. All of these should be referred to a medical practitioner for further investigation.

PREMATURE EJACULATION

This affects nearly all men at some time and is often caused by anxiety about performance or over-excitement. This can be treated by methods such as the "squeeze technique," where the head of the penis is squeezed firmly just before climaxing, to stop ejaculation. Intercourse can be resumed once the urgency of orgasm has receded.

DELAYED EJACULATION

If you are unable to ejaculate, despite achieving an erection and having intercourse, the cause may be alcohol, stress, tiredness, having already ejaculated recently, or a deeper psychological reason. If this is an ongoing condition, it should be referred to a doctor.

POTENCY

Impotence affects ability to achieve and maintain an erection (see p.45). It can be caused by stress, too much alcohol, anxiety, tiredness, or pressure of expectation. Treatments include counseling and specialist sexual therapy.

LOW SPERM COUNT

This may be caused by a variety of factors including smoking, wearing tight trousers, or the testicles getting too hot. See your doctor for tests or a referral to a fertility clinic.

Premature ejaculation can be distressing for both partners. Breathing techniques, taught by a qualified Tantric yoga practitioner, can help a man delay ejaculation.

COMPLEMENTARY THERAPIES

YOGA

Yoga can help men learn to control ejaculation, especially by practicing Tantric sex techniques, which use breathing to prolong sexual arousal (see p.244).

COUNSELING

Psychological or psychosexual counseling may help identify the cause of premature ejaculation (see p.243).

ACUPUNCTURE

Two out of three men can have their fertility restored by acupuncture. Low sperm count and poor sperm motility is seen as due to a deficiency of kidney chi (see p.230).

CHINESE MEDICINE

Recommendations would vary according to the individual, but usually eucommia bark, ginseng, dodder seeds, and mulberry would be prescribed (see p.225).

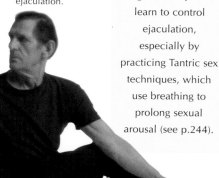

IMPOTENCE

*B*eing impotent means being unable to achieve or keep an erection. It's a fairly common condition, which strikes most men at some time during their life. Despite the fact that it affects so many men, it is something men don't like to admit, discuss, or seek guidance for. There are various contributory factors including stress, drinking too much alcohol, anxiety, tiredness, and the pressure of expectation.

Loss of sexual interest can devastate a relationship. Causes may be physical, such as illness or a reduction in the male or female sex hormones, or emotional. Talking to your partner is essential.

Stress and anxiety at work commonly lead to reduced libido or loss of sexual desire.

As men grow older, there may well be a natural falling off in their ability to have or maintain an erection, and there may also be an increase in the time taken to recover between ejaculations. Impotence should never be regarded as normal, and any experience of it should be reported to a doctor.

THE CONVENTIONAL APPROACH

There are certain sexual techniques which can enhance erection quality. For instance, the majority of men suffering from impotence report that fellatio (oral sex) helps them to maintain an erection, due to the vacuum-type effect that stimulates blood flow to the penis.

The drug viagra has been successful in treating impotence in the USA, although reports of serious side effects make it a controversial choice and it is currently unavailable on the NHS in the UK. There is also a new oral medication for impotence, sildenafil, available in the USA.

Exercise of the pubococcygeus (PC) muscle can help men maintain a firm erection. To find this muscle, the next time you urinate, stop the flow midstream. The muscle you "squeeze" to stop the flow is the PC muscle. You can try squeezing this muscle regularly and see how it improves your erection.

The condition can also be treated by talking to a trained counselor (see p.243) or by specialist sexual therapy.

If there is a medical reason for impotence, such as damage to blood vessels or nerves, the surgical insertion of an artificial penile implant which acts as a pump may be recommended.

COMPLEMENTARY THERAPIES

CHINESE MEDICINE

A Chinese herbalist will treat weakness of the kidneys and liver, and stagnation of Liver Chi. Cibot root (*Cibotium barometz,* or *Gou Ji*) may be prescribed.

HOMEOPATHY

A homeopath will prescribe according to the man's sexual and medical history (see p.226).

HERBAL MEDICINE

Saw palmetto berries help to tone and strengthen the male reproductive system.

ACUPUNCTURE

An acupuncturist will seek an underlying cause for the impotence, and treat it accordingly. Acupuncture can be effective, depending on the cause and severity of the condition (see p.230).

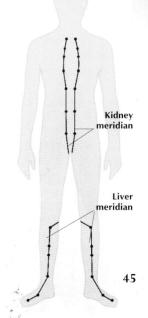

Kidney meridian

Liver meridian

An acupuncturist may treat an impotent man by releasing the flow of energy (Chi) in the liver and kidney meridians.

45

MIDLIFE CRISIS

*D*uring their 40s and 50s, most men experience some symptoms *of what is now known as the male menopause. Although these symptoms may be unlike those of female menopause, in the sense that they don't include hot flashes or night sweats, they can include headaches, memory loss, depression, exhaustion, lethargy, loss of confidence, loss of decision-making abilities, and a general feeling of being run down. It is not yet really understood why this happens.*

The overall level of the male sex hormone testosterone does not decrease significantly until men are in their 60s, but it may be that testosterone stops working efficiently when men are middle aged, due to some as yet undetermined factor. Or midlife crisis might be a purely psychological condition.

THE CONVENTIONAL APPROACH

Men who are currently being treated with testosterone replacement therapy report (in about 80% of cases) a marked upturn in their general well-being and a reduction in male menopause symptoms. It is still too early, however, to evaluate the results properly.

If your symptoms are psychological, there are some measures you can take to alleviate them. Regular exercise is always beneficial at any age and this, coupled with a regime of healthy eating, will keep you both mentally and physically energized. Don't be afraid to express your feelings—talk to your partner about any worries you may have. If you are still working try and find ways to reduce stress levels (see p.182). Seek reassurance from your partner if you are worried about your sexual performance. Be aware that this period of your life is a time of reevaluation, and that some changes may be necessary (see p.211). Embarking on new areas of study or taking up a new interest, for example, will ensure that you stay mentally active and alert.

Keeping fit and healthy and taking up a new interest such as sport can prevent feelings of uselessness common in men after retirement.

Immersing yourself in a new hobby is rewarding and may provide an opportunity to make new friends.

Retirement can be a major crisis point for men who have defined themselves solely in terms of their work. Psychotherapy can help men who have difficulties in expressing their feelings.

COMPLEMENTARY THERAPIES

PSYCHOTHERAPY

There are many forms of psychotherapy available. One school of thought follows the humanistic approach, emphasizing the essential goodness we all possess and the belief that we all have choices in life. It helps us to realize our full potential, eventually allowing us to appreciate our true feelings and giving us the ability to express them freely.

PSYCHODRAMA

The midlife crises that affect many people can often be effectively acted out in a psychodrama group. Painful and frustrating aspects of our lives may never get expressed or displayed. This can cause internal turmoil, and adversely affect our general well-being. Psychodrama forms part of the Gestalt school of psychological therapy, and can be used to unlock many doors to the past. It can give you the ability to discover and practice fresh ways of relating to others.

PROSTATE PROBLEMS

The prostate is a walnut-sized gland that sits just under a man's bladder and surrounds the urethra. It secretes semen, which carries sperm made in the testes to the penis just before ejaculation. These secretions help vitalize the sperm, providing essential nutrients including potassium, zinc, glucose, and vitamin C.

There are two main problems that can affect the prostate gland:
• Prostate enlargement, known as benign prostatic hyperplasia (hypertrophy)—BPH.
• Prostate cancer.

Enlargement of the prostate gland is treated by medication or surgery—transurethral resection of the prostate (TURP). A thin instrument called a resectoscope is passed up the urethra, and a wire loop cuts away the overgrown prostate tissue. Or a microwave beam to can be used to burn out the tissue. Alternatively, a drug called finasteride is given to shrink the prostate, by preventing hormonal action. TURP is a safe procedure with few side effects—occasionally it causes problems with ejaculation.

Prostate cancer is a much more serious condition, affecting older men, and has very similar symptoms to BPH. This is why it is essential to have any urination problems checked immediately by a doctor.

Routine screening is now available. A simple blood test looks for prostate-specific antigen, which is raised if there is a cancerous tumor. Alternatively, digital rectal examination or ultrasound scans are used.

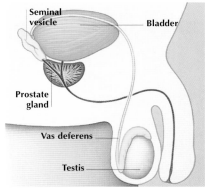

The prostate secretes substances that form the seminal fluid during ejaculation.

CAUTION
Consult a doctor if you have any of the early-warning symptoms.

EARLY-WARNING SYMPTOMS
Prostate cancer can be successfully treated with surgery, radiotherapy, and hormone treatment if it is diagnosed early enough. First symptoms of prostate cancer and BPH are:

A FEELING THAT YOUR BLADDER HASN'T QUITE EMPTIED

NEEDING TO URINATE FREQUENTLY DURING THE NIGHT

OBSTRUCTION OF NORMAL URINE FLOW

FREQUENT BLADDER INFECTIONS

BLOOD IN THE URINE

COMPLEMENTARY THERAPIES

HERBAL MEDICINE
Saw palmetto berries, the bark of pygeum, nettles, and willow tea improve urine flow.

NATUROPATHY
For BPH, increase the amount of zinc in your diet: eat grains, legumes, pumpkin seeds, seafood, and lean meat. Or take a daily 15mg supplement. Alternate hot and cold compresses, applied behind the scrotum, may bring relief and increase blood flow (see p.223).

ACUPRESSURE
Pressure applied around the Bladder, Large Intestine, and Spleen meridians is known to bring relief (see p.230).

DID YOU KNOW?
Scientists at the biotechnology company Zeneca have discovered a way of growing tomatoes with high levels of lycopene, a chemical which has been found to reduce the risk of prostate cancer. Lycopene is also responsible for stimulating the sex lives of older men with tomato-rich Mediterranean diets. You need to eat between five and ten servings of tomatoes a week in order to benefit.

Tomatoes

Saw palmetto berries

47

AGING PROBLEMS

Everyone inevitably ages and people usually become aware of a decline or loss of bodily function sometime around the age of 60. Some men age much faster than others. This is probably due to a combination of factors, including genetic reasons, a breakdown in the body's immune system, or a build-up of toxins in the body due to poor diet, neglect, and a lack of regular exercise (see also p.144).

SIGNS OF AGING

Longer healing process, loss of muscle strength, increase in joint stiffness, loss of height, wrinkled skin, reduction in bone density, impaired lung efficiency, increased bruising, gray hair, hair loss, impairment of vision, hearing loss, impairment of short-term memory.

The factors that are known to speed the aging process include smoking, regular exposure to strong sunlight, excessive drinking, lack of exercise, and a poor diet.

Conversely, the aging process can be slowed down by maintaining a healthy lifestyle and eating habits, taking regular exercise, cutting down on smoking and alcohol, and relaxing regularly. A positive approach to life is also beneficial, keeping you physically and mentally active and alert. Body function should also be closely monitored—ill-health is not a guaranteed sign of aging and any deterioration of health should be reported to a doctor immediately.

George Vaillant of Brigham and Women's Hospital in Boston claims that emotional stability is the key to longevity. He says that people who are not inclined to extremes of euphoria and depression have a better chance of long life than those who merely avoid fatty foods, alcohol, and other drugs. Vaillant studied the lives of 63 ex-Harvard students who graduated in 1942, dividing them into three groups: "squares" who showed few signs of emotion, "distressed" men who had wild emotional swings, and an intermediate group. Only 5% of squares died before the age of 75, compared with 25% of the intermediates and 38% of the distressed. Even when smoking and drinking habits were taken into account, squares still enjoyed better health. "A personality tendency to preserve a consistent mood that is largely free of psychological distress promotes physical health much more than exercise or eating habits," Vaillant said.

COMPLEMENTARY THERAPIES

T'AI CHI

Improves all-round flexibility and helps maintain good health (see p.245).

T'ai chi is suitable for all ages. In China, it is regularly practiced by men of advanced years.

ACUPUNCTURE

Though the aging process cannot be stopped, it can be slowed down. An acupuncturist will probably balance your body every three months, to improve general health (see p.230).

AUTOGENIC TRAINING

This is an excellent stress reducer (see p.242).

HOMEOPATHY

A homeopath will need to take a thorough history before prescribing a treatment for slowing the aging process (see p.226).

CHINESE MEDICINE

A Chinese herbalist will probably prescribe ginseng (*Panax ginseng*) as a nutritive tonic, as well as jujube (*Zizyphus jujuba*).

NUTRITIONAL SUPPLEMENTS

Valuable foods include brewer's yeast, wheatgerm, nuts, liver, sunflower seeds, wholegrain products, and fruit and vegetables containing antioxidants. Or take between 1–25mg each of cod liver oil and vitamin B1 (the larger quantity if you suffer from depression, loss of appetite, poor memory, emotional and neurological problems, low energy levels, or are over 60).

HAIR LOSS

We are losing hair all the time, usually at a rate of between 50 and 150 hairs a day. It grows back within three months. About 10% of our head hair is in this phase of regrowth at any one time.

If the figure of 10% is exceeded, permanent hair loss can be established. Hair loss is much more common in men than women, due to a hereditary condition called male pattern baldness. This manifests as hair loss that starts around the temples and crown, causing a receding hair line. Most men will encounter it as they grow older. However it doesn't have to be all bad: hair loss can be seen in a positive light—well-known actors Yul Brynner, Captain Picard of Star Trek, and Kojak are all considered highly attractive.

MINOXIDIL

Hair loss can be slowed down by using a lotion form of the drug minoxidil, originally developed for high blood pressure. Once treatment has topped however, the hair loss everts to its former rate. Minoxidil also helps to promote regrowth in some cases, though this is often fairly sparse. The drug is also quite expensive, and not all men respond to it.

The lotion form of the drug minoxidil can help to restore hair growth.

CARE

To give it the best chance of remaining attached to your scalp, look after the hair that you've got. Mistreating your hair by over-vigorous brushing or combing, tying the hair back too tightly in a ponytail, or using a very hard brush, won't help. Use a mild shampoo, and a low heat on the blow-dryer.

ILLNESS

Some hair loss may be caused by a fungal infection. A doctor will need to prescribe antifungal drugs to alleviate the problem. Sudden hair loss can be the result of illness, stress, major surgery, rapid weight loss, or even exposure to radiation. Once the contributory factors have been dealt with, the hair growth should return to normal.

Thinking positively about oneself, and adopting a philosophical approach, can work wonders in overcoming the negative feelings about hair loss.

Brush your hair with easy, gentle strokes.

Chinese herbal treatments are often given in a formula containing more than one herb.

COMPLEMENTARY THERAPIES

ACUPUNCTURE

Hair loss is considered to be caused by a Liver and Kidney deficiency, and treatment would involve "tonifying" both organs with extra Chi (energy) to restore balance (see p.230).

CHINESE MEDICINE

The practitioner is likely to prescribe fleece-flower root, mulberry fruit, and wolfberry fruit—all to be taken internally (see p.225).

Fleece-flower fruit

Mulberry fruit

Wolfberry fruit

WEIGHT AND HEALTH

A balanced diet can improve your general fitness, restore or raise your energy levels, nourish your skin and hair, uplift your mood, help circulation, reinforce your immune system, tone muscle and internal organs, and generally make you feel better able to cope with what life throws at you.
For most of us, maintaining a sensible weight, which is correct for our height and build, is all down to healthy eating and exercise.

It's of little value to keep starting and stopping diets, or to fast for long periods. You need a routine, sensible diet that is healthy from a nutritional point of view and one that suits your needs and likes (see p.156–p.157).

Light, frequent snacks may suit you better than heavy, infrequent meals. Provided the snacks are nutritious, it does not matter if your eating pattern is a little unconventional. Eating a big meal less than three hours before you go to bed can affect your sleep, since your system is working hard to digest the food. Do not attempt any strenuous exercise shortly after eating; it affects the digestive process.

GUIDELINES FOR HEALTHY EATING

ALWAYS TRY TO EAT SITTING DOWN at a table and don't eat alone if you can avoid it—good conversation is a marvelous appetite stimulator.

•

TAKE YOUR TIME, enjoy your food, and eat regularly—three main meals a day at set times with only light snacks in between.

•

CUT DOWN ON FAT—butter, cheese, whole milk, red meats, cream, fried foods; and eat lots of fiber—legumes, cereals, fruit, vegetables, and whole-wheat pasta.

•

EAT MORE LOWFAT FOODS—lowfat yogurts, margarine, lowfat milk, non-oily fish, steamed and baked meals rather than fried. Reduce your consumption of mood-altering foods and drinks such as sugar, caffeine, alcohol, and switch snacks from chocolate and potato chips to fruit and raw vegetables such as celery sticks.

GO FOR FRESH FOODS rather than packaged, canned, frozen, or dried and cut down on processed pies, sausages, and meats. Avoid highly refined food such as white bread and pasta and go for whole-wheat varieties instead. Buy organic food if you can.

•

SERVE SMALLER QUANTITIES AT each meal and make sure you include a fresh green salad or some vegetables at least once a day. Make cooking from fresh an enjoyable part of your lifestyle by creating tasty, simple, and colorful meals. Or go all the way—bake your own bread too.

•

LOWER YOUR SALT INTAKE to a maximum of 0.2oz (6g) a day—too much salt results in water retention, which raises blood pressure.

Too much fat in your diet from foods such as butter, whole milk, cheese and red meat, can lead to obesity and heart problems.

DID YOU KNOW?

According to Dr. Thomas Stuttaford of Leeds University, England, gaining weight is not necessarily unhealthy; it depends where you put the weight on. Extra weight distributed evenly over the body is generally much less unhealthy than a large amount of fat deposited in one area. People who develop a bulky chest and abdomen, while their limbs remain skinny, are especially at risk of developing heart disease and diabetes. Dr. Stafford says: "The risk becomes much more apparent once the abdominal girth exceeds the hip measurement." He advises men to make sure their waist measurement remains under 37in (92cm), and women to keep theirs under 31.5in (78cm).

Cooking is an enjoyable pastime. Preparing your own meals, using a variety of fresh ingredients, is the best way of ensuring that your diet meets your health needs.

INEVITABLE WEIGHT

Exercise helps stimulate endorphins, the body's mood-enhancing chemicals. But regular jogging cannot help prevent men from putting on weight in middle age, according to Dr. Paul Williams of the Lawrence Berkeley National Laboratory in California. He studied 7,000 male joggers and discovered that they put on just as much weight between the ages of 18 and 50 as men who had never jogged, with the average male gaining 3.3lb (1.4kg) for every decade of life. Dr. Williams stated, "The perception is that people gain weight as they get older, due to inactivity. Our study suggests this does not seem to be the case." He said there were physiological reasons why men put on weight as they got older, one factor being the decline in testosterone levels.

Some weight gain is to be expected as you get older. Exercise may not prevent this, but it has the benefit of stimulating your cardiovascular and respiratory systems.

COMPLEMENTARY THERAPIES

ACUPUNCTURE

Obesity is seen as dampness in the Spleen and Stomach, and treatment is carried out to correct this. More "warming" food is likely to be recommended (see p.230).

CHINESE MEDICINE

Hawthornberry, rice sprouts, and wheat sprouts, to be drunk as teas, may help to stimulate and balance the body's energies, thereby promoting weight loss.

HOMEOPATHY

Obesity can be treated with a single dose of Calcera (also known as Calcium carbonicum). Dietary changes are also likely to be recommended.

Include plenty of low-fat, fresh food in your diet, such as fruit and vegetables. Replace meat with fish or whole-wheat pasta.

Whole-wheat bread is far better for your health than bleached, white bread. It is a good source of vitamins, iron, calcium, and dietary fiber.

SECTION THREE

women's health

AND WELL-BEING

contents

Introduction

omen are often under pressure due to the various roles thrust upon them, juggling work, care of the family, and the home. Many women also feel that they must look glossy, well-groomed, and gleaming with good health at work, as well as proving themselves to be efficient. Maintaining a good level of well-being in these circumstances can therefore be quite a challenge.

IT'S UP TO YOU

This section of the book concentrates on women's health problems and issues. Simple preventive measures and complementary therapies can do much to alleviate most problems, so you will only need to seek a doctor's advice for worrying symptoms or recurring problems. By taking personal responsibility for your own health, it's possible that the only contact you will have with a medical practitioner is when you go for a regular health check.

Women fulfill many roles: as lovers, wives, mothers, and workers.

HEALTHY AND HAPPY LIVING

To actively enjoy a way of living that keeps body, mind, and spirit in good health, it helps to learn more about your body and to treat it as it deserves to be treated. It is vital to ensure that you eat a wholesome diet, and get plenty of exercise, rest, and relaxation. Don't despair if this does not reflect your lifestyle to date. The good news is that it is never too late to start. Even if you have got into the bad habit of eating too many ready-prepared, fatty, or sweet foods, and slumping in front of the television every night as a way of relaxing, you can soon retrain yourself.

Cut down on sugar and salty food, and ease into a diet that supplies less fat and more vitamins and fiber. Include plenty of wholefoods, fresh fruit and vegetables, fish, and a little lean meat, and you will soon find that your old way of eating becomes unappetizing. Balance your work and nonwork activities, so that you spend equal amounts of time engaging in restful and energetic pursuits. Time spent enjoying activities such as a session at the gym or swimming pool, a daily exercise routine, gardening, reading, listening to music, creative cooking, or following any sport or hobby you enjoy, soon makes you forget the days when you sat in front of the television because you were too tired to go to bed.

LONG-TERM WELL-BEING

Genetic inheritance can make you disposed to certain illnesses and upheavals associated with menstruation and menopause. The demands of pregnancy, birth, and breastfeeding can all affect your health. But there is much that you can do to minimize the risk of illness and keep yourself in good health throughout your life. Often women are so busy looking after the people they love, that they forget to look after themselves. Looking after yourself doesn't mean being selfish or indulgent, it is simply giving yourself the time you deserve. In the end, this means that you have more to offer others, and little, if anything, to resent.

Women lead busy lives and are often reluctant to make time for themselves, but doing so is vital.

Exercise, eat a healthy diet, and make time for pleasure to obtain optimum physical and mental well-being.

TIPS FOR HEALTH AND WELL-BEING

- Attend a clinic or have a routine health check with your doctor annually.
- Have a sight test and dental checkups at regular intervals.
- Get exercise and enough rest.
- Eat well and keep an eye on your weight.
- Don't smoke. Don't drink too much alcohol or coffee.
- Give yourself an occasional treat such as a massage or pedicure.
- Give yourself time to be alone each day, and make sure that your partner, and family, respect it.
- Don't let tasks that need doing pile up.
- Don't expect everything to run smoothly.
- Set up a domestic routine that shares out some responsibilities.

BEAUTY TREATMENTS

W hen you look good you feel good—and vice versa. We all know that being healthy is the key to this, even though good presentation helps. Take trouble over how you look, and you will inevitably start to feel good. It is also true that "beauty comes from within"— a healthy diet and exercise are essential.

Take time off to relax is time well spent: go for an invigorating walk or pamper yourself with a trip to the beauty salon.

Models drink a vast amount of water. It is a good idea to swallow at least 1.7 pints (1 liter) of plain water a day to help flush toxins from the system. Try to have a minimum of five portions of fruit or vegetables a day, and don't overburden your system with a lot of red meat and saturated fats. Reduce your intake of sugar and salt (see p.156–p.157).

SLEEP AND REST

Most of us need eight hours' sleep a night—perhaps a little more in winter, and less in summer. Insufficient sleep, whether from too little time in bed or from insomnia, takes the gloss off even those who eat well. Try to go to bed about the same time each night, and wind down beforehand with a scented bath, or by sitting in an armchair with a book or listening to music. Don't eat within two to three hours of going to bed (see p.208–p.209).

EXERCISE

Ideally, body toning exercises should be done every day, if only for 10 minutes. Stretching exercises keep the body in shape, and are best done in the morning, in front of an open window (provided that it doesn't overlook a busy road, with hazardous traffic fumes).

REDUCING STRESS

Stress shows in the face and body. It causes poor skin, wrinkles, and bad posture. There are many books and tapes on how to avoid or deal with stress (see also p.183–p.184). One of the simplest ways to begin is to accept that you *are* stressed, and ask yourself why. Often you can learn to reorganize your life and say "stop" to the sources of the stress. Allocating time to yourself is vital.

Drinking plenty of plain water every day—at least 1.7 pints (1 liter) helps to flush toxins out of the system.

Sleep truly restores health and well-being. Most people need about eight hours' sleep a night.

SUPPLEMENTS

If you have a good diet, you do not need supplements. However, some vitamins and minerals have been particularly linked to health, youth, and beauty. Those thought to contribute to healthy skin are B-complex, A, C, and E vitamins, and the minerals zinc, magnesium, and selenium (see p.164). Make sure that your diet contains an adequate supply of all these nutrients. Many people find that fish oils and nut or seed oils help to improve the condition of their skin.

MASSAGE

Massage of the neck and shoulders, back, or whole body can do wonders for your psyche as well as your body. Aromatherapy massage is particularly therapeutic (see p.231).

RELAXATION

Learn to relax completely by taking relaxation classes or using a tape. Regular dancing, swimming, yoga, and walking in the country also help you to relax and therefore look better (see p.239).

BEAUTY TREATMENTS

Cleansing, toning, and moisturizing are generally agreed to be necessary morning and evening. Nourishing the skin can be done once a week, or when you feel it is needed. There really is no need to buy proprietary preparations, tempting though advertisements and packaging may be.

STEAMING YOUR FACE OVER A BOWL OF HOT CHAMOMILE INFUSION IS CLEANSING AND SOOTHING, AND PREPARES YOUR SKIN FOR THE NOURISHING TREATMENT. ELDERFLOWER OR FENNEL CAN ALSO BE USED

ALMOND OR OLIVE OIL, AND EVEN MILK ARE ALL GOOD CLEANSERS, AS WELL AS SIMPLE, UNPERFUMED SOAP

ROSEWATER OR SPRINGWATER WITH A FEW DROPS OF YOUR FAVORITE SKIN-FRIENDLY ESSENTIAL OIL ARE GOOD TONICS. WITCH HAZEL ADDS ASTRINGENCY FOR OILY SKINS

YOU CAN NOURISH YOUR FACE WITH INGREDIENTS FOUND IN THE KITCHEN, SUCH AS EGG YOLK OR HONEY

SMOKING

As well as being a major factor in many serious diseases, smoking has a detrimental effect on the quality of your skin. Research has shown that smoking is aging (see p.172). Each cigarette reduces the amount of oxygen in the bloodstream and depletes the body of vital nutrients, particularly the antioxidants vitamin C, E, and beta carotene. The body needs these nutrients to protect the skin against sun damage and free radicals, which accelerate the aging process.

AGING

Sunlight is damaging. Overexposure to strong sun is the quickest way to make yourself irreversibly older-looking.

- Do not expose your skin to the midday sun, and restrict the amount of time you spend in the sun at any hour.
- Apply a moisturizer with sunscreen whenever you are outside, and use a high-protection cream for sunbathing and outdoor activities (See also p.33).
- Antioxidants (vitamins C, E, and beta carotene) can help prevent skin damage

There's little need to spend vast sums of money on beauty treatments. The steam from a few drops of chamomile in hot water will cleanse your face, and rosewater makes a good toner.

BREAST PROBLEMS

Among women in their mid-30s to mid-50s, breast cancer is the most common cause of death. Although little is known about preventing breast cancer, a great deal has been learned about its detection and cure (see p.140–p.141). If picked up at an early stage, it can be treated successfully in the overwhelming majority of cases.

Every woman should examine her breasts once a month to make sure there are no unusual lumps, or any area where the tissue feels different. The best time to do this is immediately after a period. After menopause, women should continue to carry out checks every month.

It is vital to consult your physician at the first detection of any of these signs. In most cases there will be a benign explanation, but the sooner medical tests are done, the more likely it is that treatment can be given successfully and with the least possible impact.

Breast cancer is the most common cancer in women, affecting about 1 in every 14 women. Causes are uncertain, though they do include genetic and hormonal factors. With early detection, the vast majority of cases are treated successfully.

CHECKING YOUR BREASTS

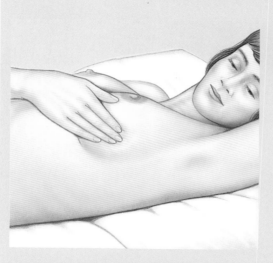

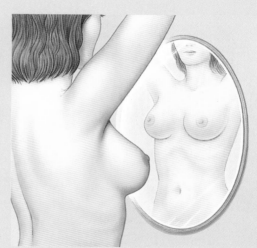

CHECK YOUR BREASTS WHILE LYING DOWN with a pillow under the shoulder blade of the side you are checking, check each breast with the opposite hand, keeping the arm raised on the same side as the breast. Feel with the flattened pads of your fingers in a circular motion starting furthest away from the nipples working your way in, in a clockwise or anticlockwise motion. Look for any lumps or swollen tissue. As you familiarize yourself with your breasts, you will be aware of any unusual changes.

LOWER ARM AND CHECK THE ARMPIT and when you have examined every area of the breast and nipple, lower your arm and check the armpit for any lump or swelling in the lymph glands.

WHILE SITTING OR STANDING examine yourself in the mirror, looking out for any changes.

THESE COULD BE

• one breast abnormally larger, or lower, than the other (however, varying breast sizes are fairly common and do not necessarily signify disease)
• change in the appearance or shape of either nipple
• any puckering or dimpling

MORE UNUSUAL SIGNS TO BE AWARE OF AT ANY TIME ARE

• discharge from the nipple
• a rash on the nipple

BREAST STRUCTURE AND FUNCTION

Until puberty, the breasts or mammary glands are the same in boys and girls. Hormones secreted by the ovaries then cause a girl's breasts to develop, as the ducts going back from the nipples branch out and fat is deposited. During pregnancy, hormones from the placenta cause milk-forming tissue to grow in the breasts and at the end of pregnancy milk is secreted.

MEDICAL SCREENING

Advice at present is that women should visit their doctor for a full gynecological checkup every three to five years. This may include mammography (breast X ray). Family planning clinics and some private medical insurance schemes, as well as your own doctor, can advise you on screening and having a mammogram. In the US, advice to women is to have a mammogram every two years from the age of 40 to 49, and annually when over the age of 50.

PREVENTION OF BREAST CANCER

At present the best advice is to watch your nutrition and alcohol intake, give up smoking and take plenty of exercise but remember that self-examination on a regular basis is far more crucial—very healthy, slim women get breast cancer.

SILICONE GEL IMPLANTS

There are reports suggesting a link between breast enhancement using silicone gel implants and autoimmune disorders, vascular disease, secondary cancers, or failure to diagnose cancer by mammogram of the enhanced breast, but to date there have not been any definitive studies undertaken.

THE PILL

Some research has suggested a link between the contraceptive pill and cancer, particularly with long-term use by women who started taking a high progestogen form of the Pill before the age of 25. These are artificial progesterone and should be avoided. Modern combined formulas use lower doses of progestogen and risks are thought to be negligible.

RISK FACTORS FOR BREAST CANCER

At present little is known about the cause of breast cancer. There is evidence that you are more at risk if:

ANY CLOSE RELATIVES HAVE HAD THE DISEASE

•

YOU ARE, AND HAVE CONTINUALLY BEEN, ABOVE NORMAL WEIGHT FOR YOUR HEIGHT

•

YOU HAD YOUR FIRST CHILD OVER THE AGE OF 30

•

YOU HAVE HAD NO PREGNANCIES

There is also evidence of links with:

SMOKING

•

DRINKING TOO MUCH ALCOHOL

•

A HIGH-FAT DIET

•

EARLY PUBERTY

•

LATE MENOPAUSE

•

EXPOSURE TO IONIZING RADIATION (X RAYS)

•

HORMONE REPLACEMENT THERAPY (HRT)

Breast cancer treatments include removal of the lump (lumpectomy), hormone or radiation therapy, and chemotherapy. Removal of the whole breast is rare. Counseling helps to overcome accompanying stress.

GYNECOLOGICAL PROBLEMS

Because some serious gynecological problems—diseases affecting the female reproductive system—have no symptoms in the early stages, routine checkups are vital. Always see your doctor if you have unusual symptoms such as pain, vaginal discharge, or nonmenstrual bleeding. Early treatment is the best way to a complete cure.

Various disorders can affect women during the course of their reproductive life, and the reproductive organs are particularly vulnerable. Exercise, safe sex, and regular health checks are positive preventive measures.

It is strongly advisable to have a regular annual gynecological checkup, including a smear test. Recommendations about how frequently you should have a test vary from once a year to every five years. This will depend partly on factors such as your age and the results of previous tests.

As well as a smear test, a checkup will include a pelvic examination, where the practitioner feels for any abnormal tissue that may indicate vaginal or cervical infections, or damage to the uterus. Your breasts may also be checked for any possible abnormality and your blood pressure may be taken.

CERVICAL CANCER AND UTERINE CANCER

Cervical cancer is a serious disease that causes many deaths. Although it takes up to 10 years to develop, it can be detected early on by a Pap smear test, before symptoms are apparent (see p.140–p.141). At this stage the cancer can be treated successfully. This is also the best way to prevent uterine cancer, which usually starts in the cervix.

PROLAPSE OF THE UTERUS (COLLAPSED UTERUS)

This condition affects many women to some degree, especially after giving birth. It causes dull pain in the lower back or abdomen, urine incontinence, and constipation. It is caused by muscular weakness, which leads to displacement of the uterus. Your doctor will recommend pelvic floor exercises to strengthen the muscles, and may prescribe an internal device (ring pessary) to give support. If the condition does not improve, you may be sent to a specialist, who may recommend surgery.

CERVICAL CANCER

This disease is most likely to affect women over the age of 35, and incidence increases with age. The following factors slightly increase the risk:

BEGINNING TO HAVE INTERCOURSE WHEN VERY YOUNG

•

SUFFERING FROM GENITAL HERPES OR WARTS

•

SMOKING, AND PASSIVE SMOKING

•

THE AMOUNT OF SEXUAL PARTNERS YOU HAVE HAD

PELVIC INFLAMMATORY DISEASE

This is an inflammation of the ovaries, fallopian tubes, or uterus. The many possible causes include reaction to an IUD, abscesses, infections such as chlamydia (caused by a microbial parasite) introduced via the vagina, and post-abortion or post-miscarriage infection. Symptoms may arise suddenly (acute) or can affect a woman in the long term (chronic). There may be abdominal and lower back pain, fatigue, vaginal discharge, or non-menstrual bleeding, and, in acute cases, a sudden fever. Always consult your doctor if you experience these symptoms. Failure to treat them can lead to irreversible damage that will cause infertility. Immediate treatment may be necessary, especially in acute cases. Initially the doctor will probably prescribe antibiotics and painkillers, but in some cases surgery may be required.

TOXIC SHOCK SYNDROME

This is a very rare form of blood poisoning, which can flare up quickly and violently as a reaction to using an internal tampon. The main symptom is sudden fever with a very high temperature. To prevent it, make sure that you change your tampon regularly (every four to six hours), and preferably use sanitary towels overnight.

FIBROIDS

Fibroids are benign uterine growths, which can vary a great deal in number and size. If the fibroids do not cause problems, your doctor may recommend no treatment. Large fibroids can press on the bladder, or cause discomfort during intercourse. Some fibroids cause heavy or prolonged periods. If necessary, fibroids can be removed surgically.

ENDOMETRIOSIS

This is a condition in which fragments of the lining of the uterus become attached to tissue in the ovaries, fallopian tubes, or elsewhere, causing fibrous cysts to develop. Symptoms are similar to those for fibroids. Hormone treatment or, occasionally, surgery may prove necessary.

VAGINITIS

Vaginitis is a sore, inflamed vagina, usually caused by a microbial or bacterial infection. Eating plenty of vitamin C (see p.162–p.163) and live yogurt (up to three pots a day) can prevent and control many infections. If the irritation is caused by vaginal dryness, use a lubricant for sexual intercourse. Avoid scented bath products; add a few drops of a cleansing and disinfecting essential oil such as tea tree to the bathwater. In some cases, temporary abstention from intercourse may speed recovery.

WARNING

Genital infections and pelvic inflammatory disease can lead to infertility if not treated.

COMPLEMENTARY THERAPIES

There are some complementary therapies that may help when coping with serious diseases such as cancer, while medical treatment is being received.

NUTRITION Strengthen the immune system by making sure that your diet is high in vitamin C. Garlic is particularly powerful.

VISUALIZATION and relaxation techniques can help to deal with the stress and fear that are inevitable while undergoing treatment for the disease (see p.239).

COUNSELING Talking to a trained counselor can help you to come to terms with your feelings and feel better able to cope (see p.243).

CYSTITIS

*C*ystitis is inflammation of the lining of the bladder, usually caused by infection. It is very rarely indicative of a serious problem, and luckily there is much that can be done to prevent and treat attacks of this annoying complaint.

Drink plenty of plain water (about 1.7 pints/1 liter a day) at all times: this is vital to flush out the toxins and keep the bladder infection-free. Avoid drinking coffee, alcoholic drinks, and strong tea, which all stimulate the bladder. If you take them, drink extra water to compensate.

HOME REMEDIES

STRICT HYGIENE IS IMPORTANT Always clean the area from front to back and use mild, unscented soap. Try urinating immediately after sexual intercourse if sex seems to trigger your cystitis.

A COURSE OF ANTIBIOTICS TENDS TO LOWER IMMUNITY TO INFECTION This can be remedied by taking vitamin C supplements or (preferably) by increasing vitamin C in the diet (see p. 162–p.163).

THE CONTRACEPTIVE PILL has been linked to the condition through a connection with yeast intolerance. Eating live yogurt every day, and applying it externally, can solve this problem.

DRINK CRANBERRY JUICE WHENEVER YOU FEEL THIRSTY, make it with warm water.

DURING AN ATTACK, drink up to 3½ pints (two liters) of plain water a day to flush the bladder.

Cystitis is miserable. Despite discomfort when urinating, drinking plenty of water will flush out the bladder and relieve the symptoms quickly.

SYMPTOMS OF CYSTITIS

Although cystitis can affect men, it occurs more frequently in women. This is thought to be partly because a woman's anatomy makes it easier for bacteria and microbes to reach the urethra. Culprits include the bacterium *E. coli*, which is present in the feces, and *Candida* infections affecting the vagina or anus. Local irritation caused by tight clothing, synthetic underwear, scented products, and vigorous sexual intercourse, may also be to blame. A frequent urge to pass urine, and the resulting sharp pain experienced while doing so, characterize the condition. In some cases there may be blood in the urine. Accompanying low backache, abdominal pain, and general lethargy are very debilitating.

WARNING

Bladder infections can sometimes pass to the kidneys. Severe or frequent cystitis demands medical attention, especially if there is abdominal pain or blood in the urine.

COMPLEMENTARY THERAPIES

ACUPUNCTURE

Cystitis may be linked to chills or debility, or to no obvious causes. Acupuncture (see p.230) can tone the body and restore internal balance.

HOMEOPATHY

There are several remedies that may be effective for cystitis. It is best to consult a qualified homeopath to find the best remedy for you (see p.226).

HERBAL MEDICINE

Tea made from marsh mallow root (anti-inflammatory, soothing) or horsetail (astringent, cleansing) are recommended.

YEAST INFECTIONS

Yeast infections can be difficult to shake off, and is often a sign that diet or way of life needs to be adjusted. In its more invasive form, the yeast parasite Candida albicans infests the gut (see p.123) and a condition known as candidiasis occurs.

Yeast infection (thrush) can occur inside the mouth, on the penis, and—especially in babies—around the anus. A vaginal yeast infection causes a thick white or yellow discharge and an intense itching or burning sensation.

Like cystitis, yeast infections are often linked to taking antibiotics or the contraceptive Pill, and to being generally slightly under the weather. Often the two infections go together.

REMEDIES

Because this is a fungal infection (*Candida albicans*), a doctor may prescribe an antifungal cream. Many home remedies can be extremely effective, and measures can be taken to prevent attacks.

DIET

Diet should be considered as the first line of prevention and cure. Avoid eating sweet, starchy foods, which encourage the organisms that cause yeast infections. Live yogurt promotes a healthy intestinal flora, which discourages *Candida*, and garlic and olive oil attack it. Mushrooms, bread, and yeast products should be avoided during an attack. Eat at least two small pots of live yogurt a day, and as much fresh fruit and vegetables and whole grains (preferably organically grown) as you can. Drink only pure water for a while, and lots of it.

HOME REMEDIES

- Applying live yogurt to the vagina is soothing, and will combat the *Candida* (immerse a tampon in plain live yogurt and insert it into the vagina).
- Wear loose-fitting cotton clothes so that air can circulate and so avoid the warm, damp conditions that encourage *Candida* growth.
- Do not use scented bath oils or soaps, and never use vaginal deodorants.

Garlic and olive oil attack *Candida*; live yogurt encourages healthy bacteria. Yogurt can also be applied internally.

COMPLEMENTARY THERAPIES

HERBAL MEDICINE

Dilute echinacea or marigold tinctures to bathe the area. Marigold (*Calendula officinalis*) has antifungal properties. *Echinacea angustifolia* helps the body to fight infection by building up the immune system.

Echinacea

HOMEOPATHY AND ACUPUNCTURE

A homeopath may prescribe one of several remedies, depending on the patient's overall picture. An acupuncturist will look at the symptoms in a holistic way, giving treatment to rebalance the whole body (see p.226 and p.230).

AROMATHERAPY

Tea tree oil is an excellent antifungal agent. Mix 20 drops of the oil with 3fl.oz (100ml) warm distilled water. Soak a tampon in the blend and insert it. Change it at least once every 6–8 hours.
Add 10 drops of geranium oil to your bathwater and soak for about ten minutes daily.

Aromatherapy bath

PMS

Premenstrual syndrome (PMS) or tension (PMT) are terms for the various physical and emotional changes that many women experience before menstruation. This is now seen as a medical issue, rather than just mood swings.

Energetic exercise or sport can help to counteract the mood swings and tensions associated with the premenstrual period.

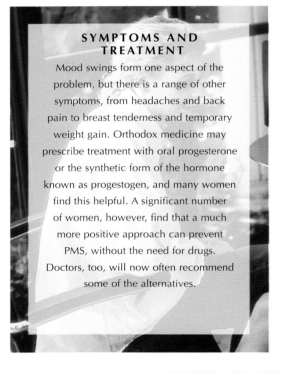

SYMPTOMS AND TREATMENT

Mood swings form one aspect of the problem, but there is a range of other symptoms, from headaches and back pain to breast tenderness and temporary weight gain. Orthodox medicine may prescribe treatment with oral progesterone or the synthetic form of the hormone known as progestogen, and many women find this helpful. A significant number of women, however, find that a much more positive approach can prevent PMS, without the need for drugs. Doctors, too, will now often recommend some of the alternatives.

Knowing your own cycle is the first step to prevention. This enables you to prepare for mood swings that may make you overre-act to certain situations. It also means that you can adapt your diet and daily activities to prevent problems such as edema (fluid retention) and headaches.

Follow a low-salt, low-sugar diet with the accent on wholefoods, and don't drink coffee or alcohol, especially in the week before a period is due. Cravings for chocolate and sweets usually disappears if you eat whole-wheat pasta, shellfish, whole-wheat bread, nuts, and peas.

Rest, relaxation, and adequate sleep in the days leading up to a period are also valuable. Exercise daily. Swimming is particularly good; as it relaxes and tones the whole system. Take steps to avoid stress before a period. Warn your partner not to take your mood swings and intolerance personally!

COMPLEMENTARY THERAPIES

Fluid retention is one of the more uncomfortable symptoms of premenstrual syndrome. Various herbal remedies, including dandelion tea (a diuretic) have beneficial effects.

HERBAL MEDICINE

There are several herbal remedies that can be tried. Balm relaxes tension. Valerian calms irritability. Chamomile is antispasmodic, and treats painful symptoms. Couch grass or dandelion tea, taken up to 5 times daily in the days before a period, relieves fluid retention.

SUPPLEMENTS

Mineral and vitamin supplements have been found to help. GLA (a form of linolenic acid found in evening primrose oil) has been extensively researched. Many women report great improvement after taking regular supplements of evening primrose oil (from 250mg to 2,000mg a day). Alternatively, try vitamin B_6 (100mg daily), 3% natural progesterone cream (¼ teaspoon daily), and magnesium (up to 500mg daily). Take for the 10 days preceding a period.

OTHER SOLUTIONS

The Alexander Technique, osteopathy, and acupuncture can all help to restore balance in the body, and assist well-being (see p.230, 233, 234).

MENSTRUATION

Few women go through life without experiencing menstrual problems at some time, but generally these are not serious. Through getting to know your body and its needs, you can ensure that menstruation is no more than a minor inconvenience.

Periods seldom maintain a regular 28-day cycle throughout a woman's reproductive life. Many factors can affect their occurrence. However, if your periods are irregular, scant, and interrupted, or heavy and painful, you should see your doctor. Occasionally, these symptoms indicate that something is amiss.

Emotional factors, weight change, and unrelated illness may affect the regularity of periods, and if so these need to be dealt with. Absence of periods could mean that you are pregnant.

PAINFUL PERIODS

Period pain is usually associated with heavy periods. A hot-water bottle placed over the abdomen is an old remedy for relieving the pain. Yarrow, shepherd's purse, and lady's mantle infusions can reduce the severity of both heavy periods and pain, especially if you take them for a few days before your period is due. Difficult though it is to force yourself, exercise helps enormously. Cycling, swimming, and brisk walking are all beneficial.

THE MENSTRUAL CYCLE

From the time of the first period (menarche) until the menopause, a woman has a short period of fertility once every 28 days or so, when one of the two ovaries releases a ripened egg (ovum) into the fallopian tubes that lead into the womb (uterus). If this egg is not fertilized, the uterus sheds the lining it has been preparing and the woman has a period. One theory is that this bleeding acts as a way of cleansing the uterus. This cycle is governed by the release of the hormones estrogen and progesterone.

Exercise and evening primrose oil can help to alleviate cramping and other painful menstrual symptoms.

About once a month, an ovary releases an egg into the fallopian tubes. If it is not fertilized by a sperm, the egg and uterine lining pass out of the body as menstrual flow.

Regular exercise throughout your cycle often helps to prevent symptoms altogether. (See also p.155.)

Avoiding tea, coffee, and alcohol, and going to bed early during the week before your period is due, can help prevent PMS. It will also increase the likelihood of the period passing more smoothly.

COMPLEMENTARY THERAPIES

NUTRITION

Heavy menstrual bleeding may leave you needing iron supplements. See p.163 for good dietary sources of iron.

SUPPLEMENTS

Evening primrose oil may be effective in regulating periods, as well as helping to make them pain-free.

HERBAL MEDICINE

Chamomile tea, a natural analgesic, soothes pain.

MASSAGE

A regular massage with melissa or lavender oil (diluted in a carrier oil) can help to regulate scant, infrequent periods.

ACUPRESSURE

The Liver 2 point is found between the first and second toe, on the edge of the web of skin. In Traditional Chinese Medicine, the liver controls the blood. Stimulating the liver channel can help relieve period pain, bloating, and headaches.

Iron supplements

SEX PROBLEMS

*M*any people feel that too much emphasis is placed on sex in our society. From being a taboo subject, it has become something we are all supposed to talk about freely and enjoy regularly. The positive side of this change in attitudes is that women no longer need to suffer in silence if they have sexual problems. There is plenty of help available. The down side is that we may imagine everyone else has a thrilling sex life and that we are abnormal if we do not.

If you and your partner are both happy with the frequency (or infrequency) and nature of your sexual activity, there is no problem. If you feel there is something missing from your sex life, there are plenty of self-help books which can help. If you have a serious physical or psychological problem, your doctor will be able to investigate possible physical causes, and refer you to a suitable counselor or specialist if necessary. If you want to talk over any problems in your relationship with a sympathetic and constructive person, make an appointment with an appropriate counseling or advisory organization.

LOSS OF DESIRE

Keeping your sexual relationship alive, once you have fallen into the inevitable daily routine of living together, is a challenge. Yet a happy sexual relationship can nourish all the aspects of your life as a couple, and a poor one can spill over into it in a damaging way.

Make sure that you and your partner still have time alone together. Meals out and weekends or nights away (while someone looks after the children, if you are parents) give you a chance to enjoy each other's company in the same way as you did when you first met. When at home, create situations in which you feel relaxed and sensual. Good food, candles, a real fire, and a warm bedroom help to set the scene. Above all, be prepared to talk, laugh, and relax.

Maintaining a sexual relationship means making time for each other. An intimate evening with good food, wine, and candlelight can help to create an atmosphere conducive to lovemaking.

Loss of libido, or sexual desire, is often caused by an inability to switch off from daily problems, particularly work-related stress. Once you are wound up by a stressful day at work it can take time to settle down in the evening. Relaxing in bed with your partner, talking to each other, and setting aside time for lovemaking, can help.

BEATING STRESS

Fatigue, stress, and poor vitality can contribute to sexual difficulties. Take a look at the way you live and make sure that you have good nutrition, adequate rest, sleep, exercise, and fresh air, and time for hobbies and interests.

Exercise is said to increase sexual desire. Many couples discover that exercising together brings them closer.

HOW TO BEAT STRESS

- Cut down your intake of alcohol.
- Eat at least five good portions of fresh fruit and vegetables a day.
- Exercise regularly. This increases the body's production of serotonin and endorphins, substances that bring about a so-called "feel-good" effect. Daily walking, cycling, swimming, or running are all beneficial.
- Have a weekly body toning session together at the gym, or take lessons in yoga or t'ai chi, which have a calming effect mentally as well as physically.
- Practice relaxation, either by joining a class, or by using one of the many books or tapes available.
- Try taking a three-month course of ginseng, which both tones and relaxes the whole system.
- Eat plenty of oats, which in folk medicine have a high reputation as a strengthening food, and are good for anyone who is feeling "run down."

COMPLEMENTARY TREATMENTS

AROMATHERAPY

Use a few drops of sandalwood, or other reputedly aphrodisiac oils such as ylang ylang, rose, jasmine, clary sage, black pepper, cinnamon, and ginger (up to three together) mixed with a carrier oil for a slow, relaxing massage. Massaging your partner restores physical intimacy in a non-pressurizing way and can lead to renewed desire. Sandalwood, in a burner, is a delightful room fragrancer.

ACUPUNCTURE

Acupuncture may assist in restoring balance, harmony, and vitality to your life, and resolve any underlying problems that may be contributing to sexual tensions. Homeopathy may be useful for the same reason.

Oil burner

HYPNOTHERAPY

A qualified hypnotherapist may be able to treat sexual problems that involve anxiety (see p.238).

NATURAL PROGESTERONE

3% natural progesterone cream (¼ teaspoon daily) is considered beneficial.

NUTRITION

A nutritionist can give detailed advice on improving vitality through diet, and may recommend taking zinc supplements. Zinc is beneficial for the reproductive system.

Zinc supplement

CONTRACEPTION

*I*deally, both partners should take responsibility for birth
control. Unfortunately, many of today's effective
methods still rely on the woman taking responsibility
for contraception, such as oral contraceptives, hormone
implants, IUDs, the cap, and the female condom.

Your doctor or family planning clinic will advise
you on contraception. For most women, birth control needs to be effective, simple to use, free from
side effects and reversible. And of course it must
not detract from lovemaking.

WHAT IS THE PILL?

Oral contraceptives contain minute, carefully balanced quantities of hormones that trick the pituitary gland into behaving as though the woman is
already pregnant, and this prevents the ovaries
from ripening more eggs each month.

Early forms of the Pill were implicated in a variety of diseases and unwanted side effects including
breast and uterine cancer, thrombosis,
headaches, and bloating. Modern "low
dose" forms have lower risks, and may
even offer protection against some forms
of cancer. There is a slightly greater risk
of a clot in the veins (thrombosis),
which is potentially life-threatening
(see p.22). The Pill has fewer than six
failures per 100 women per year.
Nevertheless, many women feel unhappy
about taking a synthetic drug, and there is much
evidence of minor but irritating side effects
such as greater susceptibility to *Candida* infections.

BARRIER METHODS

The male condom or sheath, female condom, and
cap have gained in popularity since the
1980s amid concerns about HIV. The
condom *must* be used as a protective measure against sexually
transmitted diseases.

Condoms or sheaths
have no side effects
and offer protection
against sexually
transmitted diseases,
such as AIDS.
The contraceptive
pill is virtually
100% effective.

Fear of pregnancy
can damage
lovemaking:
effective
contraception is
essential. The type
of contraception to
choose depends on
what suits you best.

Condoms

Contraceptive pills

HORMONE IMPLANT

In the 1980s, an implant was developed to go under
the skin and deliver measured doses of synthetic
progesterone. For a while this was taken up as an
alternative to the Pill: there was no need to remember to take it, and its success rate was almost 100%.
But problems have developed with the use of these
devices, not least occasional difficulty in removing
the implant, and it is now less popular.

INTRAUTERINE DEVICES

IUDs (small metal or plastic loops, or T-shaped
devices inserted into the uterus) prevent the
implantation of a fertilized ovum. The disadvantage
is that this can be seen as a form of abortion. IUDs
have the same success rate as the Pill, but were
found to be associated with serious side effects such
as pelvic inflammatory disease and are now not
widely used. However, research into safe forms of
IUD is being carried out.

NATURAL BIRTH CONTROL

Women who have regular periods are increasingly
using natural methods, especially if they can
accept the slightly higher risk of contraceptive
failure. These methods are based on avoiding
intercourse around the time of ovulation—the
fertile period—each month. The chief natural
method is known as the "rhythm method," "safe
period," or "calendar method," and involves
recording your menstrual cycle, so that you can
calculate when you will be fertile (roughly 11–16
days before each period). Others include taking
your temperature, which peaks slightly at ovulation,
and noting the changes in the mucus produced by
the cervix. These methods can be combined.

FERTILITY

The period in which you are fertile (and therefore able to conceive) is a day or two each side of the fourteenth day of your cycle, counting the first day of your period as the first day of the cycle. This is the optimum time for making love, if you are hoping to conceive.

If you do not become pregnant, despite making love in your fertile phase, there are many steps you can take. Diet and relaxation are important for both partners. Anxiety is often a cause of infertility. You should both stop smoking and keep your alcohol consumption down. (Two glasses of wine or one pint of beer or lager for a woman, and three pints of beer or lager for a man, should be the daily *maximums* at any time. When you are attempting to conceive, restricting your intake to this amount *per week* is recommended). Discourage your partner from wearing tight jeans and underwear, which overheat the scrotum and affect the production of healthy sperm.

See also Gynecological problems, p.60–p.61.

COMPLEMENTARY THERAPIES

HERBAL MEDICINE

A qualified herbalist may be able to suggest a number of remedies to balance the system and improve fertility (see p.224).

ACUPUNCTURE

This focuses on the kidney and liver areas, which are linked to hormones and menstrual cycle.

SUPPLEMENTS

There is much evidence that nutritional therapy works. Vitamins A, B$_{12}$ and E may be helpful for your partner, and you may need extra vitamin B$_{12}$, zinc, magnesium, and vitamin C. It is best to consult a qualified nutritionist for advice about your diet and possible supplements.

Some nutritionists think that infertility is caused by mineral and vitamin imbalances in the diet. Foods rich in vitamins B$_{12}$, E, and A are recommended.

Confirmation of a wanted pregnancy is a joyful experience, particularly for those couples who may have had to wait for many years to achieve conception.

TACKLING INFERTILITY

If you have been trying to conceive for a while, your doctor can arrange for you and your partner to have a range of tests to check whether there is anything organically wrong. Depending on the results of the tests, there are many forms of treatment available.

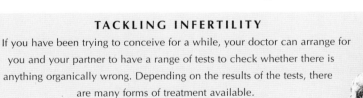

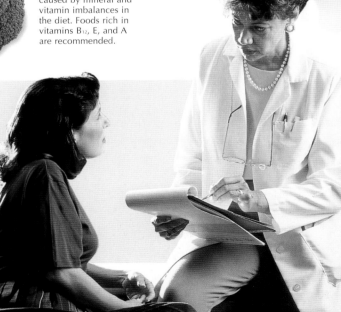

A variety of factors can cause infertility, including hormonal problems, stress, and physical or genetic factors.

PREGNANCY

During the nine months of pregnancy the body undergoes amazing changes while providing for the developing child. There may be some unwanted side effects, but apart from these the mother-to-be really does bloom.

MEDICAL CARE

Once you know that you are pregnant—and home pregnancy testing kits are reliable—see your physician who will arrange regular checkups. These will normally be once a month for the first seven months, once every two weeks in the eighth month, and once a week in the final month.

At each examination your abdomen will be felt and your blood pressure taken. Blood and urine tests will be taken to detect complications such as anemia, kidney infection, and diabetes so they can be treated.

A scan (ultrasound test) will monitor the development of the baby around the 14th and 32nd weeks of the pregnancy. In the US an ultrasound scan may be recommended in certain cases but it is not routine procedure. Older women may be advised to have an amniocentesis, which detects Down's syndrome.

You will have a chance to discuss options for the birth and to make your own "birth plan."

POSSIBLE SIDE EFFECTS

The list of side effects may be dispiriting, but most of these problems can be dealt with easily.

FATIGUE
•
MORNING SICKNESS
•
CONSTIPATION
•
SLIGHT INCONTINENCE

SUSCEPTIBILITY TO YEAST INFECTIONS
•
BACKACHE
•
TOOTH AND GUM PROBLEMS
•
VARICOSE VEINS

Despite the side effects of early pregnancy, many expectant mothers can look forward to a period when they blossom and glow with health.

Sipping ginger tea or nibbling ginger cookies will help counteract morning sickness.

SELF-HELP PREVENTION OF SIDE EFFECTS

TO PREVENT NAUSEA try eating little and often. Avoid rich, fatty, and spicy foods, and drink plain water. If you have morning sickness, nibble a dry biscuit and sip a weak herbal tea before getting out of bed. Ginger is a great preventive and cure for nausea.

TO PREVENT CONSTIPATION make sure your diet provides plenty of fiber, and drink plenty of plain water. Get some form of exercise each day.

TO AVOID INCONTINENCE, spread out your fluid intake over the day. Don't drink diuretics such as tea, coffee, and alcohol.

PROBLEMS WITH TEETH stem from your increased need for calcium. Many physicians prescribe calcium supplements, and you can help yourself by drinking plenty of milk and eating dark green leafy vegetables.

TO PREVENT YEAST INFECTIONS, try plain live yogurt, in the diet and applied to the vulva.

VARICOSE VEINS SHOULD BE PREVENTED by your healthy diet and exercise regime. Wearing support pantyhose is sensible if you are susceptible to varicose veins.

REST AND STRETCHING EXERCISES will help prevent backache. You should also watch your posture.

PREPARING FOR THE BIRTH

Have an exercise plan for your pregnancy, and stick to it. You need to get at least 20–30 minutes exercise every day. Walking and swimming are particularly good forms of exercise, and tone the body in preparation. Women who cycle generally enjoy doing so until a very late stage in pregnancy.

Prenatal classes will prepare you for the birth itself, teaching you to relax and use your abdominal and pelvic floor muscles, and are a good way to meet other women going through the same experience. Many people find yoga helpful (see p. 244). Relaxation classes, whether or not specifically designed for pregnant women, give mental as well as physical calm. If you want to continue with yoga, other exercise classes, or sports that you normally enjoy there is generally no reason why you should not do so but consult your physician and let your instructor know that you are pregnant.

A regular exercise plan is beneficial for expectant mothers—walking, swimming , and even cycling can be enjoyed even during the latter stages of pregnancy.

COMPLEMENTARY THERAPIES

HERBAL MEDICINE

During pregnancy it's unwise to take any medication, even herbal, without medical advice. Gentle herbal infusions of chamomile or peppermint can still be drunk as teas and are safe and pleasant for everyday use. For the final stage of pregnancy only, raspberry leaf tea is widely recommended as a uterine tonic and has been used to ease labor. Take two to three cups daily during the last month.

MASSAGE

If you enjoy using essential oils, dilute them to half the usual strength. Consult one of the many aromatherapy books for advice on which oils you can safely use. Beneficial oils for use in massage include chamomile, clary sage, jasmine, and rose. Professional massage or aromatherapy massage can be valuable during pregnancy, provided the masseur knows that you are pregnant and is qualified to treat pregnant women (see p.231).

Yoga is an ideal form of exercise, particularly for the latter stages of pregnancy, as it promotes mental calm as well as keeping the body supple.

ACUPRESSURE

Found just two finger-widths above the crease of the wrist, the powerful point known to the Chinese physicians as Neiguan or Pericardium 6 (P6) is helpful in the relief of morning sickness.The point can be stimulated easily by finger pressure that is applied with increasing force as the waves of nausea and sickness rise. The same point can be used for symptoms such as irritability, vomiting, and palpitations that may also be experienced by those in early pregnancy.

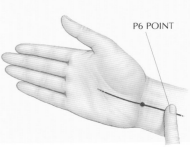

P6 POINT

MOTHERHOOD

E *ating, resting and exercising sensibly during pregnancy not only help to*
ensure that you feel well before the baby is born, but will also help you face
the demands of looking after a newborn baby. Following these guidelines
will prepare you for the demanding time you will face after the baby is born.

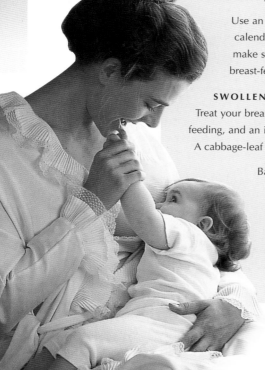

The birth of a first child can be overwhelming for a new mother. It is a source of immense pleasure, but can also be emotionally and physically draining.

Breast milk increases on demand: the more the baby feeds, the more milk you will have. When feeding, make sure you and the baby are comfortable, and that the baby feeds for as long as he or she needs.

Every mother will tell you that birth is a shattering experience, involving great emotional and physical upheaval. Afterward it is necessary to adjust to all the changes involved in looking after the new baby, including nights of broken sleep.

BREAST-FEEDING

Many mothers prefer to breast-feed their babies if they possibly can, rather than bottle-feeding. This provides the best nourishment, as substances in the milk protect against a wide range of infections and diseases. Breast-fed babies are less likely to suffer from gastroenteritis and allergies, and there is also evidence that they develop better after weaning. Breast-feeding can be a fulfilling and relaxing experience, which encourages bonding between mother and child, and makes the baby happy and relaxed too. Unfortunately, some women cannot breast-feed for all sorts of reasons. If your baby is allergic to cow's milk try goat or soy milk instead, and check the labels of formula milks for nutrient content.

PROBLEMS OF BREAST-FEEDING
Here are some simple ways to remedy common problems.

SORE NIPPLES
Learn to relax. Make yourself comfortable while feeding your baby, in quiet, stress-free surroundings

Let your nipples dry in the air after feeding

Use an herbal ointment such as calendula, comfrey, or chamomile but make sure the nipples are clean before breast-feeding

SWOLLEN BREASTS (ENGORGEMENT)
Treat your breasts with a warm compress before feeding, and an ice-cold compress after feeding. A cabbage-leaf poultice is a soothing folk remedy

Bathe the breasts in warm water containing a few drops of rose or rose geranium essential oil

UNHAPPY BABY
Caffeine can make the baby restless, so drink as little tea and coffee as possible. Alcohol can have the same effect and can also give the baby colic

Try different feeding positions until you find one that seems to suit your baby the best

INSUFFICIENT MILK
Make sure that you have a nutritious diet, and in particular drink plenty of fluids

Milk supply increases on demand, so make sure that the baby is in a comfortable position and can suck properly

There are many folk remedies. Drinking herbal teas made from aniseed, borage, caraway seed, fennel, and milkwort all help to ensure a good supply of milk. A medical herbalist can give recommendations

ACCEPTING HELP

Despite all the pleasures and happiness your baby will undoubtedly bring, you are bound to find that coping with a new baby is also a demanding experience. If this is your first child, you will be finding your feet. Take all the advice you can get— from your doctor, health visitor, mother, friends, relations —but more than anything, trust your own instincts.

All the evidence shows that baby and mother alike flourish when they have close physical contact. You can't cuddle your baby too much. Look at her, smile at her, and talk to her as often as you can. But at the same time, don't forget that you need time and space to yourself, and the baby can form relationships with other people, such as her father, brothers, and sisters, and grandparents, at a very early stage. Encouraging the other people in the baby's life to share in looking after her will help them to feel involved in caring for the new, helpless but rapidly developing person, and allow a loving relationship to grow. It will make for a happy baby and a confident child, and enable you to take much needed time for yourself.

Motherhood should be fun. Taking time to play with your baby gives you pleasure and helps the baby's development and well-being.

Older children may be jealous of the new arrival. Give them plenty of attention, both before and after the birth.

GUIDELINES TO KEEP YOU SANE

Becoming a mother is both a pleasure and a traumatic experience. Here are some tried and tested guidelines to help keep you sane.

BE TOGETHER Plan evenings out together with your partner; be nice to each other; support each other; look after each other.

BE ORGANIZED Work out a baby duties rota for you and your partner.

HAVE A LIFE Spend time not talking about the baby. Keep up your outside leisure interests.

CHANGE YOUR LIFE Change your needs to be in line with the baby's. Sleep when the baby sleeps.

NOTHING LASTS Whatever stress and tension you are going through, remember that the sleepless nights are only temporary.

TALK ABOUT IT Becoming a mother generates a lot of feelings. You need to talk about and express them.

SUPPORT Don't be afraid to ask for whatever support is needed or available.

BE AWARE Your children's needs change as they grow older—keep up to date on current theories and advice.

73

MISCARRIAGE

*I**t is important not to be so afraid of miscarrying that you mollycoddle yourself during
your pregnancy, but at the same time it makes sense to be aware of the dangers.
It is thought that about 15% of all pregnancies miscarry, but in most cases this is
because of congenital abnormalities.*

The most frequent cause of miscarriage is an
abnormality of the fetus. Alternatively, there may
be a fault in the placenta, which nourishes the fetus
in the uterus. In many cases, a miscarriage prevents
a malformed baby from developing. It is believed
that in many cases, what is simply assumed to be a
late period is actually a very early miscarriage.
Miscarriage is most likely to take place up to the
thirteenth week of pregnancy, and up to one in
seven pregnancies ends in this way. The most likely
time for a miscarriage is the time when a period
would have occurred.

Having a miscarriage is bound to be a sad or even
traumatic event, involving grief and feelings of loss.
The emotional support of partner, family, and
friends is vital in helping the mother adjust to her
experience. But it is important for the mother to
remember that her partner will also be feeling a
sense of loss and sadness, which he may find hard to
express. She must be prepared to share her grief
with him (see p.213).

THE RISK OF FURTHER MISCARRIAGES

About eight out of ten women who have had a miscarriage go on to have a completely normal second
pregnancy. A doctor will only consider it necessary
for tests if a woman has had a second miscarriage.
Hormonal difficulties or uterine problems may be
to blame, and these can be remedied.

PREVENTING MISCARRIAGE

Six months before you start trying to conceive,
begin to prepare your body. Eat a sensible diet and
take plenty of exercise to improve your breathing
and circulation. Do not smoke, and reduce alcohol
and caffeine intake to a minimum.

When you have conceived, there are further
measures to take. Continue to take regular, gentle
exercise during your pregnancy. Avoid taking medication. Ensure that you get adequate rest, especially around the time a period would have been
due. Calcium, zinc, vitamin D, and folic acid
(400mcg a day, starting six months before conception and continued into early pregnancy) are linked
to the development of a healthy baby. Check with
your doctor before taking supplements.

Miscarriage, the
loss of an infant
during pregnancy,
is devastating and
both parents need
to grieve. The
mother in particular
needs support and
understanding from
her partner.

SIGNS OF THREATENED MISCARRIAGE

The main sign of a threatened miscarriage
is loss of blood. There may also be pain.
If you have vaginal bleeding, you should
rest and tell your doctor. If the bleeding is
heavy, call an ambulance and lie down
while you wait for it.

MATERNAL CAUSES OF MISCARRIAGE

SMOKING

•

ACCIDENTS (SUCH AS
HEAVY FALLS OR
ROAD ACCIDENTS)

•

ACUTE ILLNESS OR
GENERAL ILL-HEALTH

•

SHOCK

•

VITAMIN DEFICIENCY

POSTPARTUM DEPRESSION

Your hormones are in a state of flux, you have a disturbed sleep pattern, you have just been through a draining experience physically and emotionally, and you may have other children and a partner all expecting to be at the center of your world. You've been building up to this for months and now you may feel let down, unable to cope, or just plain exhausted. No wonder you sometimes want to sit down and cry. Doing this may help, but you also need to pick yourself up. Postpartum depression is a medically recognized condition, so talk to your health-care advisor if you experience it.

Good tonic herbs for the first weeks after the birth include angelica and cloves, or cinnamon with ginger. Raspberry leaf tea is a useful uterine tonic, which also encourages milk supply.

DIET

If you are breast-feeding, you need at least 500 extra calories a day. Make sure that you eat plenty of cereals and legumes, nuts, fruit (particularly bananas), and vegetables and salads, especially watercress, chicory, and dandelion leaves.

EXERCISE

Postpartum exercises will help you get back into shape, prevent prolapse, and tone the muscles that have been under great strain during pregnancy. The exercises will give you a valuable daily break and regaining your pre-pregnancy shape and suppleness will make you feel better in yourself.

A healthy diet and regular meals will build up your stamina and help you to cope with the exhaustion that can contribute to postpartum depression.

CONVENTIONAL TREATMENTS

Antidepressant treatments may be indicated in protracted cases.

COMPLEMENTARY THERAPIES

HERBAL MEDICINE

St. John's wort extract is one of nature's most effective antidepressants. It comes from the herb *Hypericum perforatum*. A daily dose of 300mg taken three times a day, has been shown to be the most effective in recent clinical studies.

HOMEOPATHY

If your depression fits into one of the classes listed below, use the associated remedy. Depression alternating with bad temper: Nux vomica. Tendency to weeping episodes, and seeking solitude: Natrum mur. Easily upset and resentful: Staphysagria. Under a deep black cloud: Aurum met. Feeling like you just don't care: Sulfur.

AROMATHERAPY

Certain essential oils work in a similar way to antidepressant drugs, providing an uplifting effect. Have a massage, using one or a combination of the following oils: melissa, orange, lavender, ylang-ylang, geranium, lemon, tangerine, and neroli.

NUTRITIONAL THERAPY

Take a good multiple supplement containing the B-group vitamins and trace elements such as zinc and selenium. Avoid drinking too much tea or coffee and eating sugary foods.

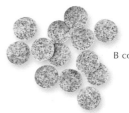

B complex vitamins

MENOPAUSE

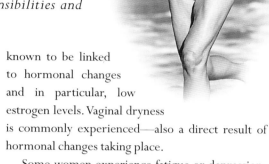

*M*edically, the term "menopause" refers to a woman's final period, but the expression also refers to what is commonly known as "the change." Menopause is a time of readjustment, and it can be a very positive time, when a woman launches herself into an active period of her life, free from many of the responsibilities and problems of earlier days.

Many women feel a fresh surge of energy around the time of menopause and take up a new exercise, such as jogging.

During the menopause, the ovaries stop producing eggs, estrogen levels decrease, and menstruation gradually ceases.

The age at which periods cease, and the length of time this takes, varies a great deal from person to person. The usual age is from 50 to 55, but it may be earlier or even later. Some women experience almost no menopausal symptoms and have their last period quite suddenly, while others are aware of symptoms for several years, and may continue to have infrequent periods for a long time. In the US, it is common to take estrogen with a lower dose of progesterone daily during this time (HRT).

Almost everyone experiences a change in menstruation. Periods become irregular, and may sometimes be more frequent, scanty, or heavier than usual.

Annoying symptoms of menopause, which many women experience, include hot flashes and night sweats, known to be linked to hormonal changes and in particular, low estrogen levels. Vaginal dryness is commonly experienced—also a direct result of hormonal changes taking place.

Some women experience fatigue or depression, acutely dry skin, itching eyes, weight gain, and other symptoms: their causes are not yet understood.

WARNING

If you experience unusually painful or heavy periods, you should consult your doctor.

EAT YOURSELF WELL

Your diet can play a vital role in getting you through the menopause and keeping you healthy afterward. Avoiding hot and spicy foods can help to reduce hot flashes, and cutting down on alcohol, tea, and coffee is also beneficial. To guard against the bone-thinning associated with postmenopausal women, you should make sure your diet supplies plenty of calcium, found in milk, cheese, and other dairy products, green leafy vegetables, and tofu. Vitamin E (from wheat germ, whole grains, dark green leafy vegetables, and nuts) is said to relieve menopausal headaches and other symptoms, and the body needs vitamin D (from fish oils, and exposure to sun) to help absorb the calcium essential for strong bones.

SUPPLEMENTS

If your diet is good you should not need supplements, but for those who dislike dairy products, and in soft water areas, a calcium supplement may be beneficial. Calcium citrate, a tetrahyde form, is needed, and a balanced preparation containing vitamin D (to aid absorption), boron, and magnesium is most suitable (see p.164).

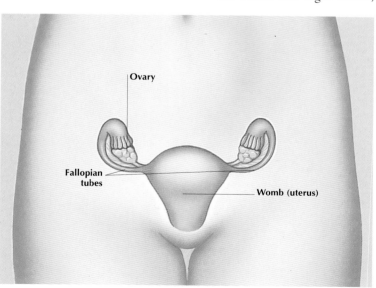

Ovary

Fallopian tubes

Womb (uterus)

HORMONE REPLACEMENT THERAPY

Hormone replacement therapy (HRT) is now frequently prescribed for women with menopausal symptoms. Current therapy is known as cyclical HRT, and involves a combination of the hormones estrogen and progesterone, in a sequence similar to that of the menstrual cycle, for three weeks in every four.

Although (particularly in the US) HRT is taken by many women after menopause is complete, it is often prescribed for a short time during the transition toward menopause, and immediately afterward. It banishes hot flashes and vaginal dryness, and there is evidence that it reduces the severity of osteoporosis (lack of bone density, which occurs in many post-menopausal women). HRT also gives some protection against heart disease when taken long-term. However, it is also statistically linked with a number of dangers, such as an increased risk of cancer. Your doctor may advise against HRT. If you decide to go ahead with HRT, you should have frequent checkups.

The use of natural progesterones is becoming increasingly popular. These substances are generally beneficial (the progestogens that are typically used in HRT are chemicals that imitate the body's natural progesterone).

Hormone replacement therapy (HRT) can relieve some physical symptoms, such as hot flashes, and may offer protection against osteoporosis and heart disease.

EXERCISE

Research has shown that regular weight-bearing exercise (a minimum of 30 minutes of brisk exercise such as walking, running, or playing tennis) at least three times a week, has two beneficial effects. The first is that it encourages the release of hormonelike substances that give you a feeling of well-being, and the second is that it strengthens the bones. All forms of regular exercise also help to keep you slim and fit, and it is even thought by some researchers to delay the effects of aging, partly by increasing the efficiency of oxygen delivery around the body.

DRESS CODE

If you suffer from hot flashes, wear cotton underwear and make sure that your clothing is made from natural fibers such as cotton, wool, or silk. When night sweats are a problem, minimize discomfort by wearing cotton nightclothes and sleeping on cotton bed linen.

Stretching and other exercises help to keep muscles toned, joints supple and weight under control, all of which encourage a sense of well-being.

COMPLEMENTARY THERAPIES

AROMATHERAPY

An aromatherapist might recommend a massage with rose essential oil. Geranium and clary sage are other beneficial oils. Any form of massage is relaxing and revitalizing (see p.228).

HERBAL MEDICINE

It is best to seek the advice of a qualified herbalist—there are numerous herbs that can help, depending on the symptoms. Oats can be taken for fatigue and chamomile for irritability, but a combined treatment will probably be recommended.

HOMEOPATHY

A homeopath will consider your particular case before prescribing individual remedies. Lachesis may be prescribed for hot flashes and palpitations, Pulsatilla for mood changes, and Sepia for hot flashes and vaginal dryness.

ACUPUNCTURE

Acupuncture restores balance to the body, and is often effective for hot flashes and night sweats (see p.230).

NATURAL PROGESTERONE

Try using 3% natural progesterone cream: ¼ teaspoonful twice a day can be of great help.

Oats   Chamomile

SECTION FOUR

children's
WELL-BEING

contents

Introduction

Young children have a wonderful ability to shake off illness.

Young children fall prey to innumerable short-lived illnesses and have the wonderful ability to recover rapidly every time. It's often their parents who suffer—from disturbed nights when the child needs to be nursed or comforted, to eventually catching the bug themselves. Unfortunately the same illnesses often take hold more firmly in adults, and are harder to shake off.

TREATING CHILDREN'S AILMENTS

This section covers some of the most common childhood ailments and general problems, and how to deal with them at home. Most parents feel confident that they know their child and can tell when symptoms warrant a physician's attention. For many routine problems, parental care will be sufficient, but there are times when calling a doctor is imperative. As a general rule, the younger the child, the more threatening symptoms such as vomiting and diarrhea, coughs, colds, and fevers can be. If an emergency arises it may be necessary to take your child straight to the hospital (see p. 95).

A FIRST-AID KIT

For emergencies it is a good idea to learn first aid (see p. 96–p. 97) and to keep some medical supplies at home. A first-aid kit should contain the following: a first-aid book, a thermometer, all the materials needed for dealing with cuts and grazes

A loving home environment, a good diet, and plenty of fresh air do much to safeguard the well-being of children.

(gauze, lint, and bandages in sterile packs, adhesive dressings, roll of adhesive tape), support bandages for sprains, scissors, tweezers, safety pins, child-strength aspirin or acetaminophen (paracetamol), antiseptic ointment, a bottle of disinfectant, and calamine lotion. Other very useful additions to these conventional first-aid materials are chamomile ointment (soothes many skin conditions), tea tree oil (an antiseptic, healing, and antifungal oil), lavender oil (good for burns), Bach's Rescue Remedy™ (calming in emergencies), arnica cream or tincture of arnica (for bruises), and calendula cream (for sore skin, stings, and minor wounds). Once you start using complementary medicines, you will gradually find your own favorite remedies, including homeopathic ones.

Every home should have a first aid kit, containing basic equipment such as bandages, scissors, and child-strength painkillers.

COMPLEMENTARY THERAPIES

Because they are so gentle, specific complementary remedies can be very good for minor illnesses in children, and the most useful are mentioned in the entries in this section. Complementary therapies that may be helpful include:

- Acupuncture (e.g. to treat eczema and digestive disorders).

- Alexander Technique (for postural problems associated with asthma; to prevent postural problems, for example as a result of playing a musical instrument and spending long hours in one position practicing, or carrying a heavy bag of schoolbooks).

- Herbal remedies.

- Homeopathy (used alone or in conjunction with orthodox remedies for a wide range of chronic and acute conditions).

- Massage and aromatherapy.

- Osteopathy (especially to correct postural changes associated with asthma; also good for sports injuries).

Whenever possible, select your therapist on personal recommendation. Your physician may also be able to recommend a competent practitioner. Always check a therapist's qualifications, and make sure that he or she belongs to a recognized professional association and is insured.

Peppermint relieves wind and colic and is particularly useful for soothing digestive problems in children.

INFANCY PROBLEMS

*I**f you are a new parent, your baby's every symptom can be a worry. Your doctor or a baby clinic can usually be relied on for good advice. If your baby is feeding, putting on weight, and is generally content, there is probably nothing wrong. This section deals with the most common problems of infancy.***

Many children have to visit the hospital at some time during infancy. Provided a parent remains with them, the experience need not be frightening.

DIAPER RASH

Diaper rash is the direct result of wearing diapers. It sounds obvious, but one way to cure it is to let your baby go without diapers as much as possible.

Since this is difficult, the best solution is to change the baby's diaper as soon as you know that it is damp, and to use one-way liners that help to keep the skin dry.

The chief cause of the rash is the ammonia produced by the action of bacteria on the baby's urine, trapped in the diaper against the baby's delicate skin. Rubber pants worsen the problem by holding in moisture. Wash and dry the baby's bottom every time you change the diaper, and apply traditional zinc oxide cream or zinc and castor oil ointment. Do not use talcum powder, which sticks to the skin and absorbs moisture. Leave your baby without a diaper when in the crib, with a layer of old towels to catch accidents. Breast-fed babies are less prone to diaper rash than bottle-fed ones, but it is not known why.

Fathers can, and should, play an active part in caring for babies. During bottle-feeding, it is important that the baby does not gulp too quickly, taking in air that may cause colic.

HERBAL REMEDIES

• Use distilled witch hazel for washing the baby's skin as an alternative to soap and water.
• Chamomile or calendula cream can be used to calm the rash and protect the skin.

CRADLE CAP

Many babies have an encrustation of yellowish scaly patches over their scalp, known as cradle cap. This is absolutely normal and harmless, and is thought to be due to an overproduction of sebum. The condition is not infectious. Loose scales can be softened with olive oil and will then brush out. Do not try to pick them off because this can cause infection.

WHEN TO CALL THE DOCTOR

Call your doctor if your baby:

HAS A TEMPERATURE OF 100°F/37.7°C OR MORE, WHICH IS NOT BROUGHT DOWN BY SPONGING WITH TEPID WATER, OR ADMINISTERING ACETAMINOPHEN

•

HAS SEVERE VOMITING OR DIARRHEA THAT LASTS FOR MORE THAN A FEW HOURS

•

HAS A SEIZURE OR IS UNCONSCIOUS

•

HAS DIFFICULTY IN BREATHING

COLIC

If your baby seems to cry for no reason, and normal remedies such as feeding, changing, soothing, and cuddling all have no effect, he or she could have colic. A baby with colic may cry until red in the face and draw up the legs as if in pain. Colic is most likely to affect babies under three months old.

Even though there is little medical evidence, it is widely believed that one cause of colic is gulping in air while feeding. Always check that the baby is well "latched" to your breast or the bottle, and try to feed before the baby becomes so hungry that he or she gulps down the milk. If you are bottle-feeding, ask your doctor or childcare advisor for advice on nipple type and feeding method.

Reaction to certain foods is also thought to be involved. Many babies are allergic to cow's milk in formula feeds. This tends to happen in families where allergies are common. Breast-fed babies are less prone to colic than those that are bottle-fed, but they may still react to something in the mother's diet that disagrees with them.

When ingested by the mother, some of the most common foods and drinks that may cause a reaction in a baby are coffee, alcohol, onions, and vegetables and legumes that cause flatulence in adults (such as green bell peppers, beans, lentils, and sprouts).

Colic is most common in the evening or at night. For parents, trying to pacify a screaming baby, seemingly in terrible pain, can cause a buildup of tension that makes the whole problem worse. If possible, mother and father should take it in turns to comfort the baby, to give each person a break. Hold the baby upright and gently rub the back.

Colic is a severe abdominal pain that is notoriously difficult to treat. It may help to put the baby over your shoulder and gently pat his or her back to release gas before putting the baby down to sleep.

HOME REMEDIES

- The traditional remedy of "burping" a baby after a feed (and during an attack) by patting her on the back, is well worth trying in order to prevent colic.
- If colic is a regular problem, try giving your baby a warm bath just before the time it usually strikes.
- Babies over four weeks old can be very gently massaged, using 1 tsp/5ml of an oil suitable for use on the face, such as almont carrier oil, mixed with 1 drop of chamomile oil.
- Lie your baby face-down on your lap, with her tummy positioned over a warm hot-water bottle that has been wrapped in a towel.
- To avoid tension, allow plenty of time for preparing the baby for bed.

Winding, or "burping" the baby after feeding can ease the discomfort of colic. You can do this by holding the baby upright, while gently stroking or patting her back.

83

TEETHING

Teething can be a very trying experience for baby and parents. The first teeth are cut at five or six months, and teething continues until the child is about 18 months old.

A baby who is teething will probably cry a lot, since the gums can be extremely sore just before a tooth pushes through. The gums will be red and swollen, and the baby will produce a good deal of saliva.

As babies grow, the release of growth hormone into their system stimulates the eruption of new teeth. Growth hormone also has the ability to upset the child's general well-being, making him or her more fretful and picky at mealtimes. It is not uncommon for a teething baby to lose their appetite for food altogether until the teeth have cut through, preferring to drink their milk instead.

A cool teething ring (you can put one in the refrigerator for a few hours, but not the freezer) can be soothing for the baby, as can anything to chew on. Just rubbing the gums with a cool finger can also help relieve inflamed gums. If your baby has trouble sleeping, try putting a few drops of calming lavender oil on to the bedlinen at nighttime.

Most babies find teething uncomfortable. They may be irritable, dribble, and cry. Biting on something, such as a cool teething ring, can ease discomfort. Teething is unlikely to cause illness.

WARNING

Other signs can indicate that the baby is teething, such as a red face, slight facial swelling, or rash, rubbing of the ears, and general irritability. However these signs can also be symptoms of illness. Tummy trouble is often thought to be connected with teething, but this is not the case. Keep a check on the baby's general feeding and sleeping habits, and consult your doctor if symptoms are not clearly connected to the emergence of a new tooth.

CARING FOR TEETH

It is never too soon to instill the habits of dental hygiene in your infant. As soon as the first tooth comes through, brush it (with the baby sitting on your lap, and while supporting her head). Use a baby's very soft toothbrush and no toothpaste.

Good dental hygiene should begin as soon as your baby's first tooth appears. Do not put sweet solutions on to a pacifier. Encourage even a young baby to hold and use a toothbrush.

Baby's toothbrush

Homeopathic cures for teething include Aconite, for discomfort and pain, and Pulsatilla for comfort.

VOMITING

*T*hrowing up is part of childhood, and although it may be unpleasant, it is not usually serious and is soon forgotten. The younger the child, the more seriously all symptoms must be taken, unless they pass very quickly.

Vomiting is the result of an irritation of the stomach lining. It can be caused by food allergies, eating contaminated food, overeating, and viral infections such as gastric flu. Migraine (rare in children), a head injury, and appendicitis may also lead to vomiting. Parents can usually tell whether the vomiting is serious or or not. If it persists, or if it's accompanied by a bad headache, stiff neck, sensitivity to light, or high fever, call a doctor without delay; these symptoms may be indicative of meningitis.

MOTION SICKNESS

Children with motion sickness can be helped by the following measures:

SUCKING A HARD CANDY

•

LOOKING AT THE HORIZON

•

EATING GINGER, IN THE FORM OF
CRYSTALLIZED GINGER OR GINGER COOKIES

HOME REMEDIES

- It is particularly important to give your child liquids after he or she has vomited, since the body will have lost fluid. Make sure that the child does not gulp the drink down quickly but sips it slowly, otherwise it may cause vomiting again.
- If bedding has to be changed, make sure the child is kept warm and comfortable while you do this.
- As your child's appetite begins to return, gradually introduce light soups with strips of toasted bread floating on top, purées of fruit or vegetables, and plain or fruit yogurts. Avoid fats, meat, and foods with strong flavors until you are sure the symptoms have passed.
- Live yogurt will help to normalize the digestive tract.

THE CONVENTIONAL APPROACH

If your child has vomited repeatedly, the doctor may prescribe oral rehydration powders, which are mixed with pure water according to the instructions (see the recipe for rehydration fluid on p.95). This mixture replaces the body's lost salts, sugars, and fluids in a balanced way, speeding recovery.

An infusion of peppermint or chamomile may ease feelings of motion sickness. Make up a drink of it for the child to sip during the journey.

COMPLEMENTARY THERAPIES

HERBAL MEDICINE

Chamomile infusion is soothing and will help a child who is distressed.

ACUPRESSURE

Stimulating an acupuncture point on the front of the wrist (on both arms) helps. Specially designed bands apply pressure to this point, and are available from most drugstores.

HOMEOPATHY

A homeopath might prescribe Veratum alb. for a child with vomiting and diarrhea accompanied by cold sweats. Several remedies may be applicable, depending on the precise clinical picture. A homeopath can select the right one for your child (see p.226). A proprietary homeopathic remedy for motion sickness is available from most health outlets and pharmacies.

Chamomile

Herbal infusion

FEVERS

*N*ormal body temperature may vary from child to child, and from one part of the day to another. It's normal for body temperature to rise during the day and drop at bedtime, for example. A fever may come on suddenly or gradually, with flushing, hot skin, aches, and pains.

It is not unusual for a child's temperatures to fluctuate a great deal. Although a normal temperature is around 98.4°F/37°C, there is generally nothing to worry about if your child's "normal" temperature is a little lower or a little higher than this, within the range of 96°F/35.6°C to 99°F/37.2°C. If your child's temperature goes above 100°F/37.7°C, this is considered to be a fever.

Feverish symptoms will become increasingly noticeable as the child's temperature climbs. The child may be restless and sweating, and have hot skin (especially on the forehead) and flushed cheeks. He or she may also want to go to sleep (which can generally be encouraged).

Fever is usually a sign of an infection and is a natural reaction. Temperature elevates as white blood cells, the body's first line of defense, fight off the invading viral or bacterial agents, which are causing the infection. In children, quite minor infections can cause very high temperatures for a short time. Other signs, such as vomiting, lethargy, and loss of appetite must also be taken into account when deciding whether the fever is serious.

TEMP GUIDE

Call doctor (104°F/40°C)

Fever
(above 100°F/37.7°C)

Normal (96°F/35.6°C – 99°F/37.2°C)

If your child's temperature continues to rise above 100°F/37.7°C, then you must seek urgent medical advice.

WARNING

A temperature of 100°F/37.7°C in babies or a temperature of 104°F/40°C in children can be serious. Call your doctor immediately for advice (or if a high temperature is not brought down by treatment).

Both conventional and complementary practitioners advise sponging a feverish child all over with tepid water.

HOME REMEDIES

- **BATHING** If the fever doesn't subside, sponge the child gently all over with tepid water, or let her sit in a tepid bath if she feels well enough.
- **KEEP INDOORS** Keep the child indoors in a warm room, but it is not necessary for her to be kept in bed.
- **LOTS OF SLEEP** If the fever is high, the child will naturally want to sleep, and this should be encouraged.
- **DO NOT FORCE CHILD TO EAT** Do not worry if the child's appetite is poor for a few days, and do not try to force her to eat.
- **PLENTY OF FLUIDS** Make sure that the child has plenty of fluids, such as plain water, fruit juices, and herbal infusions.

Give your child plenty of fluids, or small cubes of fruit with a high water content, such as melon.

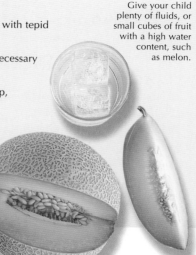

CHICKEN POX

*F*ew children grow up without experiencing this infectious childhood illness. It takes from two to three weeks to develop, but a child can pass on the infection two or three days before the tell-tale pustules show, and up to ten days afterward. Chicken pox is more irritating than debilitating, and there's almost no risk of serious complications developing.

There is little that can be done to prevent chicken pox, but the way it is treated can greatly help to minimize the irritating effects and prevent scarring. Discuss with your doctor the possibility of having your child vaccinated.

Pustules tend to develop on the body first, followed by the face and limbs. These develop into small, fluid-filled blisters. The virus responsible for chicken pox can also cause shingles, a disease which is particularly painful for the elderly.

HOME REMEDIES
- Simple calamine lotion is the traditional treatment for soothing chicken pox. The lotion has an immediate cooling effect, but needs to be reapplied frequently.
- Add 1–2 cups of bicarbonate of soda to warm (not hot) bathwater.

Chicken pox causes small, itchy red pustules that become fluid-filled blisters. To ease the itching, place your child in a warm bath to which you've added tea tree oil and witch hazel or chamomile oil.

WARNING
Reye's disease is an extremely rare but dangerous disease that very occasionally develops in a child who is recovering from chicken pox. Never give aspirin (even junior aspirin) to a child with chicken pox; it is thought possible, though as yet unproven, that this provokes Reye's disease. Call your doctor immediately in cases of sudden, severe, repeated vomiting, seizures, spasms, severe lethargy, or unconsciousness.

SYMPTOMS
In many children a sudden outbreak of red, blistering sores on the trunk and face is the only symptom. Occasionally the child may be a little off-color before the sores develop, and may be slightly feverish or complain of a headache. The sores can spread down the trunk and onto the legs, becoming extremely hot and itchy. When the lesions have eventually crusted over, the child is no longer infectious, but he or she will find it very difficult not to scratch off the crusts.

COMPLEMENTARY THERAPIES

AROMATHERAPY
Mix 2–3 drops of tea tree oil with 1tsp (5ml) of witch hazel and add to warm (not hot) bathwater. (This can even be used on babies.) Bathe the child every few hours. In many cases, there will be an amazing difference in 12–24 hours. If the skin (or the child) needs soothing, use 1 drop of chamomile oil and only 2 drops of tea tree in the bath. Use tea tree or lavender, in a vaporizer, for their antimicrobial properties. Lavender is preferable if the child seems stressed or restless.

HERBAL MEDICINE
Soothing chamomile ointment cools the skin and aids healing.

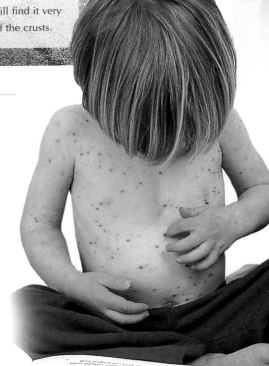

Discourage your child from scratching chicken pox because this can cause minor infections or scarring. Apply soothing calamine lotion or chamomile oil to the skin to ease discomfort.

MEASLES

*M*easles is uncommon now that many children have been vaccinated against it. Until the age of 12 months, children have natural resistance to the measles virus. Having measles once gives life-long immunity to the disease.

HOME REMEDIES
- Give your child plenty of fluids, including glucose/fruit drinks for energy, while appetite is poor.
- Sponge your child using tepid water.
- Freshly squeezed lemon juice and honey in hot water makes a comforting and healing drink.
- Apply calamine lotion to the rash if it is hot or itchy.
- A light diet will help while your child recovers.

Measles is usually accompanied by a high fever, which can distress your child. Complications are rare, provided the child has been immunized, but a child with measles needs comforting.

The first sign of measles is called the catarrhal stage and is like a cold, with a runny nose and eyes, and a raised temperature. This is followed by a sore throat, which usually lasts for only a few hours. Sickness and diarrhea may also occur.

Before the rash of measles appears, Koplik's sores can be seen inside the mouth. These are little white spots inside the cheeks, and are a sure sign that your child has measles.

MEASLES RASH

The measles rash proper can take up to a week to develop, and is preceded by a sudden fall in temperature. The rash starts behind the ears and then goes onto the neck and forehead, before covering the whole face and spreading downward onto the trunk. The small red sores often run together, to form blotchy brownish red patches.

The rash usually causes a bout of high fever, which can make the child feel miserable, however, the rash itself is not itchy. The cold symptoms will be at their worst at this point, and the eyes may be sensitive to light.

IMMUNIZATION

It is advisable to have your child immunized against measles, partly because complications, although fairly rare, can be serious. Measles also weakens the immune system, and leaves the child vulnerable to other infections. Immunization does not give total protection but if the child does catch measles, the symptoms are not severe.

WARNING
In rare cases measles can carry the risk of complications, including middle ear infection, pneumonia, and, more rarely, inflammation of the brain tissue (encephalitis). Consult your doctor if the fever is very high, or if it recurs when the symptoms have disappeared.

COMPLEMENTARY THERAPIES

HERBAL MEDICINE
Measles can weaken the immune system. Garlic or echinacea can be given to strengthen it. Chamomile or calendula infusion can be added to the bathwater to calm body and mind.

AROMATHERAPY
A chest massage with three drops of tea tree oil in 1 tsp/5ml of light carrier oil will ease cold symptoms. Three drops of lavender oil (chamomile for babies and young children) can be added to the bathwater to soothe and calm.

HOMEOPATHY
Homeopathic remedies can be very effective (see p.226). Your homeopath may suggest Morbillinum, Bryonia, Stramonium, Aconite, or Pulsatilla.

MUMPS

This is a viral infection which is mostly likely to affect children from four to 14 years old. Its severity varies from child to child. Although catching mumps gives immunity for life, it can involve more serious complications, so it is well worth having the child immunized to prevent it.

It takes from two to three weeks for the symptoms to develop after exposure to the infection. The first symptoms are flu-like, with shivering and a raised temperature. The throat and ears are affected, with a sore throat, difficulty in swallowing, and pain in the head and neck.

Full-blown symptoms are an extremely tender and swollen jaw on one or both sides of the face, and pain on opening the mouth and swallowing, making it troublesome to eat. Your child will have very little appetite. Temperature further increases at this stage too, and your child will have bouts of shivering and feel alternately hot and cold. Call your doctor if symptoms are severe.

Children over the age of 12 months can be vaccinated against mumps. The vaccination is usually given in conjunction with vaccines for measles and rubella.

WARNING

Mumps can lead to meningitis. Although this is usually mild, it is potentially serious. Always call your doctor if your child is vomiting, or has a stiff neck or headache. Inflammation of the brain tissue (encephalitis) has similar symptoms and is another serious, though very rare, complication.

HOME REMEDIES

- Sponge your child with tepid water if feverish.
- Give your child plenty of fluids.
- Cool drinks, soups, purées, and ice cream will soothe the throat.
- A cold compress can help ease a swollen face.

TEENAGE BOYS

Catching mumps after puberty carries the added risk that a boy might develop orchitis, a painful inflammation of the testicles that can lead to sterility.

COMPLEMENTARY THERAPIES

AROMATHERAPY

Lavender oil will treat all the symptoms simultaneously. Try a few drops in a vaporizer, on a handkerchief or pillow, and in the bath. It will soothe a headache, earache, inflammation, and fever.

NUTRITIONAL SUPPLEMENTS

Extra vitamin C, in soluble tablet form, will help the immune system to fight the infection.

HOMEOPATHY

Homeopathy is effective for mumps (see p.226). Remedies include Rhus tox., Aconite, Belladonna, Mercurius sol., and Pulsatilla.

Soluble vitamin C

RASHES AND SKIN ALLERGIES

*R*ashes and allergies can be difficult to treat by orthodox means, but many complementary therapies can help to ease symptoms. Luckily, rashes are often a passing phase that the child grows out of. For diaper rash, see p.82.

For most itchy rashes, bathing in a solution of sodium bicarbonate, or applying calamine lotion, is soothing. Wearing loose cotton clothing will prevent a rash from getting any worse and may even prevent it from occuring in the first place. Never squeeze the pustules or blisters of a rash because this can cause bacterial infection.

HEAT RASH

This rash of hot, itchy red sores appears in the elbow, knee, and groin creases and also on the face and neck. It affects babies and young children, usually when they are too warm. Make sure that the child's clothes are not too tight; the rash is most likely to develop where sweat gets trapped. Cotton clothing, because it is cool and absorbent, can be helpful. Reduce the heat of the skin by bathing it in cool water mixed with a drop of chamomile oil. Applying some calamine lotion will also soothe the rash.

Children develop a variety of rashes, some caused by allergies, others by heat or infestation. Loose-fitting cotton clothes, rather than synthetic fabrics, are kinder to the skin and can prevent rashes.

NETTLE RASH (URTICARIA)

Nettle rash (urticaria) consists of a patch of raised blisters on reddened skin, causing itching and burning. It is usually an allergic reaction to some substance that has come into direct contact with the skin, but the allergen may also be something inhaled from the air. A rash can also indicate a food allergy, most commonly to milk and dairy products. Sometimes heat (such as from bathwater), or stress can trigger the rash. Try to ensure the child is not exposed to the allergen. A doctor may prescribe an antihistamine.

Angioneurotic edema, or giant hives, is a rash of large swellings which may affect the back, lips, eyelids, or throat. It needs medical treatment.

MILIA

This rash, also called miliaria, resembles a sprinkling of millet seeds. Tiny white bumps appear over the nose and across the face. It may be described as prickly heat, but only rarely is it itchy or troublesome. Except in tropical conditions, when adults can develop milia, it usually only affects babies and very young children and is caused by blocked sweat glands. Normally no treatment is needed, but the child should wear cotton clothing, and the bedroom should be warm but not hot. Apply calamine lotion if the rash is itchy.

SCABIES

This contagious itchy rash, which also occurs in adults, is caused by an infestation of the scabies mite. In children it is most likely to affect the palms of the hands, the soles of the feet, and the webbing between the fingers. It is best to seek medical advice, although eucalyptus, tea tree, and lavender oils are claimed to be effective.

Eucalyptus, tea tree oil, and rosemary all have antiseptic qualities and can be used in the treatment of scabies.

Many foods cause allergic reactions. If your child develops one, keep a diary of the foods your child eats so that you can eliminate the culprit from his or her diet.

ECZEMA

This consists of dry, itchy red patches that may become scaly or weep. They occur in the skin folds, and in patches on the face or on any part of the body (see p.126). The cause may be a food allergy (often to wheat or dairy products) or skin contact with an allergen such as perfume, metal, or the fur of household pets. The best remedy is to avoid the allergen. Eczema can be eased by a diet that supplies plenty of vitamins C and B-complex, and by taking supplements of evening primrose oil. However, a specialist's advice may be needed. The complementary therapies of acupuncture, herbalism, and homeopathy may help. Rosewater with a drop of lavender or chamomile oil can soothe the rash. Eczema often occurs in children who are asthmatic (see p.121).

KEEPING A NOTE OF ALLERGIES

Sometimes it is very easy to discover which food triggers an allergic response. The most common food allergens are milk, wheat, and yeast-based foods. However, some reactions to foods may take up to 48 hours to become apparent, so keeping a careful diet diary can be helpful (see p.215).

Lavender is antiseptic and relaxing. Applied as an oil, it calms the skin and can be used for ringworm and athlete's foot.

Lavender

RINGWORM AND ATHLETE'S FOOT (TINEA INFECTIONS)

Ringworm is a contagious and intensely itchy fungal infection, which produces a ring-shaped rash. It can occur on the scalp, causing a temporary bald patch, and may also affect the trunk, fingers, groin, or armpits. It can be passed to people by family pets or farm animals. It's closely related to athlete's foot (which manifests itself as soft white flesh between the toes, surrounded by areas of tender red skin that can be hot and itchy). It can also cause discolored, ridged nails.

Both these forms of tinea infection thrive in moist, warm conditions. Treat by washing and drying the area carefully at least once a day, using strict hygiene to prevent spreading (do not share towels, combs, etc., and wash them in very hot water). Give your child at least one container of live yogurt a day. For athlete's foot, apply tea tree oil. Wear cotton or wool socks and change them every day. For ringworm see your doctor, who may prescribe antifungal cream. Tea tree, lavender, or lemon eucalyptus oil, and calendula cream can calm the skin. Vinegar also helps: add two tablespoons to a footbath.

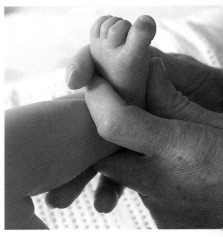

Athlete's foot causes peeling and cracking between the toes. Keeping those areas clean and dry will discourage the fungus.

COUGHS, COLDS, AND CONGESTION

Young children seem to be even more prone to respiratory infections than adults. As with other minor infections, they almost always throw them off with remarkable speed. These infections can usually be treated at home, but it is wise to consult a doctor if your child has a chronic condition or suffers repeated infections.

Babies' symptoms should be taken seriously; they can quickly lead to complications. See your doctor if your baby is not feeding or sleeping properly because of a cough or cold.

See your doctor if your child develops a middle ear infection, perhaps as a result of a cold. Untreated infections can cause hearing or balance problems and should be dealt with quickly.

It is said that there is no cure for a cold and it must just run its course. Symptoms can either pass quickly or linger, depending on the child's general health and the treatment you give. Instead of using proprietary medication from the pharmacist, try to treat your child's cold with natural remedies whenever possible. Herbal teas are a soothing way of supplying much-needed liquids. Essential oils can be used for inhalation (in a bowl of steaming water, from a vaporizer, or sprinkled on the pillow at night) and gargling (for older children). A diet rich in vitamin C (from fresh orange and lemon juice, and fruits and vegetables in general) aids the immune system.

CHILDREN AND SMOKING

It is harmful for a child to inhale smoke. Many of the children who have frequent respiratory complaints are reacting to their parents' cigarette smoke. Give up smoking, or if you cannot do so, protect your child from your tobacco fumes by not smoking in his or her presence.

MIDDLE EAR INFECTION

In young children, infections can quickly spread from the throat down the Eustachian tube to the middle ear. Middle ear infections can be dangerous and can lead to deafness if they are not treated. The main symptom of an infection is an earache, usually with a high temperature. An older child will tell you she has earache; a baby will cry and rub her ears. Because of the dangers, you should consult your doctor the same day if symptoms don't pass. Meanwhile, keep the child's ear warm (but do not put cotton wool in the ear) and give her warm, comforting herbal infusions to drink.

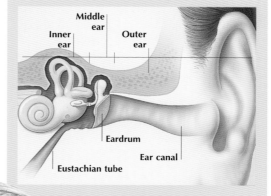

Middle ear infection is the result of viruses or bacteria reaching the ear from the throat via the Eustachian tube which connects the two. The infection then develops into earache or fever.

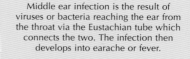

HOME REMEDIES

- Apply petroleum jelly or chamomile ointment to a sore nose.
- Make a decongestant massage oil by mixing 5 drops of myrrh, pine, or sandalwood essential oil with 50ml almond oil. Gently massage the chest, neck, and upper back.
- Give your child plenty of fluids, such as herbal infusions and fruit juices diluted with water. Hot lemon and honey is especially beneficial, and palatable.
- Because they can be mucus-forming, try cutting milk and cheese from the child's diet for a few days.
  - Get your child to inhale a benzoin preparation available from your pharmacist, who can make a suitable recommendation.
  - Give your child an extra pillow at night—being slightly raised helps alleviate coughing.
  - Ensure that your child gets plenty of vitamin C, either from fresh fruit and vegetables, or by taking a supplement.

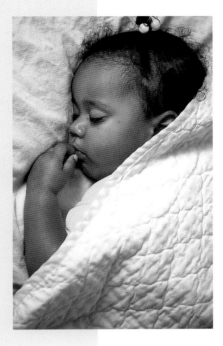

Sleep helps to restore physical well-being and aids recovery from illness. A warm drink of lemon and honey at bedtime encourages sleep and helps to soothe coughs.

Petroleum jelly

COMPLEMENTARY THERAPIES

AROMATHERAPY

Many essential oils have antiseptic properties and can help to clear the respiratory tract and soothe a sore throat. Among the best are: tea tree (balsamic, expectorant), eucalyptus (decongestant, expectorant), and pine (balsamic, decongestant, expectorant).

Use the oils in a vaporizer in the child's room, or for steam inhalation (up to 3 drops per bowl of hot water). Older children can use tea tree as a gargle (2 drops in a glass of warm, boiled water).

Other useful antiseptic oils, especially good at night, are: lemon (soothing, lowers fever), lavender (decongestant, soothing), sandalwood (expectorant, soothing).

Sprinkle a few drops on a handkerchief left on the child's pillow.

HERBAL MEDICINE

The following herbal infusions (drunk hot) are useful for treating children's colds:
- Elderflower—for chills, feverish colds, congestion, and sinusitis.
  - Peppermint—for feverish colds.
- Hyssop—for coughs and colds (good at night as it relaxes airways, calms, and helps to clear phlegm).
  - Lime blossom—for colds with a headache (encourages restful sleep).

Peppermint sprig

Peppermint is one of the most widely used of Western herbal remedies. Often drunk as a tea or infusion, it can be used for feverish colds.

HOMEOPATHY

A qualified homeopath may be able to prescribe a suitable remedy for your child, after taking into account his or her individual symptoms and personality picture (see p.226). *Pulsatilla* is a remedy given for many children's complaints.

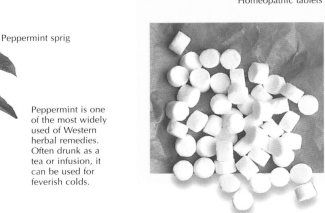

Homeopathic tablets

93

PREVENTING ACCIDENTS

*U*nder-fives are most likely to have accidents in the home. Children over this age become more adventurous, are not supervised as closely, and are also at risk in the street and playground. You need to be aware of accidents "waiting to happen" and to train your growing child to acquire this awareness.

At home, lock dangerous substances such as medicines and cleaning materials, as well as any sharp objects, in a cupboard.

IN THE HOME

KEEP ALL MEDICINES, BLEACH, CLEANING FLUIDS, FABRIC CONDITIONER, AND DANGEROUS OBJECTS (SCISSORS, KNIVES, SCREWDRIVERS, KNITTING NEEDLES) OUT OF REACH.

•

DO NOT ALLOW SMALL CHILDREN ACCESS TO BUTTONS, BEADS, DRIED BEANS, OR ANY OTHER OBJECTS THAT THEY COULD SWALLOW OR PUT UP THEIR NOSES.

•

KEEP FOOD SUCH AS PEANUTS AND PIECES OF RAW CARROT AWAY FROM VERY YOUNG CHILDREN WHO WILL CHOKE ON THEM.

•

DO NOT LEAVE YOUNG CHILDREN PLAYING ALONE IN A ROOM.

•

CONSIDER FITTING STAIRGUARDS, WINDOW LOCKS, AND SAFETY COVERS ON ELECTRIC OUTLETS.

•

DON'T LEAVE ELECTRICAL CABLE TRAILING ACROSS THE FLOOR.

•

USE STRONG FIREGUARDS AROUND OPEN FIRES AND HEATERS.

•

KEEP SAUCEPAN HANDLES TURNED INWARD.

•

DON'T LEAVE HOT DRINKS WHERE THEY CAN BE KNOCKED OVER.

•

CHECK THE WATER TEMPERATURE BEFORE THE CHILD GETS INTO THE BATH.

•

HAVE UNBREAKABLE GLASS FITTED ON PATIO DOORS AND LEAVE THE DOORS WIDE OPEN IF CHILDREN ARE LIKELY TO BE RUNNING FROM THE YARD INTO THE HOUSE.

•

IF YOU OWN GUNS, MAKE SURE THEY ARE LOCKED IN A SECURE AREA AND AMMUNITION IS STORED SEPARATELY.

IN THE STREET AND PLAYGROUND

INSTALL A LOCKABLE GATE SO YOUR CHILD CAN'T RUN INTO THE STREET.

•

TEACH CHILDREN NEVER TO RUN INTO THE ROAD AFTER A BALL. DISCOURAGE PLAYING IN THE STREET.

•

TRAIN YOUR CHILD IN ROAD USE, BOTH AS A PEDESTRIAN AND A CYCLIST.

•

INSTIL AN AWARENESS OF THE DANGERS OF MOVING SWINGS AND SEESAWS.

IN THE GARDEN

STORE GARDEN CHEMICALS SAFELY. NEVER USE RECYCLED DRINKS BOTTLES FOR STORING DANGEROUS SUBSTANCES.

•

KEEP PONDS AND SWIMMING POOLS NETTED OR FENCED FOR SAFETY.

•

DO NOT GROW POISONOUS PLANTS.

Moving swings and horseplay in the playground can cause serious accidents. Teach your child to use playground equipment properly and keep a careful watch on his or her activities.

MEDICAL EMERGENCIES

*I*n an emergency, you will need urgent medical help. Look at the box on this page and call your doctor or take your child to hospital if any of the symptoms applies. When children are very young (in particular) an episode of sickness and diarrhea can quickly cause dehydration, and this presents a serious threat to their health. The rehydration fluid shown on this page can be made simply and speedily in sudden cases of severe vomiting and diarrhea.

WHEN TO CALL THE DOCTOR

Call your doctor if your child has diarrhea, vomiting, a high temperature, and is extremely lethargic; also if the condition has not improved in 24 hours, or if any of the symptoms are very severe. You will also need medical attention in the following cases:

VERY HIGH TEMPERATURE (OVER 102°F/39°C)

•

TEMPERATURE OF OVER 100°F/38°C FOR MORE THAN THREE DAYS

•

RAPIDLY CHANGING TEMPERATURE

•

BREATHING DIFFICULTIES

•

SEVERE ABDOMINAL PAIN

•

DISTURBED VISION AND HEADACHE

•

STIFF NECK AND HEADACHE, WITH RAISED TEMPERATURE

•

DROWSINESS WITH COLD SKIN AND LOWERED TEMPERATURE (BELOW 95°F/35°C)

•

SEIZURES

•

HEAD INJURIES

•

UNCONSCIOUSNESS

•

INFANTS WHO HAVE DIARRHEA OR VOMITING FOR MORE THAN A FEW HOURS.

If the condition seems serious and you are unable to contact your doctor, take your child to the hospital. If the condition seems life-threatening, call an ambulance, or rush your child to the hospital without delay

REHYDRATION FLUID

In a scrupulously clean container, mix 1 tsp/5ml salt and 1 tbs/15ml sugar with 1 pint/600ml of just-boiled water. Allow this to cool and give your child 1 tsp/5ml every 15 minutes.

Salt, sugar, and boiled water are the basic ingredients for a rehydration fluid, which should be used to counteract dehydration caused by vomiting or diarrhea.

Trust your instincts: get medical help quickly if you are seriously concerned.

ACCIDENTS AND FIRST AID

*A*lways be prepared for accidents. A little first-aid knowledge could save a child's life. The best way to learn how to give first aid is to enlist on a course such as those given by the Red Cross or the Emergency Medical Services. It is wise to keep a first-aid kit in a safe, accessible place. This should contain an illustrated booklet on what to do in an emergency, as well as key telephone numbers such as that of your doctor and local hospital.

Make sure you know how to cope with cuts, grazes, and nose-bleeds. Find out what to do when there is a life-endangering threat such as choking, poisoning, or burns. Call the emergency services immediately in the event of a serious accident.

Most of the injuries you will have to deal with will be minor, but if you encounter a serious accident, keep calm. Taking quick emergency action could be vital. The checklist on this page tells you the steps to take while waiting for professional help to arrive. For information on recovery position, kiss of life, and cardiac massage, see opposite.

Keep a first-aid box in an accessible place, stocked with conventional equipment and some complementary remedies. If possible, take a first-aid course or invest in a first-aid reference book. Keep emergency telephone numbers handy.

EMERGENCY CHECKLIST

POINTS TO CHECK		WHAT TO DO
Is the child conscious?	no →	Put in recovery position
Is the child breathing?	no →	Give mouth-to-mouth resuscitation
Is the airway clear?	no →	Clear, by tipping back head and cleaning inside mouth with finger
Is the child's heart beating?	no →	Give heart massage
Is there bleeding?	yes →	Staunch bleeding or compress bleeding wound

Take your child to your nearest hospital emergency department if you have any doubt about the seriousness of an injury. A bone may have fractured or broken.

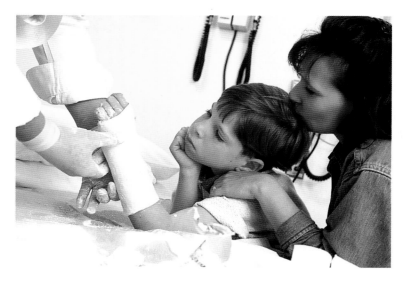

EMERGENCY AID

BLEEDING
Staunch heavy bleeding by pressing firmly (with a clean cloth if available) to keep the gash closed as much as possible. If anything is embedded in the flesh and causing bleeding, do not attempt to remove the object (this can cause more damage).

BURNS
Apply copious cold water while waiting for emergency help.

CHOKING
For a baby or young child, hold the child upside-down and firmly tap the back (preferably get someone else to do this while you hold the child). For an older child, hold the child from behind and press your fingers vigorously inward just under the ribs (Heimlich's maneuver).

INJURIES

Do not attempt to move someone who may have fractures or internal injuries, unless it is vital. Stay by him to check that he is breathing and not choking on vomit (if necessary clear his mouth with a finger). Do not give an injured person anything to eat or drink, in case surgery is needed.

MOUTH-TO-MOUTH RESUSCITATION AND CARDIAC MASSAGE

This is most likely to be needed after an electric shock, or when a child has almost drowned.

Step 2

Step 1

1 Lie the child flat on his back. Tilt the head back, clear the mouth, make sure the airway is clear.

2 Pinch the child's nose lightly. Place your mouth over his and breathe out gently.

3 Raise your head and watch the chest rise. When the chest falls, repeat step 2.

4 If the heart is not beating, press your hand repeatedly on the breast bone quite sharply (depending on the size of the child), slightly faster than once a second. (Use two fingers for a baby.) Do this 15 times, then give two breaths.

5 Alternate blowing air into the mouth and giving chest massage, until the heart starts beating.

6 Continue with the mouth-to-mouth if the child's breathing fails again.

WARNING

Do not attempt to give artificial respiration unless you are quite sure that the child is not breathing. Do not give cardiac massage unless you are SURE that the heart is not beating. If the child is breathing (however lightly or irregularly), the heart will still be beating.

RECOVERY POSITION

An unconscious or semiconscious child, who is breathing and whose heart is beating, should be placed in the recovery position and kept warm until medical help arrives. This makes sure that he or she can breathe easily and will not inhale vomit. The position can only be used when fractures or internal injuries are not suspected. Learn how to put a child in the recovery position and teach your children how to do it too.

1 Turn the child's head toward you, tilting it slightly backward to aid breathing. Then slide the arm nearest to you down his side, and ease his hand under his buttock. Bring the other arm over his chest. Cross the leg furthest from you over the nearer leg at the ankle.

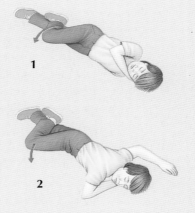

2 Support the child's head with one hand while you turn him toward you, using his clothing to gently pull him over at the hip.

3 Adjust his position so the head is still well back. The upper arm and leg should be bent to prevent him from rolling forward, and the straight arm and leg will prevent him from rolling backward.

4 Cover him with a coat or blanket, and wait with him until help arrives.

Babies can also be put into the recovery position but since their limbs are lighter they are more likely to roll backward and possibly choke if the airways become blocked. After you have placed the infant in the correct position, hold him in place by gently supporting the back and upper leg until the emergency services arrive.

BEHAVIORAL PROBLEMS

*F*ew parents get by without having to deal with some kind of behavioral problems in their child. Problems may be worse when the child's emotional security is threatened, but they may also be a normal and inevitable phase in development.

Temper tantrums are common in growing toddlers. The best method is to ignore the child during the tantrum but be on hand if reassurance is required.

HEAD BANGING

This is usually a short phase, common in toddlers, and generally nothing to worry about. The child will bang his or her head rhythmically on the side of the crib, or on the wall by the bed or some chosen object. Frustration, anxiety, or desire for attention may be the cause of this behavior.

LEARNING TO CONTROL

Try to help your child to feel a sense of achievement if you notice frustration building. This may happen when they start to perceive how complex their world is, and how little they can do to control it. Playing with constructive toys and learning to manipulate objects, with your encouragement, gives a feeling of being in control.

Make sure there are toys to play with and books to look at in the crib or bed, so your child has something to do when she wakes up. It could be pure toddler boredom that is the cause.

Many temper tantrums arise as a result of boredom—make sure that your child has enough constructive toys to keep them occupied.

Alternatively, anxiety or need for attention may be at the root of this behavior, particularly if the child has had a major change in routine, experienced an event such as the death of a pet, or acquired a new sibling. Feeling secure is all-important. Make sure that you have time for your child so they can feel reassured that their world is safe and they matter just as much as before.

TEMPER TANTRUMS

Temper tantrums affect many two- to three-year-olds and can seriously disrupt their parents' composure. The sweetest and most rational children are just as prone. Generally the tantrum involves wanting or not wanting something, and screaming about it. In some cases this may carry on until the child is out of breath, or they may deliberately hold their breath until they are blue in the face.

REASONS FOR TANTRUMS

Being tired, hungry, or overexcited can create the conditions for a tantrum and an incident such as being thwarted in favor of a sibling can provoke it. Deep down the reason is that the child is learning how to be independent, while skills (such as handling objects, emotions, and relations with other people) lag far behind.

Ignoring tantrums is usually the best way to handle them. Make sure the child can't get hurt while allowing her the freedom to give vent to her feelings. If you feel your child needs reassurance it may be best to hold her firmly during the tantrum. Occasionally you may be able to distract the child by diverting the child's attention to something else.

You may find that tantrums take their toll on you. You need to be calm—relaxation or yoga (see p.239 and p.244) will give you the mental calm to cope. It will also help to see if your child's tantrums fall into a pattern. For example if they occur when you are shopping, you may be able to arrange for her to be looked after while you go shopping alone. Dodging the issue is a perfectly good way of coping with this phase of child development.

HYPERACTIVITY

This rather loose term can cover a range of behavior disorders. Some children are truly hyperactive from birth, being restless and out of control, and unable to concentrate. This leads to difficulties in relating to other children, which exacerbates the original problem, causing aggressive, disruptive behavior, and in turn problems in school. Seriously hyperactive children may often be clumsy, insomniac, destructive, and subject to violent moods. In such cases professional help is needed.

At the more usual end of the scale a so-called "hyperactive" child simply needs to run around and make more noise than other children. Tolerance and understanding, and even a little assistance and guidance are all that's needed in these cases. Providing the opportunity to let off steam and encouraging constructive play are beneficial. The child may simply be bright and in need of plenty of mental stimulation.

SPECIALIST CARE

Psychiatric problems, brain damage, and epilepsy can be involved in hyperactivity and a specialist's care may be needed in such cases.

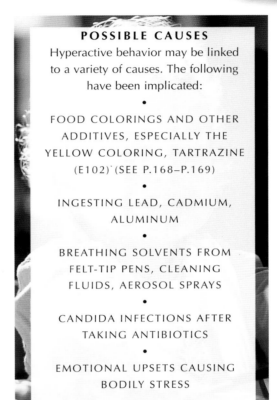

POSSIBLE CAUSES
Hyperactive behavior may be linked to a variety of causes. The following have been implicated:

FOOD COLORINGS AND OTHER ADDITIVES, ESPECIALLY THE YELLOW COLORING, TARTRAZINE (E102) (SEE P.168–P.169)

INGESTING LEAD, CADMIUM, ALUMINUM

BREATHING SOLVENTS FROM FELT-TIP PENS, CLEANING FLUIDS, AEROSOL SPRAYS

CANDIDA INFECTIONS AFTER TAKING ANTIBIOTICS

EMOTIONAL UPSETS CAUSING BODILY STRESS

Hyperactive children are constantly on the go, so give them plenty of opportunity to run around and burn off that extra energy!

COMPLEMENTARY THERAPIES

HERBAL MEDICINE
An infusion of chamomile, catnip, hops, or limeflower at bedtime is calming.

ALLERGY TESTING
You may notice that hyperactive behavior is linked to diet. Try an exclusion diet, in which you eliminate likely candidates. Do not exclude dietary staples.

SUPPLEMENTS
Where the effects of illness or stress are suspected, give a daily multi-mineral and vitamin tablet and one evening primrose oil capsule.

OTHER REMEDIES
You could find joining a support group invaluable.

By joining a support group and getting to know parents of other hyperactive children you can support each other and discuss strategies for coping with your child's behavioral problems.

SLEEP DISORDERS

*O*ften, a child's sleep disorders have the capacity to affect the parents more than the child. Disturbed nights are a serious threat to parental well-being!

Few parents manage to get through their child's early years without experiencing the tribulations of their offspring's sleep problems, ranging from inability to get to sleep and waking during the night, to sleepwalking and early waking. There are two parts to attacking the problem: finding out the cause of the sleep disorder, and working out a strategy to cope with it.

SLEEP PATTERNS

Just like adults, babies and children have their own individual sleep pattern, or lack of pattern. If your baby is not distressed when he wakes up in the night, the best thing to do, if you can, is to take turns with your partner in settling him off to sleep again. This ensures that you get your rightful share of sleep. A young child is more likely to wake up at an inconveniently early hour, than to make a habit of waking up during the night. As long as this is the only problem, you can stop him disturbing you by leaving him toys to play with and books to look at when he wakes up.

ANXIETY AND NIGHTMARES

Nightmares, waking up during the night in need of comforting, and difficulty in getting to sleep are signs that something is wrong. It could be that the child is about to fall prey to an infection, or that he needs emotional reassurance. The birth of a new brother or sister, a change of home, going to a new school, or the death of a grandparent can all cause anxiety. During the child's waking hours, do everything you can to make him feel safe, secure, and loved.

Sleep patterns vary with age. Most young babies, provided they are fed, tired and comfortable, sleep soundly. But from about six months, most children wake easily and disturbed nights are common.

Children need a peaceful bedtime routine, at the same time each day. Leave a nightlight in the room if your child is scared of the dark.

Disturbed sleep can make a child insecure and unhappy. Reassurance from parents during the daytime will help calm and prepare the child for a good night's sleep.

COMPLEMENTARY THERAPIES

FLOWER REMEDIES

Bach Flower Remedies can safely be given to children. Rescue Remedy can calm a child who is upset (see p.227).

HERBAL MEDICINE

Chamomile infusion will calm a crying child. The same infusion in a warm bath will help prepare the child for a restful sleep. Giving 50–100mg of kava kava per day is also recommended.

AROMATHERAPY

Babies over four weeks old and young children alike respond well to a gentle bedtime massage. A few drops of chamomile essential oil in a carrier oil reinforce the soothing effect of the massage. Add mandarin oil to the bedtime bath (1 drop for babies, 2–3 for children).

HOME REMEDIES

A nourishing drink of warm milk and honey is good before bed, or to comfort a child who has had a bad dream.

NUTRITIONAL SUPPLEMENTS

You can also try 1,000mg tryptophan, 1,000mg GABA, or 1,000mg taurine at bedtime.

BEDWETTING

*I**t is unrealistic to expect your child to be dry at night as soon as he or she is toilet trained. Accidents will continue to happen for several years. There's no point pressurizing children who wet their beds by making them feel as though they have been bad. Instead, reassure them.*

Creating a fuss about bedwetting will usually make the problem worse. The best way to cope with it is to treat it as a minor practical problem, and remember that the child will eventually grow out of it. Use a waterproof undersheet to protect the mattress, and bedlinen that's easily washed and dried. Or, for under-fours, continue to use a diaper at night.

REVERSION TO BEDWETTING

If a school-age child, who has learned to be dry, starts wetting the bed at night, this is likely to be a sign of stress. It could also be that the new regime is so tiring that your child is sleeping more soundly and not noticing the need to empty the bladder. You must treat the matter very tactfully, since the child will probably feel ashamed of incontinence, and will feel even more anxious. Be reassuring, don't discuss the matter in front of other members of the family, help your child to deal with any anxieties, and the problem should soon pass.

WHEN TO SEE THE DOCTOR

Bedwetting is perfectly normal in young children, but if it becomes very troublesome, or if your child is also incontinent during the day, see your doctor; this can occasionally indicate a problem in the urinary tract, or even diabetes (see p.138).

Don't be angry with a child who wets the bed. Handle the situation delicately and reassure the child that all is well.

Bedwetting is usually temporary. In older children (aged four to seven), it may be the result of anxiety, perhaps caused by starting school or the arrival of a new sibling.

COMPLEMENTARY THERAPIES

HERBAL MEDICINE

Traditionally an infusion of horsetail, St. John's wort or American cranesbill, sweetened with honey, is believed to help, especially as a bedtime drink. All are astringent, and honey is anti-inflammatory. They may also have a placebo effect.

HOMEOPATHY

Pulsatilla or Silica, which treat emotional states related to bedwetting, may be useful.

Honey and herb infusion

GOING TO SCHOOL

*W*hen a child begins school, it can be a wrench for the parents as well as the child. This significant step marks a crucial stage in the child's growth toward independence, and could be the first time a child experiences outside influences without the protection and guidance of a parent.

Starting school is a major event in a child's life. For most children, it is the first time that they have been separated from their parents for long periods.

The first days at school are stressful, but most children soon settle comfortably into the daily routine. Encouragement and interest from parents helps the settling-in process.

A child who has already been in daycare or to a nursery will be more accustomed to interacting with children and adults outside the safe world of home. This child will find the transition to full-time school fairly easy. But for any child, the first few weeks at school can be demanding and stressful, even if he is enjoying it.

SIGNS OF STRESS

Hair-pulling, fidgeting, stammering, nightmares, reversion to bedwetting when previously dry, loss of appetite, and digestive upsets such as a tummy ache, feeling sick, or having constipation, can all be signs of stress in a child. Help to prevent stress by making sure that you still spend time alone with your child and get him or her to talk to you about school experiences. Minor matters such as using the school washrooms or remembering the correct peg or desk, can assume great importance, and encouraging your child to talk to you about his anxieties is often all that is needed. Always handle the discussion diplomatically, offer plenty of reassurance, and never belittle fears or worries.

If you are unable to work out what's wrong, you may find that talking to your child's class teacher helps. If you suspect that your child is being bullied, you must report it to the school principal. You only need to consult your doctor if the signs of stress continue to afflict your child over a long period. The doctor may consider referral for counseling or some form of psychotherapy.

LICE

Outbreaks of head lice frequently occur in schools. Lice like clean scalps and short hair just as much as less hygienic heads, and are as active as they ever have been. The tiny white eggs or nits are visible in the hair, while the grayish lice—the size of a pinhead—travel to the scalp, where they bite and cause itching. You can buy a special comb to remove the nits, and instead of using a proprietary scalp treatment, try making your own from olive oil and essential oils.

HOME SCALP REMEDY

Mix 1tsp/5ml each of lavender oil and tea tree or eucalyptus oil, 15 drops each of geranium and rosemary oil, and 10 tsp/50ml olive oil. Apply to the scalp, and leave overnight (or for at least an hour) before washing off with tea tree shampoo. Apply daily for five days, then once every three days, for two more weeks. Use the nit comb daily.

Lice are an unfortunate fact of school life. Hair should be washed with a blend of herbal oils and combed thoroughly to remove nits.

GOING ON VACATION

*T*oday, many previously inaccessible destinations have become popular vacation resorts. Such different environments can present a challenge to your child's health, and it makes sense to be prepared for the consequences of exposure to unusual food and the bacteria that thrive in warmer climates.

Before you book your vacation, do some research. Your family doctor or tour operator should have an up-to-date list of prevalent diseases and any vaccinations needed. Also check that your travel insurance is suitably comprehensive.

Once you have arrived, check out the local facilities and availability of medical care should you need it. Ask your travel representative if an English-speaking doctor is available 24 hours a day. Keep a note of any emergency telephone numbers the representative provides.

DIGESTIVE UPSETS

In general it is advisable to use bottled water for drinking and brushing your teeth. Think twice about food you have not encountered before, and in tropical countries, avoid salads and ice cream.

WHAT TO PACK

A pack of first-aid remedies can be very useful if you are traveling with young children.

GENERAL FIRST-AID SUPPLIES

STERILE DRESSINGS

•

PLASTERS AND ANTISEPTIC WIPES

•

INSECT REPELLENT

•

IF TRAVELING IN DEVELOPING COUNTRIES, ASK YOUR PHYSICIAN FOR A SUPPLY OF DISPOSABLE HYPODERMIC NEEDLES AND SYRINGES, TO ENSURE YOU HAVE STERILE EQUIPMENT AVAILABLE IF NECESSARY

•

TWEEZERS

•

EYEWASH

Wristband for motion sickness

THE CONVENTIONAL APPROACH

For sickness and diarrhea, short courses of antibiotics may be required. Antinausea medications for motion sickness are available over the counter. Antihistamine creams can be used for itching caused by insect bites. Protect children from the sun by using a high-protection factor sunblock.

The dangers of sunburn are well known. Children's skin is particularly vulnerable.

GENERAL COMPLEMENTARY REMEDIES

	Homeopathic	Herbal	Other
Vomiting and diarrhea	Arsenicum album	Golden seal	Activated charcoal biscuits
Motion sickness	Cocculus		
Insect bites	Urtica	Witch hazel	
Heat rash	Merc. sol.	Propolis cream	
Bruising and sprains	Arnica ointment		
Minor burns	Urtica		
Sunburn	Chamomile (see also p.128)		

SPECIFIC REMEDIES

OINTMENTS: Arnica (for bruising and sprains), St. John's wort or witch hazel (for insect bites), nettle (for skin problems), and chamomile (for sunburn —see also p.128).

When traveling with children, it's a good idea to take some basic complementary remedies to deal with eventualities such as heat rash, diarrhea, and sprains.

restoring

WELL-BEING

 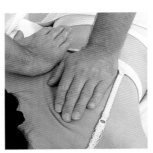  

contents

Introduction

The lifestyle you choose will have a profound effect on your well-being. Fresh air and movement are better aids to health than inactivity and poor diet.

When circumstances place stress on our body's reserves, illness often results. Disease can be regarded as a useful signal that all is not well, and that the homeostatic (balance) mechanisms are in need of attention. As long as 4,000 years ago, ancient writings discussed restoring harmony to the body during disease. The Chinese concept of Yin and Yang highlights this desire for balance (see p.230). Modern medicine appears to have turned its back on ancient wisdom in favor of powerful drugs that frequently suppress the body's own powers of healing. Although drugs may destroy the disease, their effects may disrupt body systems and vitality. It may be preferable to opt for a more natural method of treatment.

Complementary therapies such as massage and osteopathy are holistic treatments that take the whole person into account: body, mind, and lifestyle.

MAKING A DIFFERENCE

In selecting a natural treatment, consider the aspects of your lifestyle that require the most attention. There's little point in taking a homeopathic remedy and hoping for a miraculous cure if you are a heavy smoker living on a diet of convenience food that is devoid of nutrients. To make a real difference to your health, and to gain the full bene- fit of your internal healing energies, a holistic treatment plan is required. This takes into account all aspects of lifestyle, food and drink intake, exercise, emotions, and

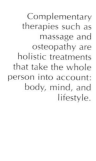

stresses. Hippocrates (c. 460–370 B.C.E.), the so-called "father of modern medicine," was immortalized by his phrase "Let food be your medicine." In more recent times, Thomas Edison was quoted as saying, "The doctor of the future will give no medicines, but will interest his patient in the care of the human frame, in diet and in the causes of disease."

Both visionaries focus on the patient assuming an active part in healthcare and maintenance: positive well-being is yours for the taking, but you may need to work diligently for it. Many people expect that delegating health problems to a physician and obediently swallowing pills will completely restore their well-being. This expectation, however, arises from living in a society where healthcare is oriented toward doctors and empirical science.

Obesity and heart problems are endemic in the Western world. It is vital to teach children the importance of a healthy diet from an early age.

HOLISTIC TREATMENT

Holistic healthcare requires you to take an active role in your own health. You may need to change your diet and eating habits, or to undertake a program of exercise and relaxation. You may wish to try a complementary therapy—in which case an understanding of your health problem will allow you to make an informed choice about which one to try. The "tools" for natural healing include osteopathy, acupuncture, massage, remedies from the botanical world (herbal and Chinese medicine), homeopathic remedies, and nutritional supplements that redress dietary deficiencies.

PROBLEMS AND TREATMENTS

The section that follows outlines some of the most common health problems present in clinical practice. It gives a selection of treatment options from both holistic and conventional areas of medicine. However, the information cannot replace the advice of a qualified health professional, who should be consulted before embarking on a self-prescribed treatment plan.

There are times when we all need to visit the doctor but responsibility for health also lies in our own hands.

107

DEPRESSION

*O*ccasional depression is a natural human response, but it has been estimated that nearly one in four people will need treatment for depression in their lifetime, with the risk being slightly higher for women than men. Depression tends to run in families and evidence suggests that in more severe cases there is an inherited factor.

Modern psychology describes depression as a mood or emotional state that is marked by sadness, inactivity, and a reduced ability to enjoy life. However, true depression is very different from simple grief, bereavement, or mourning, which are normal emotional responses to the loss of loved ones. The natural history of depression is extremely variable from person to person; it may be fleeting or permanent, mild or severe, acute or chronic. When a person is found to be experiencing alternating states of depression and mania (extreme elation of mood), he or she is said to suffer from a manic depressive disorder, also known as a bipolar disorder.

CAUSE

Although a single factor has not yet been identified to cause depression, there are two main areas of interest which have been formed in an attempt to explain this condition. One area is psychological, while the other focuses on the activity of certain biological substances in the brain known as biogenic amines. Monoamines, such as serotonin, melatonin, dopamine, adrenaline, and noradrenaline, are produced from building block proteins in the body. An imbalance in the supply of these building blocks, or in their conversion into monoamines, can result in depression.

There is mounting evidence to show that a low level of substances such as phenylalanine and tyrosine in the body may be responsible for the depressive states in some people. Phenylalanine is converted into a substance called phenylethylamine (PEA), which has an amphetaminelike activity in the brain. It has been found that depressed individuals have low levels of

One in four people will experience some level of depression at some stage during their life regardless of their age.

SYMPTOMS
Although there are varying degrees of depression, it is generally described as being much more intense than feeling low in spirits for a short period of time. Depression commonly results in a number of symptoms including a feeling of despair, general lack of interest and concentration, poor sleep, and low appetite, with every task seeming like a great burden. Other symptoms include tiredness, weight loss, lack of energy, waking early, aches and pains, no sex drive, feelings of worthlessness, irritability, and often suicidal thoughts.

PEA. It is also interesting to note that this substance is found in high concentrations in chocolate, a favorite comfort food in depression sufferers.

THE CONVENTIONAL APPROACH

Depending on the type of depression, various antidepressant medications are commonly prescribed. Drugs from the tricyclic group of medications (such as amitriptyline and prothiadine) are often the first choice in the treatment of depression. More recently, a relatively new range of medications known as selective serotonin re-uptake inhibitors (SSRIs) have been widely used (such as Prozac and Seroxat). These new drugs appear to offer fewer adverse side effects than traditional antidepressant medications.

COUNSELING

Simply talking through your feelings with an unbiased person often helps to resolve your worries. Try to find someone you can trust to share your feelings with, perhaps a friend, relative, or a health professional. It is worth trying to find a self-help group where you will meet people with similar problems who can empathize with you (see p.243).

Don't suffer in silence—talking it over often helps, whether it be with a qualified therapist or a group of friends or other sufferers.

COMPLEMENTARY THERAPIES

Get regular exercise to beat depression. This releases endorphins, the brain's "feel-good" chemicals that give you a natural high.

NUTRITIONAL THERAPY

It is worth supplementing your diet with amino acids. The D and L forms of phenylalanine are commonly available as the supplement known as DLPA, which has been successfully used by many sufferers—discuss using DLPA with your physician.

L-tyrosine is another beneficial amino acid for depression. Try taking 1,000mg L-tyrosine supplement twice daily, about half an hour before food. After one month, it is recommended to halve this dose.

It is important to consult a health professional before starting nutritional therapy. Many prescription drugs can have dangerous interactions with amino acids and they should not be taken together (see p.222).

HERBAL MEDICINE

For centuries traditional herbal medicine has used the "sunshine herb" to battle against depression. Recently this herb, known as St. John's Wort (*Hypericum perforatum*), has been studied in Germany. The discovery that the active agent, hypericin, alters brain chemistry and improves mood supports the traditional herbal teachings. It is generally recommended that a 300mg dose (containing 0.125% hypericin) is taken two to three times daily.

HOMEOPATHY

Homeopathic remedies such as Aurum metallicum (homeopathic gold) are frequently successful in treating depression. Consult your homeopath to discover for the right one for you.

There are a variety of conventional drugs that are used to treat depression. These only relieve the symptoms, however, and do not deal with the cause.

The herbal remedy St. John's Wort, known as "Nature's Prozac" has long been regarded as a valuable antidepressant.

FEARS AND PHOBIAS

A certain amount of fear is necessary in life in order to alert us to danger and enable us to deal with it. But persistent or irrational fear can develop into a phobia, which is then classified as a mental disorder.

A sense of panic in certain situations, such as when hemmed in by crowds, is common. Only when this fear prevents normal functioning does it become a problem.

Many people are frightened of certain animals—spiders in particular. Such fears may originate in childhood.

Lavender and chamomile have relaxing qualities. Add a few drops to a tissue and inhale the scent if you sense panic rising.

Fears can range from a horror of flying, to a fear of walking into a room full of strangers. When fear is experienced, the body releases adrenaline. This causes the heart to speed up, an increase in perspiration, a dry mouth, and a slowing of the digestive system. For some, these changes can bring about an increase in performance, for instance in an exam, but for others they cause panic, such as stagefright.

PHOBIAS

A person afflicted by a phobia panics unreasonably and will go to great lengths to avoid confronting the source of his fear.

Although there are many phobias, the most common ones are abnormal fears of open spaces (agoraphobia), enclosed areas (claustrophobia), spiders, public toilet facilities, or even of eating in front of other people. Phobias are thought to be caused by an underlying problem such as a previous bad experience, or abnormal brain functioning.

THE CONVENTIONAL APPROACH

Anxiolytics are used for anxiety, phobia and panic attacks. These drugs come from the benzodiazepine family, such as lorazepam and oxazepam. Shorter-acting agents, such as diazepam, are also commonly used. Your physician can also prescribe betablockers such as atenolol.

COMPLEMENTARY THERAPIES

AROMATHERAPY

Put a few drops of a relaxing essential oil, such as lavender or chamomile, on to a tissue. When you feel panic or fear, hold the tissue to your nose and breathe slowly.

BEHAVIORAL THERAPY

The therapist will help you learn to face your fear in a controlled way.

NUTRITIONAL THERAPY

Nutrients aimed at calming the nervous system, such as the B-complex vitamins and the amino acid (natural calming agent) known as GABA are very useful. It is best taken just before a stressful event. Magnesium is also a good addition.

HOMEOPATHY

Fear that leads to tears is best treated using Pulsatilla (6C). Those fears that appear to be worse at night respond to the remedy Kali carb. (6C). A useful remedy to use in cases of school phobia is Gelsenium (6C). The "C" means "centesimal," and refers to the homeopathic potency of the remedy (see p.226).

HYPNOTHERAPY

Hypnotherapy could offer an answer to severe fears and phobias that do not respond to traditional methods. Under the careful guidance of a hypnotherapist, patients are placed in a hypnotic trance. During this time, fears and phobias can be identified, addressed, and replaced with positive thoughts. Patients can gain long-term relief from their negative and often destructive thought processes (see p.238).

EATING DISORDERS

*A*norexia nervosa and bulimia nervosa are the most common types of eating disorder. The psychological characteristics of both are similar, with 10–15% of sufferers having additional behavioral problems such as shoplifting or alcohol and drug abuse. Anorexia is ten times more common in women than men, and bulimia is seen 50 times more frequently in women.

The fear of obesity warps the eating habits of anorexia sufferers, who are even distressed by the possibility of being the normal weight for their height and shape. A marked distortion of their particular body image results in obsessive behavior over food and eating and drives their relentless pursuit of thinness.

BULIMIA NERVOSA

This condition is characterized by occasional bingeing and vomiting, but also includes other symptoms such as depression (see p.108). Bulimic patients tend to be a little older than those with anorexia (starting between 17 and 18, compared to between 13 and 14 for anorexics). A bulimic's day revolves around eating, avoiding meals and carbohydrate foods, and drinking black coffee. By evening, the craving for carbohydrates triggers a bingeing and vomiting episode. Some bulimic patients can consume a staggering 26,000 calories in a single day, most of which is never absorbed.

THE CONVENTIONAL APPROACH

The main treatment for eating disorders is psychotherapy. Sometimes drugs are used to to help stimulate the appetite. SSRIs (selective serotonin re-uptake inhibitors) are antidepressant drugs that are used to increase the levels of serotonin in the brain.

Someone suffering from bulimia nervosa is likely to binge on junk foods and items high in carbohydrates, then induce intense vomiting to avoid weight gain.

Many people, particularly women, have a distorted view of their body size. The anorexic, however, grossly overestimates body size, even when severely emaciated.

COMPLEMENTARY THERAPIES

NUTRITIONAL THERAPY

During eating disorders, the body suffers greatly from nutritional deficiencies, especially of trace elements and the water-soluble vitamins (B-complex and vitamin C). A good multivitamin and mineral supplement should be taken daily (see p.222).

HOMEOPATHY

To help establish a healthy appetite, try Ignatia (6C) or Rhus tox. (6C) as a general appetite stimulant. Calc. carb. (6C) helps if you find meat difficult to eat. When bloating is a problem, take Nux vomica (6C), or try Lycopodium (6C).

Malnutrition, and vitamin and mineral deficiencies, are some of the serious side effects of eating disorders. Supplements of B-complex vitamins and vitamin C are recommended.

BEHAVIORAL THERAPY

The underlying problem with all eating disorders is faulty self-perception and a fear of obesity. When this gets out of control, the body's natural feeding mechanisms need support to get back on the right track. Behavioral therapy aims to restore a balanced perception, but requires the subject to be willing to make changes in her life (see p.243).

ADDICTIONS

Although the word "addiction" conjures thoughts of hard drugs, the most common addictions are socially acceptable, such as smoking, and drinking alcohol or caffeine-rich drinks. Chocoholics, too, are unlikely to be ostracized. But consuming too much of these products often results in serious health problems.

Smoking cigarettes probably has more detrimental effects on a person's health than any of the other commonly used drugs.

It has been estimated that over 4,000 toxic substances are inhaled each time a cigarette is smoked. Chemicals such as carbon monoxide bind with the oxygen-carrying substance in the blood, which reduces its ability to transport oxygen to the body's cells.

Other toxic constituents include lead, hydrogen cyanide, arsenic, nitrosamines, and even DDT (see also p.172).

Cigarette smoking is increasingly becoming socially unacceptable, but still remains a major problem. Tobacco contains nicotine, a highly addictive stimulant.

Alcoholism is a major problem in many countries. Its seriousness is often masked by the fact that having a drink with friends in a bar is considered to be an acceptable social pastime.

ALCOHOL

Alcohol is a drug that depresses the central nervous system, acting as a tranquilizer and mild anesthetic. However, alcohol intake can soon get out of hand: a glass or two at lunchtime, followed by a regular evening drink and then a nightcap, soon mounts up (see p.170–p.171).

CAFFEINE

It's often difficult to appreciate that some addictions can occur without you being aware of them. Caffeine is found in so many everyday products

SMOKING CAUSES:

- Heart disease
- Peripheral vascular disease
- Stroke
- Low birth weight
- Vitamin and mineral deficiencies
- Bronchitis
- Emphysema
- Cancer of the lung, mouth, tongue, larynx, esophagus, bladder, pancreas, and cervix
- Sinusitis
- Peptic ulcers
- Varicose veins
- Osteoporosis
- Impotence

(coffee, tea, cola drinks, chocolate, and some painkillers) that a daily intake can soon reach potentially toxic amounts. If this occurs every day, the body soon becomes addicted to the high caffeine level, and symptoms start to appear.

The main active agents in caffeine are a group of chemicals known as methylxanthines, which stimulate the central nervous system.

Another common problem associated with caffeine is the withdrawal effect that can generally be felt as a thumping headache, followed by a fatigued feeling and a craving for coffee. Nausea, vomiting, and a racing heart (tachycardia) may also be experienced (see p.171).

THE CONVENTIONAL APPROACH

Many addictions are treated using psychotherapy (see p.243), with or without drug therapy. Severe addictions need in-patient treatment and a strict detoxification program.

EXCESSIVE ALCOHOL CAN BE RESPONSIBLE FOR THE FOLLOWING:

- Gallstones
- Inflammation of the pancreas
- Stomach inflammation and ulcers
- Damage to the nervous system
- Premature senility
- Heart disease
- High blood pressure
- Vitamin deficiencies (B_1, B_2, B_3, B_6, B_{12}, A, C, D, E, and K)
- Osteoporosis
- Deficiencies of the amino acid L-methionine, zinc and magnesium
- High cholesterol levels
- Blood sugar problems
- Obesity
- Impotence
- Birth defects
- Immune suppression
- Increased risk of Candida albicans infection
- Aggravation of premenstrual problems
- Social problems
- Violent behavior

HOW MUCH IS TOO MUCH?

SUBSTANCE	RECOMMENDATION
Cigarettes	Do not smoke.
Alcohol	Men: 21 units a week.
	Women: 14 units a week.
	(1 unit = ½ pint beer, lager, or cider
	⅓ pint strong beer, lager, or cider
	1 small sherry
	1 measure of spirits
	1 small glass of wine)
Coffee	On average, a cup of coffee contains between 50mg and 200mg of caffeine.
	Keep well below 600mg per day.
	N.B. There are no official guidelines on coffee drinking.

COMPLEMENTARY THERAPIES

HOMEOPATHY

When alcohol is a problem use Quercus (6C) and Zinc met. (6C) to help reduce cravings and trembling.
To help reduce dependency on nicotine use Lobelia (6C), Tabacum (6C), and Nux vomica (6C), if nausea is a problem.

If you are trying to give up coffee use Coffea (6C) to help kick the caffeine habit and Nux vomica for the associated nausea.

NUTRITIONAL THERAPY

To help the body rid itself of the toxins accumulated during an addiction, supplement your diet with the amino acids L-cysteine, L-methionine, taurine, and glycine. Extra vitamin C, pantothenic acid and zinc are also recommended.

ACUPUNCTURE

This may be helpful for some addictions (see p.230).

VISUALIZATION

The use of relaxation and imagery can help you gain control over the inner psychological driving mechanisms behind addictions (see p.239).

During visualization, you relax and focus your mind on a chosen image, such as a beautiful tree. Learning to focus on this, while allowing positive thoughts, can help to break addiction processes.

INFECTIONS

Infections occur when the body is invaded by pathogenic (disease-causing) organisms such as bacteria or viruses. If the body has come across a "bug" previously, it memorizes the organism and produces antibodies (biological structures that enable the immune system to kill bugs) in preparation for a new attack by the bug. If, on the other hand, the bug is new to the body, white blood cells engulf the invading organism and "learn" about it, ready for the next time it appears.

Most of the symptoms felt by the unlucky sufferer occur while the white blood cells undergo this learning phase. As the disease is attacked by the white cells, the body temperature rises and sweating occurs. A rash often develops as the fever reaches a peak. Toxins are frequently eliminated during this phase, sometimes as an eruption of sores. Together with fever, joint aches and pains, muscular stiffness, and headaches are further manifestations of the illness.

The human body is remarkably adept at fighting disease. Here, white blood cells surround and attack an invading virus.

In a healthy individual, the majority of infections are self-limiting. But for the very young or very old, who are more vulnerable, special precautions need to be taken to try and prevent them from catching infections which, to them, may prove more serious. For those who find they get sick frequently, attention must be directed toward boosting the health of the immune system, our only line of defense against invading "bugs."

THE CONVENTIONAL APPROACH

Most bacterial infections are treated using either a broad-spectrum or a specific antibiotic. Viral infections are usually self-limiting.

COMPLEMENTARY THERAPIES

HERBAL MEDICINE

A tincture of elder (Sambucus nigra) can help induce sweating and speed recovery from many minor infections. During the illness, take the immune stimulant purple coneflower (Echinacea purpurea) at regular intervals to keep the white cells active and aggressive.

Elder has numerous medical uses. A tincture of either flowers or berries induces sweating, which helps to fight off infection.

HOMEOPATHY

The remedy known as Aconite (6C) should be taken within the first few hours of the illness, followed by Aesculus if backache develops, or Rhus tox. if muscular aches are felt. For prevention, homeopathic nosode therapy (remedies made from pathogens) is valuable. These act as a natural "immunization" against illness. For example, the nosode Influenzium protects against the flu.

NUTRITIONAL THERAPY

During illness, and as part of a regular prevention program, take extra vitamins A, E, C, B_2, B_6, and folic acid as well as the minerals zinc, manganese, selenium, and iron.

Vitamins

ME OR CFS

The incidence of people suffering from the long-term after-effects of viral infections often referred to as myalgic encephalomyelitis (ME), or chronic fatigue syndrome (CFS), appears to be increasing. We usually have to wait for viral infections to run their natural course, relying on the effectiveness of our own internal antiviral mechanisms, the immune system, and its special killer cells, to overcome them.

Viral particles are tiny, and many of them actually work by infecting bacteria, using bacterial cells or the body's cells to reproduce. They then burst out in their millions, ready to infect other healthy cells.

COMBATING VIRAL INFECTIONS

Once a viral infection takes a hold in your system, the white cells of the immune system are mobilized to attack the virus. If this initial cellular response is strong enough, the white cells will eliminate the viral assault. If, however, the white-cell attack is ineffective, the production of antibodies may help to strengthen the attack on the viral infection. This is known as the antibody mediated immune response. The biological battle may carry on for a long time, with neither side gaining much ground in the ensuing war. There are often sporadic bursts of viral assault, during which time the white cells defend their ground, making more antibodies, and attempting to suppress the viral advance. But because the viral particles are so small and have the ability to change their genetic makeup and characteristics, new strains of infection can occur and take hold in the debilitated system.

SYMPTOMS

During this time the sufferer will feel great lethargy and fatigue, causing a general loss of mobility and the ability to perform simple tasks. Symptoms of nausea, sleep disturbance, and an inability to concentrate are very common. People report that even walking is accompanied by muscular aches and pains and becomes a great effort. All these apparently unrelated symptoms can be linked by a process called lactic acidosis (an accumulation of lactic acid in the system).

THE CONVENTIONAL APPROACH

Because there is still great controversy over the condition, there is no accepted orthodox treatment for CFS. Some doctors believe the problem is more psychological than physiological, and prescribe antidepressants; others may use small doses of antidepressants to relieve physical symptoms.

EXERCISE
Exercise promotes healthy circulation and oxygen exchange in the cells. Even though CFS sufferers find exercise almost impossible, it's important to attempt to raise the heart rate daily as this is vital to recovery, although sufferers should not exercise to the point of exhaustion (see p.154–p.155).

COMPLEMENTARY THERAPIES

NUTRITION
Key vitamins and minerals must be included in an effective program for promoting the immune system: vitamins A, C, E, B-group (especially B_5, B_6, B_{12}, folic acid); zinc, magnesium, and selenium. Co-enzyme Q10 can help to prevent excessive lactic acid production (lactic acidosis), which may cause many CFS symptoms.

HERBAL MEDICINE
Echinacea is well known for boosting the body's resistance to infection. Goldenseal has shown remarkable immuno-stimulatory activity. These herbs are important for building up the immune system of a CFS sufferer (see p.224).

Echinacea

HEART CARE

Heart disease is a major killer of men and women alike. All body functions rely on the heart and circulatory system so it is of paramount importance to keep them healthy. A predisposition to heart disease may be inherited, but lifestyle also dictates the likelihood of suffering from it (see p.16–p.17).

Twenty minutes of strenuous exercise, three times a week, will help you maintain a good level of fitness. Cycling to work, instead of taking the car, is an excellent way of keeping fit.

Sacred to the ancient Druids, mistletoe (*Viscum album*) dilates the blood vessels and lowers blood pressure.

The benefits of garlic and onions have been known since ancient times. They are best eaten raw in salads, baked in the oven, or fried. Both guard against heart disorders.

While not all the causes of heart disease have yet been identified, smoking is one of the main factors that causes heart attacks, especially in younger people. Some of the chemicals in cigarettes cause the small blood vessels to contract and therefore interfere with the blood's ability to carry oxygen to the heart. Nicotine also increases the likelihood of cholesterol buildup on the walls of blood vessels.

High blood pressure or hypertension may go undetected unless you have regular health checks. Hypertension has a number of possible causes, including smoking and drinking a lot of alcohol.

Being overweight places a great strain on the heart. Coupled with a diet high in fat and a lack of exercise, being overweight can significantly increase your risk of heart disease.

THE CONVENTIONAL APPROACH

Modern medicine is focusing on prevention, and many different out-patient clinics are now available. Heart health depends on a combination of factors such as correct weight, stopping smoking, and keeping cholesterol low. Regular health screening has proved a good way of spotting early-warning signs of possible problems in later life.

HOW TO REDUCE YOUR RISK OF A HEART ATTACK

STOP SMOKING

•

CONTROL YOUR WEIGHT

•

CUT DOWN YOUR INTAKE OF FAT, ESPECIALLY ANIMAL FAT

•

TAKE REGULAR EXERCISE

COMPLEMENTARY THERAPIES

DIET

Try to eat more garlic and onions. Both have been shown to be anticoagulants, lowering both blood cholesterol levels and high blood pressure.

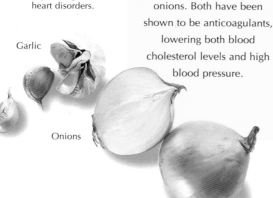

Garlic

Onions

HERBAL MEDICINE

The berries and flowers of the hawthorn (*Crataegus oxyacantha*) are very good sources of plant-based chemicals (phytochemicals). Berry and flower extracts have a powerful effect on lowering blood pressure, and can even improve the symptoms of angina.

•

Mistletoe also has the ability to lower blood pressure, and contains many chemicals that are biologically active in the heart. Mistletoe is commonly combined with hawthorn, but care must be taken because this plant is potentially toxic. It should be dispensed by a naturopath or herbal practitioner who is experienced in its use.

PALPITATIONS

*P*alpitations is the term used to describe an awareness of your own heartbeat, or the sensation that your heart is beating faster than normal, or even beating irregularly. Although an unpleasant feeling, palpitations are generally not accompanied by pain and are usually temporary.

Palpitations are usually harmless and can occur for many reasons. They may be felt after exercising, after a fever, acute or severe anemia, hypoglycemia, or in anticipation of an event such as an exam result, or in response to stress. They may even be the result of drinking too much coffee. A diet deficient in vitamin B_1 can also cause palpitations.

Ectopic heartbeats are those that are felt at rest as flutterings or thumping in the chest. These can be heard through a stethoscope as an early beat followed by a long pause before the next beat. They are not indicative of heart disease.

If palpitations are felt over several hours, recur over several days, or are accompanied by dizziness, nausea, chest pain, or shortness of breath, consult your doctor. They may be a warning sign of heart disease or an overactive thyroid gland.

THE CONVENTIONAL APPROACH

Medication is not usually given for palpitations that have no physical illness underlying them. Occasionally, relaxants (such as diazepam) are offered as a short-term help. If the heart itself is at fault, drugs aimed at normalizing heart rhythm, such as beta-blockers and digoxin, are prescribed.

WARNING

If palpitations persist over a long period, occur unexpectedly, or are accompanied by nausea or dizziness, they may sometimes indicate something more severe. You must consult your doctor, who may arrange for an electrocardiogram.

Medical treatment for palpitations may include drugs such as beta-blockers.

COMPLEMENTARY THERAPIES

NUTRITIONAL THERAPY

Taking about 30–60mg of magnesium, under your physician's supervision, will give relief in some cases. The amino acid known as GABA, which acts as a neurotransmitter, can be taken on a regular basis. It has a rapid calming action on the nervous system.

AROMATHERAPY

Relax in a soothing bath by adding five drops of an essential oil such as chamomile or mandarin (see p.228).

HOMEOPATHY

Spigelia (6C) can be taken during times of stress, supported by Digitalis (6C), but this should only be taken after consultation with a homeopath (see p.226).

Digitalis, from foxglove (*Digitalis purpurea*), increases the efficiency of the heartbeat.

Foxglove
(*Digitalis purpurea*)

ACUPRESSURE

The symptoms of palpitation were well known to the ancient Chinese. The recommended treatment was stimulation of the Shenmen or Heart 7 point (H7). This point can be found just under the wrist crease along an imaginary line running down the little finger, through the palm, and crossing the wrist crease. Steady pressure over this point can help balance the heart and reduce palpitations.

HIGH BLOOD PRESSURE

When *your blood pressure is taken two readings are noted, the systolic pressure, (the squeezing power of the heart), and diastolic pressure, which measures the elasticity of the arteries. "Normal" blood pressure is said to be in the region of 120/80 and is measured in millimeters of mercury (mmHg).*

It is advisable to have your blood pressure checked once a year after the age of 40. Hypertension rarely causes symptoms.

It has been estimated that about 80% of people with hypertension fall into a border-line category and do not require prescribed medication. Considering that it's such a common problem in the West, the cause of hypertension is still not fully understood. Only 10% of patients have the cause of their elevated blood pressure identified, the most common causes being hardening or narrowing of the arteries. This leaves about 90% of hypertensive patients unclear about the reason. In most cases high blood pressure can occur without any symptoms at all, which is why it has been termed the silent killer.

Severe hypertension is a major risk factor for heart disease, stroke, and an early heart attack. For those suffering only mild to moderate hypertension, natural remedies and lifestyle changes, particularly if you smoke or are overweight, may be all that's needed.

THE CONVENTIONAL APPROACH

There are various drugs that can be prescribed to lower blood pressure depending on the level of elevation and if any underlying cause can be detected. In most cases a mild diuretic can be given which helps to reduce the level of water and salt in the body's fluids. Alternatively, there are drugs available which alter the diameter of the blood vessels (vasodilators) or modify the heart's sensitivity to nerve stimulation (adrenergic neurone blockers).

COMPLEMENTARY THERAPIES

DIET
Follow a low-salt (sodium), high-potassium diet rich in fresh fruit and vegetables (see p.222).

Reduce salt intake; too much salt causes water retention, which raises blood pressure.

EXERCISE
This is vital, especially in mild to moderate cases. Regular exercise improves the cardiovascular system, enabling the heart to pump blood more efficiently and remove toxins from the system. Those with severe blood pressure problems must consult a health professional before undertaking any form of exercise regime (see p.154–p.155).

NUTRITIONAL THERAPY
Co-enzyme Q10 (30 mg daily) in conjunction with the minerals potassium (99 mg daily) and magnesium (250 mg daily) have been shown to help normalize high blood pressure. Calcium is also helpful.

HERBAL MEDICINE
Hawthorn (*Crataegus oxyacantha*) has a balancing effect on the heart. It also has a mild diuretic action. Garlic and onions are very effective for lowering blood pressure and should be included in the diet whenever possible. Siberian ginseng (*Eleutherococcus senticosus*) has the ability to reduce both cholesterol and blood pressure.

CHOLESTEROL

Cell membranes and hormones are made from cholesterol obtained from our diet or from internal production in the liver. The liver can make its own cholesterol to maintain the blood levels required for health. If the daily diet is high in animal (saturated) fat, the blood cholesterol level naturally rises, increasing the risk of heart disease.

The Western diet tends to include foods rich in cholesterol, such as eggs, red meat, cheese, butter, and other animal fats. Unfortunately a high cholesterol level does not present any symptoms. Symptoms may, however, reflect other disease states that have a high cholesterol level as a secondary effect. Sometimes yellow-white fatty deposits, known as xanthomas, appear around the inner part of the eyebrow area just near the nose and they may be the only external sign that cholesterol levels in the blood could be high.

For a better understanding of your cholesterol level it is wise to obtain a blood test (known as a lipid profile) that checks all the fats and their levels in the blood: cholesterol, triglycerides, and low and high density lipoproteins.

Changing your diet reduces the risk of heart disease. Trade saturated fats for fruit, vegetables, and fish.

THE CONVENTIONAL APPROACH

If dietary change has not helped, drugs that block or remove cholesterol synthesis known as reductase inhibitors can be used (lovastatin, simvastatin, atorvastatin) and fibric acid derivatives (ciofibrate and gemfibrozil). Cholesterol-lowering drugs known as anion-exchange resins may also be recommended to help bind bile acids, so stimulating the body to increase the conversion of excess cholesterol into more bile, thus making its excretion easier.

DISEASES CAUSING HIGH CHOLESTEROL

- Clinical obesity
- Sugar diabetes
- Low thyroid hormone
- Kidney disease
- Liver and gall bladder disease
- Drugs such as beta-blockers, steroids, estrogens, progestagens, and alcohol taken in excess

COMPLEMENTARY THERAPIES

DIET

Dietary changes can reduce your cholesterol level by over 10%. It is essential that your daily diet is trimmed of its fat and animal-based foods. These products come laden with extra unnecessary cholesterol. Try to eat more fresh fruit and vegetables with lean meats and fish for protein (see p.160).

Fatty foods such as bacon, butter, and fat-rich cheeses add extra cholesterol, increasing the risk of heart disease.

NUTRITIONAL THERAPY

Pantothine is the biologically active form of pantothenic acid (vitamin B_5) and is a key enzyme involved in the transportation and breakdown of triglycerides and cholesterol. A dose of 300mg is recommended, taken three times daily. Large doses of niacin may also help. For many patients folic acid is curative.

HERBAL MEDICINE

An extract from the resin of the myrrh tree *(Commiphora mukul),* known as gugulipid, has the ability to reduce blood cholesterol levels by stimulating the liver's ability to metabolize cholesterol more efficiently.
A dose of 25mg is recommended, taken three times a day.

Myrrh is a stimulant and anti-inflammatory.

Fatty foods

Myrrh resin

BRONCHITIS

*B*ronchitis can be acute or chronic, and is the result of inflammation of the airways that lead from the windpipe (trachea) to the lungs.

All living things need oxygen to survive. Pollution in the air, whether car exhaust fumes or cigarette smoke, can cause breathing problems.

Acute bronchitis is usually the result of a virus, such as the flu or a cold, which makes the lungs more vulnerable to invading bacteria. It lasts from a few days to a couple of weeks, while chronic bronchitis tends to affect those over 40 years. Smoking is the major cause.

Inflammation of the cells lining the bronchial tubes leads to an increase in the production of mucus or phlegm. In the case of acute bronchitis the sufferer will attempt to cough up the mucus which is yellow, green, or gray. They will suffer other symptoms such as wheezing, a high temperature, and pain in the upper chest. The chronic bronchitic suffers from a persistent cough, coughing up thick mucus on most days for three months or more each year. Other symptoms include wheezing, difficulty in breathing, and pain or tightness in the chest.

The lungs lie in the chest, protected by the rib cage. The trachea branches out into two main bronchi, which supply the lungs with air. These divide again into smaller bronchi, which divide into a network of bronchioles that open out into air sacs called alveoli.

Many people with chronic bronchitis will develop emphysema where the air sacs in the lungs become distended and the walls damaged, thus hindering the exchange of carbon dioxide and oxygen in the lungs. These two conditions put great strain on the lungs and leave the individual more susceptible to respiratory infections.

THE CONVENTIONAL APPROACH

The standard medical approach to bronchitis is the use of an antibiotic such as amoxycillin and bronchodilator inhalers or oral agents. In more severe cases, drugs that open up the airways are used to assist breathing.

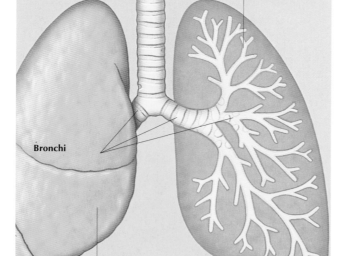

Trachea

Bronchiole

Bronchi

Right lung showing lobes

COMPLEMENTARY THERAPIES

HOMEOPATHY
Try Aconite 6C in the early stages, progressing to Sulfur 6C in the later stages especially when sputum becomes difficult to cough up and symptoms are worse at night. If a dry hacking cough is felt, the remedy Bryonia 6C is indicated, while a cough with yellow phlegm requires Hepar Sul. 6C.

AROMATHERAPY
Place a few drops of eucalyptus in a bowl of steaming water. Cover your head with a towel, close your eyes and inhale the vapors for a few minutes daily.

NATUROPATHY
Most bronchitics have food sensitivities, most commonly to milk and dairy products (see p.223).

ACUPUNCTURE
Acupuncture can be useful in treating bronchitis (see p.230).

ASTHMA

*A*sthma is a breathing condition where the airways in the lungs go into spasm. It's particularly common in children and it has been estimated that around 10% will suffer from an attack at some time with males being twice as likely to be affected. Often their symptoms will disappear by the time they become teenagers.

Asthma is often caused by a reaction to various allergens. The most common include pollens, dust mites, mold, and animal fur.

Bronchodilator drugs taken via an inhaler provide immediate relief.

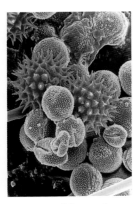

Asthma can be due to intrinsic factors such as an allergy to certain foods, particularly wheat-based products, or to substances in the air such as pollen or dust (see p.215), or extrinsic factors such as a sudden change in temperature, exercise, stress, a cold, or other respiratory infection.

During an asthma attack, the muscles of the bronchi walls in the lungs go into spasm, which causes the airways to contract. The sufferer has great difficulty taking a breath in, but finds it even harder to expel the breath, which results in wheezing and gasping for breath. The sufferer feels the need to cough but is unable to do so and in severe attacks may become pale, have an increased pulse rate, and may become extremely anxious, which exacerbates the condition.

Asthma often occurs at night starting with a tight feeling across the chest accompanied by wheezing.

THE CONVENTIONAL APPROACH

A common combination treatment for asthma sufferers is the use of an anti-inflammatory inhaler (steroid-based) with a puffer that helps open up the airways (bronchodilator). When used regularly they are very effective in helping the sufferer to control their breathing.

WARNING

A severe asthma attack can be life threatening and the sufferer should be taken to a hospital immediately if they experience severe breathlessness, are pale and clammy, or their skin becomes blue.

COMPLEMENTARY THERAPIES

HOMEOPATHY

For asthma symptoms that occur during the night try using Kali carb. 6C but if the wheezing is loud and distressing take Antim. Tart. 6C and seek medical advice.

HERBAL MEDICINE

One of nature's best cough expectorants (loosens phlegm) is Marsh mallow (*Althaea officinalis*). To help prevent the build up of phlegm try using Angelica (*Angelica archangelica*). Parsley (*Petroselinum crispum*) acts as a natural antispasmodic and helps relieve the tight chest symptoms associated with asthma.

ACUPUNCTURE

Acupuncture aims to disperse the cold and phlegm using Moxa (dried mugwort) burned on the ends of the needles to warm the lungs and the insertion of needles into specific points along the bladder, lung, and large intestine meridian (see p.230).

ACUPRESSURE

Asthma was well known in ancient China where the use of special acupressure points often gave welcome relief. One of the most popular points was known as Taiyuan or Lung 9 (L9). It can be found just under the wrist crease at the base of the thumb in a small depression between the tendons. During an attack, steady pressure over this point may help ease the chest congestion and tightness.

FLUID RETENTION

I t is very common for women to retain excess fluids due to excessive amounts of the hormone estrogen. Over the menstrual period this may be aggravated by an increase in the levels of the hormone prolactin. For some 60% of women suffering hormone-related fluid retention it is not unusual to gain over three pounds (1.4 kg) in weight.

When fluid accumulates in the body the classic symptoms of breast tenderness, swelling of the abdomen, legs, arms, hands, and face occur. Sufferers often women find that their rings become tight on their fingers.

The prolactin connection has been established in only a few studies but what cannot be contested is the implication of another hormone, aldosterone. This is vital to health but if an excess occurs in the lead up to menstruation it increases the amount of fluid held in the body.

Bloating caused by fluid retention during or just before menstruation causes discomfort, irritability, and a number of similar symptoms. But exercise helps.

THE CONVENTIONAL APPROACH

Depending on the cause, reduction of excessive body fluid can be achieved using drugs known as diuretics. These substances work by either increasing blood flow to the kidneys and so the rate of water removal or by stopping the retention of salt (sodium) by the kidneys.

PROVEN CAUSES OF FLUID RETENTION

EXCESSIVE ESTROGEN, PROLACTIN, AND ALDOSTERONE
•
STRESS
•
DEFICIENCY IN BRAIN CHEMICAL DOPAMINE
•
HYPOTHYROIDISM

WARNING

Anyone taking diuretics or those with kidney disease should take the advice of a health professional before supplementing their diet with potassium tablets.

COMPLEMENTARY THERAPIES

Bananas and raisins are rich in potassium, which helps prevent fluid retention.

Raisins

Bananas

NUTRITION

Minerals play a vital part in the regulation of body fluid. A deficiency of magnesium causes the adrenal glands to produce more aldosterone which in turn causes fluid retention. It is further aggravated due to the kidneys being unable to hold onto magnesium. 100mg of magnesium and B$_6$ daily often helps. The mineral potassium is becoming rare in our modern diets due to the tendency toward a high salt and low vegetable diet. The best advice anyone can follow is to cut out salt and eat more fruit and vegetables.

HERBAL MEDICINE

Some herbal remedies may not have the same strength as prescribed diuretics but they can be just as effective over a longer period of time. Try taking Bearberry (*Uva ursi*) extract, Boldo (*Peumus boldo*) extract, and Goldenrod (*Solidago virgaurea*) extract. Watermelon seed is also an excellent diuretic.

Boldo

CANDIDIASIS

When the yeast parasite Candida albicans *infests the gut, a condition known as candidiasis occurs. This refers to the overgrowth of candida and its general spread via the circulation to many parts of the body.*

Most sufferers complain of a craving for sugars, bread, and alcohol and have multiple allergies to food and often to perfume, tobacco, and strong odors. The bowels are upset with constipation and diarrhea.

COMMON FACTORS ASSOCIATED WITH A YEAST INFECTION

• Frequent or long-term use of antibiotics
• Use of the contraceptive pill
• Premenstrual syndrome
• Recurrent genital yeast infection in women and men
• Mental symptoms such as depression, mood swings, or confusion
• Cravings for sweet foods, bread, or alcohol
• Sensitivity to molds and dampness
• Regular use of cortisone-based drugs
• Chronic fatigue, indigestion, or food reactions
• Recurrent skin and/or nail fungus infections such as athlete's foot

As symptoms progress, depression, as well as chronic fatigue is not uncommon.

A chronic candida infestation can ultimately cause "leaky" gut syndrome, which occurs when the candida damages the cells that line the gut making large holes in the gut wall. Incompletely digested proteins are then absorbed into the general circulation, which can result in allergies. Sufferers also complain of joint pains because immune complexes (clumps of antibodies) become deposited in the joint space, irritating the sensitive lining.

THE CONVENTIONAL APPROACH

The antifungal drug nystatin is the standard medical treatment for yeast infections.

Complementary therapists believe uncontrolled candidiasis can produce a range of symptoms from chronic fatigue to joint pains and depression. Improving your diet, particularly avoiding sugar, can help to control candidiasis.

COMPLEMENTARY THERAPIES

HERBAL MEDICINE

Supplementing your diet with the herb goldenseal (*Hydrastis canadensis*), thyme oil, peppermint oil, and oregano oil extract can help eliminate candida in conjunction with dietary changes (see p.224).

HOMEOPATHY

Take the homeopathic remedy Candida albicans 6C for at least two months (see p.226).

NATUROPATHY

Acidophilus suppositories are recommended to encourage the growth of natural beneficial bacteria in the bowel.

THE EIGHT-WEEK DIET TREATMENT PLAN

Starve yeast infections of the foods on which they thrive by following the diet guidelines below for the next eight weeks.

EAT MORE OF THESE	AVOID
Vegetables	Sugar
Meats	Alcohol
Poultry	Fruit juice
Eggs	Dried fruit
Fish	Refined flour
Whole Grains	Breads
Nuts & Seeds	Baked foods
Butter	Vinegar
Oils	Pickles
Lemon	Cheese
Fresh fruit*	Mushrooms

* limit this to 2 pieces per day

IRRITABLE BOWEL SYNDROME

*I*t has been estimated that irritable bowel syndrome (IBS) accounts for over half of the gut problems diagnosed by hospital specialists with women being twice as likely as men to suffer from the condition. It often starts in adolescence or young adulthood and is thought to be exacerbated, or even caused, by stress (see p.185).

The cause of IBS is not fully understood, but one popular theory suggests that there is an imbalance in the nervous system. In times of stress, the hormone epinephrine is released which stimulates nervous activity and increases the heart and breathing rates. Changes also occur in blood glucose and fat levels and there is a general reduction in gut activity. If, over a period of time, the stress is not reduced or managed correctly, the reduced gut activity turns into a gross dysfunc- tion of normal activity. The bowel becomes unable to contract and move normally because it is under continuous unbalanced nervous stimulation.

SYMPTOMS

Irritable bowel syndrome commonly results in symptoms such as abdominal bloating, pain, cramps, fatigue, and alternating bouts of diarrhea and constipation. Sufferers often report the passage of mucus in the stool, gas, and nausea. Another common finding for some sufferers is the relief of abdominal pain by the passing of a bowel movement. For others, however, certain foods will actually induce pain.

Irritable bowel syndrome affects twice as many women as men. Adopting a high-fiber diet is a must but you should get much of your fiber in soluble form, for example, from fruit.

WARNING

It is important to seek professional advice when bowel symptoms are felt since other conditions may mimic IBS such as lactose (milk sugar) intolerance, celiac disease, diverticular disease and bowel cancer.

THE CONVENTIONAL APPROACH

Enteric-coated capsules of peppermint oil are also used medically to reduce bowel spasms, as well as bowel relaxants (colofac) and drugs which slow down gut motility (loperamide) and laxatives, such as castor oil, bisacodyl, and milk of magnesia.

COMPLEMENTARY THERAPIES

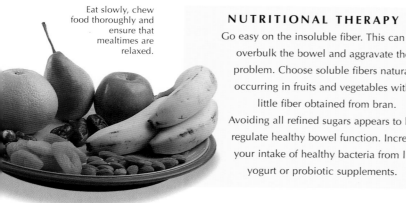

Eat slowly, chew food thoroughly and ensure that mealtimes are relaxed.

NUTRITIONAL THERAPY

Go easy on the insoluble fiber. This can overbulk the bowel and aggravate the problem. Choose soluble fibers naturally occurring in fruits and vegetables with a little fiber obtained from bran. Avoiding all refined sugars appears to help regulate healthy bowel function. Increase your intake of healthy bacteria from live yogurt or probiotic supplements.

HERBAL MEDICINE

Ask your local naturopath for a course of Roberts complex. This age-old combination of herbs has stood the test of time in the treatment of irritable bowel syndrome and contains many herbs such as American cranesbill, cabbage extract, marsh mallow extract, okra, slippery elm, echinacea root extract, and goldenseal root extract. Other natural bowel relaxants are the herbs valerian, rosemary, chamomile, and melissa.

COLITIS

*C*olitis mainly takes one of two forms; either ulcerative colitis or regional enteritis, also known as Crohn's disease, both of which are categorized as inflammatory bowel disease. Regional enteritis affects a small part of the bowel but in ulcerative colitis the entire lining of the bowel becomes inflamed and ulcerated.

Crohn's disease normally starts as an acute bout of abdominal pain with frequent bowel movements. The stool is commonly quite loose and only semi-formed. Pain tends to be colicky and localized to the lower right-hand side of the abdomen. Many sufferers report that eating can aggravate the pain. As the condition progresses, weight loss becomes apparent as nutritional deficiencies develop. Some Crohn's patients also go on to develop arthritis and eye inflammation (iritis).

Ulcerative colitis results when the lining of the colon becomes inflamed causing lower abdominal pain, frequent loose and bloody stools with fever, dehydration, and weight loss. These symptoms may grumble on for many years if proper treatment is not sought. One major potential complication with ulcerative colitis is the possibility of bowel cancer. Regular medical investigations are recommended.

THE CONVENTIONAL APPROACH

Many special drugs can be used to calm colitis. These include immune-suppressant agents and steroids, which can be taken for several months to reduce the inflammation.

Easy to digest, high-fiber foods such as bean or vegetable soups and whole-wheat bread are beneficial.

COMPLEMENTARY THERAPIES

NUTRITIONAL THERAPY

Slowly increasing your fiber intake can prove helpful for colitis but the very rough insoluble fibers such as bran can irritate the bowel. Unrefined grains and vegetables are preferable forms of fiber. Food allergies may play a key role in inflammatory bowel disease.

Legumes such as lentils and black-eyed peas are a nutritious source of fiber, and will not irritate the gut.

NUTRITION

Nutritional deficiencies of Iron, vitamin B$_{12}$, folic acid, magnesium, and potassium, vitamin C and D, and zinc are common in colitis so a broad spectrum multivitamin and mineral supplement is essential. Several clinical studies have shown that fish oils, such as high potency EPA (eicosapentaenoic acid) marine-lipid concentrate can help the inflammation associated with inflammatory bowel disease.

HOMEOPATHY

When the stools are watery try Colchicum and add Merc. Corr. If the colic pain is bad in the evening, try the remedy Colocynth mixed with Kali Sul. is recommended, while a combination of Colocynth and Natrum Sul. can help if the pains are bad in the morning.

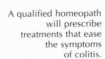

A qualified homeopath will prescribe treatments that ease the symptoms of colitis.

ECZEMA AND PSORIASIS

*E**czema, often known as dermatitis, is an inflammation of the skin. It often occurs around the back of the knees and elbows leaving the skin red, itchy, and scaly. Psoriasis is a skin disease that tends to run in families. The skin develops thick, red patches often covered by silvery scales. It usually affects the skin of the elbows, knees, back, and scalp. (See also p. 33.)***

Avoid harsh soaps as they will dry out the skin. Take warm baths or showers and use oiled or moisturizing soaps.

Eczema is thought to affect one in 12 people and can be caused by a number of factors including stress, sensitivity to certain foods, and coming into contact with chemical irritants (contact dermatitis).

PSORIASIS

Approximately 39% of psoriasis sufferers can recall a specific event that preceded the skin reaction. The stress that occurred over these events appears to act as a trigger, which makes the genetic predisposition to psoriasis run its course.

Research indicates that psoriasis may be a disorder of the immune system, where a type of white blood cell, the T-cell, that normally protects the body against infection is overproduced, triggering inflammation and excessive skin cell reproduction.

THE CONVENTIONAL APPROACH

For psoriasis, a combined drug and ultraviolet light treatment known as PUVA therapy, as well as the drug calcipotriol, can help. However, in most cases of eczema and psoriasis, steroid creams, and medications are commonly used.

FOOD NEEDS

Psoriasis skin cells need tryptophan, an amino acid only available from food. Foods high in tryptophan include barley, chocolate, cocoa, eggs, pasta, nuts, scallops, bread, cheese, fish, flour, ice cream, and meat. White mean contains less tryptophan apart from turkey, which is considered the best source.

COMPLEMENTARY THERAPIES

ACUPUNCTURE

Acupuncture can help both eczema and psoriasis (see p.230).

NUTRITIONAL THERAPY

Vitamins A, E, and C, zinc, and evening primrose oil are recommended. 200mcg selenium and 50 mcg zinc taken for a month followed by a lower dose of 15mg zinc and 50mcg selenium for a further month should balance skin cell production. Gamma linolenic acid (GLA) and omega-3 and -6 oils are needed for healthy skin.

HERBAL MEDICINE

The herb, *Coleus forskohlii* (from the mint family) helps to balance skin cell turnover. Correct liver function is vital and milk thistle extract *(silymarin)* is of great value. The active agent in licorice, Glycyrrhetinic acid, exerts a powerful anti-inflammatory action on the skin.

HOMEOPATHY

Sulfur is the most common homeopathic remedy used for eczema. Homeopathy can also help psoriasis (see p.226).

HYPNOTHERAPY

Hypnotherapy and healing can be very useful for skin conditions such as eczema and psoriasis.

Whole-wheat bread and cheese are rich in tryptophan.

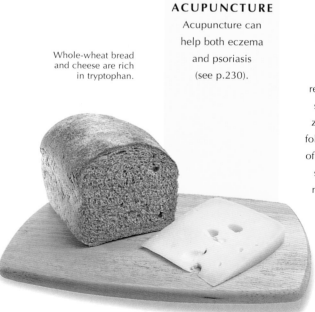

ACNE

*A*cne is the most common of all skin problems and occurs mostly on the face and to a lesser extent on the back, chest, and shoulders. The onset of acne usually occurs in puberty and approximately 70% of adolescents between the ages of 12 and 20 are affected at some point.

Puberty triggers massive changes in the growth and sex hormones. This results in an imbalance of oil (sebum) production that normally keeps the skin supple, and an excess production of keratin (a proteinlike substance). The combination of excess keratin and sebum consequently blocks the pores, which are then unable to discharge the sebum to the surface. Instead, it is left trapped deep within the skin where it turns into a toxic, rancid substance and causes inflammation and redness. This in turn produces acne. White cells then accumulate in an attempt to clear the debris and the mixture then becomes pus. This raises the internal pressure of the pimple and the surrounding tissues distend which stimulates pain endings and leads to discomfort (see also p. 33).

It is often hard for the sufferer to resist squeezing the infected area to get rid of a pimple. However, this drives the infected matter deeper into the tissues and causes a cystic sore, which may then leave a scar.

ACNE AND DIET

To provide the skin with all the factors needed for healing, follow a healthy diet high in fresh fruit and vegetables, fresh water, and fiber and low in sugar and salty foods. Avoid junk food, such as potato chips, and candy, cookies, and carbonated drinks.

THE CONVENTIONAL APPROACH

For girls, the contraceptive pill is often offered to balance the hormones. In most cases a mild antibiotic (minocyclin) is given. In stubborn cases the drug roaccutane is prescribed but it has potentially serious side effects. Topical antibiotics (clindamycin, retin-A, and benzoyl peroxide) may also be given.

Cut out dairy products and eat plenty of fresh fruit. Vitamin C is particularly beneficial for acne sufferers.

COMPLEMENTARY THERAPIES

HYDROTHERAPY

Try alternate hot and cold applications to the face. This has the effect of stimulating the circulation and encouraging the healing process. Adding some Calendula (*Calendula officinalis*) extract can have soothing benefits.

HOMEOPATHY

Calendula (*Calendula officinalis*) extract can have additional soothing benefits to the hot and cold applications. In general, apply the hot face cloth for no longer than 5 minutes followed by a cold face cloth for 1 minute. Repeat this procedure 2–3 times daily.

HERBAL MEDICINE

A number of herbal remedies have been traditionally used to treat acne. Alfalfa (*Medicago sativa*) for example contains many key nutrients required for healthy skin. Red clover (*Trifolium pratense*) extracts are recommended if the skin is inflamed and irritated, while the herb Burdock (*Arctium lappa*) can relieve dry skin and soothes any eruptions of pimples.

SUNBURN

This occurs due to overexposure to the sun without adequate protection and at best results in red, painful and inflamed skin. Over a period of time it can lead to aging of the skin and a predisposition to skin cancer.

SUNBURN CAUTION

Seek professional advice
- if the skin blisters
- if skin becomes infected
- if the pain and swelling do not ease within 5 days
- if the sunburn covers more than 10% of the body

DO NOT APPLY BUTTER OR OIL-BASED CREAMS TO BURNED AREAS

It is important to protect yourself from the sun, even in cooler climates. On hot days, seek shade and use appropriate sunblocks.

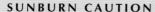

There are three types of ultra-violet radiation and these are classified into UVA, UVB, and UVC. The Earth's atmosphere absorbs most of the UVC rays so it is the UVA and UVB rays that cause detrimental changes to the skin.

Damaging UVA rays will penetrate the skin more deeply and cause more permanent damage to the skin in the form of aging, wrinkling, and loss of elasticity.

Only a small amount of UVB is necessary to cause skin damage. Exposure to UVB rays has been shown to cause more than 90% of skin cancers, so protection against these rays is essential.

BUILT-IN PROTECTION

The body produces a brown pigment, melanin, which is responsible for your tan, while this pigment blocks out some of the damage incurred, skin changes are inevitable. Fair-skinned people have less melanin than dark-skinned and so have a greater risk of burning.

If sunburn occurs, a layer of chamomile lotion, covered with a cold, damp cotton cloth is cooling. Vitamin E also aids healing.

HOME REMEDIES

- If you are unfortunate enough to get severely burned, seek professional advice immediately.
- For a minor burn apply a cold water poultice to the area immediately or rinse in cold water for 3–4 minutes to prevent blister formation. Apply after-sun cream to soothe and moisturize the skin.
- Break open a 400iu vitamin E capsule and apply directly to the skin to aid healing.

Vitamin E capsules

PREVENTION

- UVB rays are predominant between the hours of 9am and 3pm, so it's wise to decrease your exposure during these hours.
- A sunscreen with a sunlight protection factor (SPF) of minimum 15 should be applied every 2 hours to all areas exposed to the sun.
- Snow reflects the sun and can cause snowblindness and sunburns. Use a sunblock and wear goggles.

ALOE VERA

This plant extract is one of the simplest and cheapest sunburn treatments available. The fresh gel-like juice extracted from the leaves offers the most therapeutic benefits. Simply apply the natural gel to the inflamed area and leave it to soak in. This can be repeated as needed. Keep any spare aloe vera extract in the refrigerator.

THE CONVENTIONAL APPROACH

People with severe sunburn may need hospitalization and fluid replacement. In most cases, avoiding sunlight and applying lotion will suffice.

FATIGUE AND EXHAUSTION

*W*hile tiredness may just be the symptom felt at the end of a busy day, persistent fatigue can be a warning sign indicating illness or that we are pushing ourselves too far. Whatever the cause, exhaustion is a definite sign that we need to rethink our lifestyle.

There is a wide variety of causes of fatigue and exhaustion which can include illness, continual lack of sleep, low blood pressure, thyroid gland imbalances, anemia, stress, and pregnancy.

It has been estimated that around 40% of cases of fatigue are caused by psychological or lifestyle factors. This is not surprising considering that in the modern Western world we try to fit more into shorter periods of time than ever before and, together with an increased workload, this causes great pressure on the human spirit and body. Stress tends to accumulate to the point where the sufferer feels low, tired, and under pressure (see p.185). While relaxation may seem the obvious answer, often people are too busy, harassed, and wrapped up in their problems to take the time to relax. When they do, often they find it difficult to sleep as the mind is preoccupied with worries. Lack of physical exercise is also a contributory factor, regular exercise will increase your energy, help you unwind, and improve sleep.

THE CONVENTIONAL APPROACH

So long as there is no underlying cause for the tiredness your doctor may tell you to try and reduce your stress levels or take a vacation, which is good advice. A general tonic may be prescribed.

Chronic tiredness may be a sign of illness; it may also reflect an exhausting lifestyle and lack of rest.

COMPLEMENTARY THERAPIES

HERBAL MEDICINE

The use of stimulatory herbs can offer temporary relief from tiredness. Try taking ginseng extracts or ginseng tea. Other herbs such as cayenne can be effective when you simply feel run down (see p.224).

HOMEOPATHY

Arnica 6C is one of the best remedies for exhaustion. When circulation is also poor and requires stimulation try taking Carbo Veg. 6C.

TRADITIONAL CHINESE MEDICINE

A practitioner will identify the symptoms as originating from an imbalance in the life energies (Yin and Yang). The use of medicinal herbs and Chinese acupuncture help to rebalance the energies.

DIET

Even though it's tempting to eat high sugar foods followed by a strong coffee for the quick boost of energy, in the long run you will only overstress an already stressed system. Try to eat wholesome foods and complex carbohydrates such as grains and legumes (see p.156–p.159).

To boost energy levels, avoid sugary snacks. Instead, eat more nutritious slow-release carbohydrates such as rice and pasta.

BACK PAIN

Back pain is common and most people will eventually complain of some degree of discomfort from it during their life. It has been estimated that 60% of adults suffer from back pain, 30% of whom become chronic sufferers. Those most commonly affected include professional drivers and manual workers. Low back pain is the most common work-related disorder and in economic terms the most costly (see also p.32).

Back pain may be sharp or dull, diffuse, and poorly localized. Sharp pains are very suggestive of nerve involvement especially if the pain travels or shoots down the legs (sciatica). A disk injury is typically worse when sitting and is felt to be easier when standing or keeping mobile, while muscular spasm is felt to be the reverse. Muscular spasm is an almost universal back pain symptom. It can be very difficult to control. When the body senses intense pain its natural reaction is to "splint" the affected area with a spasm.

Massaging relaxes muscles and eases aches and pains. Visit a practitioner, or ask a friend to massage you.

Lifting or carrying heavy objects puts great strain on the back and can cause problems. Back-packs are one way of distributing weight more evenly.

CAUSES IN ADULTS

POOR WORKING POSTURE AND INADEQUATE/
INFREQUENT WEIGHT TRAINING

•

EXTENDED PERIODS WORKING IN A FIXED POSITION

•

POOR CAR SEAT DESIGN

•

"SOFT" LIFESTYLE, LACK OF EXERCISE, SAGGING
MATTRESSES, AND BADLY DESIGNED HOME SEATING

•

WEAK ABDOMINAL AND BACK MUSCLES

•

INADEQUATE VITAMIN C

CAUSES IN CHILDREN

POOR SEATING

•

LACK OF SCHOOL LOCKER
SPACE THEREFORE VERY HEAVY
SCHOOLBAGS

•

LONG PERIODS OF SLOUCHING
IN FRONT OF THE TV

•

EXCESSIVE USE OF
HOME COMPUTERS AND
COMPUTER GAMES

Poor posture and slouching will cause a backache. Sit upright, with your feet firmly on the ground, and use a chair that supports the lower back.

MEDICAL INVESTIGATIONS

One of the most frequently requested tests is the X ray but unfortunately this test is very limited. X rays only show bone and don't give much indication of the condition of the soft tissues, such as nerves and muscles.

Modern imaging techniques to identify problem areas include magnetic resonance imaging (MRI) and computerized tomography (CT). Both have revolutionized the diagnosis of low back pain. These methods can show bone as well as all the soft tissue structures that can generate pain. MRI also has the additional benefit of being a radiation-free technique.

THE CONVENTIONAL APPROACH

For most back pain simple painkillers (aspirin or acetaminophen [paracetamol]) or the heat from a hot water bottle wrapped in a towel and placed on the back will bring relief. Sleeping on a firm mattress that supports the back is also recommended. For more serious cases, a course of nonsteroidal anti-inflammatory drugs (NSAIDs), such as ibuprofen, may be needed, with or without a muscle relaxant. However, these drugs can upset the digestive tract.

The spine is a mobile and flexible structure that supports the entire skeleton. It contains the spinal cord, which links brain and nerves—32 pairs of nerves radiating out from the spine.

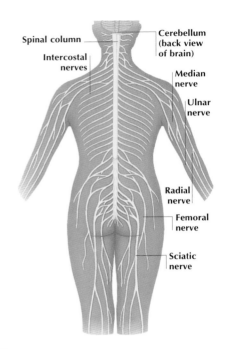

Spinal column
Intercostal nerves
Cerebellum (back view of brain)
Median nerve
Ulnar nerve
Radial nerve
Femoral nerve
Sciatic nerve

COMPLEMENTARY THERAPIES

OSTEOPATHY

Manipulation of the bones in the back by an osteopath can give great relief to backache sufferers. Gentle mobilization is preferable during a backache, especially when the condition is acute and very painful. Many osteopaths will advise that an ice pack (a bag of frozen peas is best) is needed in the early stages of a backache in order to minimize the reflex muscle spasm (see p.233).

ALEXANDER TECHNIQUE

The effect of posture cannot be underestimated in the long-term treatment of back pain. A method of postural re-education, known as the Alexander Technique, aims to teach people body awareness and an appreciation of postural stress and strains.

ACUPUNCTURE

The ancient Chinese technique of inserting ultrafine needles into the body has stood the test of time. Modern research now confirms that the nerve stimulation caused by acupuncture can help reduce muscle spasm and bring rapid relief from back pain (see p.230).

The Alexander Technique aims to put you in touch with your body and re-educate you about posture. When lifting a heavy object, for instance, bend your knees and keep a straight back.

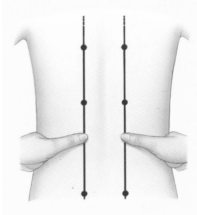

ACUPRESSURE

Many well documented points can be used, such as those known as Shenshu Bladder 23 (B23) and Yishe Bladder 49 (B49). To find them, place your hands around your waist so that your thumbs sit close to your spine. Count up 3 finger widths from the crest of your pelvis and 3 finger widths out from the spine to find B49. Counting 2 finger widths in toward the spine from this position finds B23.

HEADACHES AND MIGRAINES

A headache may be defined as any type of pain arising from the scalp and the tissues around the brain. It has been estimated that 98% of the Western world suffer from nonserious headaches on a regular basis. Migraines affect around 10% of the population and although some people will only suffer from an attack once a year, on average sufferers experience an attack once a month, which can last anything from a couple of hours to a few days.

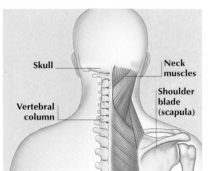

Persistent tiredness, poor posture, and stress can cause muscular stiffness and pain in shoulders and neck, leading to headaches.

One of the most common causes of headaches is muscular tension in the neck. As the pressures of daily life mount, stress hormones are released. These make the muscles tighten, drawing the shoulders up around the ears. When the stress diminishes we are often left "stuck" in this position without being aware of it (see p.184–p.185).

Another stress-related symptom is grinding the teeth at night. Headaches can result from the biting down action and contraction of the muscle groups over the temporal region of the skull. Some headaches are commonly felt in the morning and may be due to the blood sugar levels dropping in the night, leaving the brain starved of its primary fuel. A snack before bed can help prevent this.

To avoid stiffness and muscular tension at work, stretch regularly or get up and walk around for a while.

CAUSES OF SERIOUS HEADACHES

HIGH BLOOD PRESSURE

•

TUMOR

•

MENINGITIS

•

HEAD INJURY

•

LIVER DISEASE

•

ANEMIA

ANCIENT REMEDY

Documented evidence for the treating headaches can be traced to ancient Egypt. Trepanning, (drilling or cutting a hole in the head) was used to release pressure or perhaps let demons out.

POSSIBLE CAUSES OF NONSERIOUS HEADACHES

MUSCULAR SPASM

•

SIDE EFFECTS OF MEDICATION

•

GRINDING TEETH

•

DEPRESSION (SEE P.108–P.109)

•

ARTHRITIS (SEE P.146–P.147)

•

HYPOGLYCEMIA (LOW BLOOD SUGAR)

•

SPINAL PROBLEMS IN THE NECK

•

EYE STRAIN.

•

FOOD SENSITIVITIES

MIGRAINES

Migraines tend to be characterized by a throbbing, severe pain, usually on one side of the head as blood vessels in the brain contract and expand. These types of headaches are sometimes accompanied by visual disturbances, such as double vision or blind spots along with nausea and vomiting. Depending on the individual, a migraine attack can last for either a few hours, or in acute cases, several days.

TYPES OF MIGRAINE

Typically there are two types of migraine: 80% begin as headaches that slowly increase in intensity until it becomes a throbbing pain, which is made worse by movement or noise. An estimated 20% are preceded by a visual aura that includes an area of visual blindness and flashing lights half an hour before the throbbing pains. They can also cause temporary weakness on one side of the body. Some sufferers have been known to become sensitive to certain sounds or smells before an attack.

THE CONVENTIONAL APPROACH

For simple headaches the use of painkillers (analgesics) such as acetaminophen (paracetamol) or aspirin are normally sufficient to relieve the pain. When migraines are a problem, special drugs that help to regulate the blood flow (such as ergotamine) can help. The new choice is a drug that blocks the action of serotonin (5-HT blocker). Known as sumatriptan, this drug has revolutionized the treatment of migraine for many sufferers.

CAUSES
Although there seems to be an inherited factor to migraines, around 70% of sufferers are women which suggests that hormones may play a key role.

A migraine can be temporarily disabling. It usually begins with a headache that develops into a throbbing pain. It may be preceded by visual disturbances.

COMPLEMENTARY THERAPIES

NATUROPATHY
The naturopathic approach will include the identification of food sensitivities and the use of traditional herbal remedies such as valerian and passiflora. To help stabilize blood sugar levels, the trace mineral Chromium is an effective nutrient (see p.223).

OSTEOPATHY
Osteopathic treatment aimed at releasing tight spinal joints and muscles can give great relief (see p.233).

NUTRITIONAL THERAPY
Try avoiding dietary stimuli such as cheese, red wine, beer, chocolate, oranges, and coffee, which can set off an attack (see p.156). Large doses of riboflavin are excellent.

HERBAL MEDICINE
Common tansy (*Tanacetum vulgare*) and feverfew (*Chrysanthemum parthenium*) are a traditional remedy for migraines. They slow the expansion of the blood vessels, preventing the throbbing head pain. Feverfew must not be taken during pregnancy.

Feverfew

Cheese

Some migraine sufferers find it helpful to avoid cheese, red wine, and chocolate.

Chocolate

Red wine

SOFT TISSUE INJURIES

The skeletal framework of the body is supported by muscles, ligaments, tendons, and connective tissues, which are known collectively as the soft tissues. During sporting activities it is the soft tissues that carry most of the strain and receive considerable stress, especially in contact sports such as football, hockey, and certain martial arts.

To avoid injury, always do some warm-up and stretching exercises as part of your exercise or sport routine.

Most sports injuries occur accidentally but a large proportion can be avoided. Warming up properly beforehand is essential since all soft tissues benefit from a good blood supply. Your level of general fitness is another important factor to consider. If you spend most of your working day sitting at a desk you cannot expect your soft tissues to withstand the unaccustomed forces associated with sports.

Running injuries are common and can be avoided. To prevent leg strain, run in an easy fashion, arms low, body moving smoothly. Land heel first.

ACTIVITIES CAUSING INJURY

OVERSTRETCHING MAY LEAD TO MUSCLE DAMAGE (STRAIN)

•

IMPACT CAN CAUSE BRUISING

•

OVERTWISTING CAN RESULT IN LIGAMENT DAMAGE (SPRAIN)

•

REPETITIVE INJURY CAN CAUSE TENDON INFLAMMATION (TENDONITIS)

STRAINS

Stretching injuries are very common and are most likely to occur when warming-up exercises have not been performed adequately. Muscular tears tend to occur in the belly (middle) of the muscle or where the muscle joins onto its tendon. These injuries need prompt treatment to prevent chronic changes occurring in the soft tissue.

BRUISES

When the body is damaged by an impact, bleeding occurs within the tissues involved. This is commonly seen as a bruise, when a bluish-black mark appears on the skin that then turns reddish-yellow before eventually disappearing. More serious bleeding results in a hematoma, which represents a larger accumulation of blood from a broken blood vessel, often clotted. Like most soft tissue injuries, the appropriate first aid can make all the difference. However, a hematoma that occurs in the brain can be dangerous and cause permanent brain damage.

SPRAINS

Twisting injuries occur when the joint (commonly the knee) is placed under great strain during a rotational movement such as a tennis player changing direction quickly with the foot firmly placed on the court. During this type of injury the ligaments, which are designed to resist such movements, are damaged or torn.

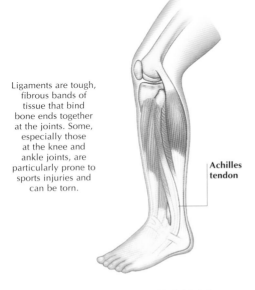

Ligaments are tough, fibrous bands of tissue that bind bone ends together at the joints. Some, especially those at the knee and ankle joints, are particularly prone to sports injuries and can be torn.

Achilles tendon

THE CONVENTIONAL APPROACH

Depending on the type of injury, medications ranging from simple painkillers such as acetaminophen (paracetamol) through to steroids may be given. But the basic first-aid approach must be followed first—apply ice and elevate the leg.

RSI

Overuse injuries occur when repetitive stresses are placed on the joints. This type of injury is often seen in racket sports such as tennis, or in the use of computer keyboards. The friction that occurs irritates the tendons that pass across the joints resulting in inflammation and pain on movement. If left untreated, serious disability can occur.

FIRST AID FOR SOFT TISSUE DAMAGE

During the acute stage or at the sports site always apply ice immediately and if possible try to elevate the damaged area. If swelling does not immediately occur (suggesting bleeding into a joint) also apply compression to the damaged area and of course avoid physical activity until the injury can be fully assessed (see also p.95). If the injury occurred over 24–48 hours ago the most acute stage has been missed. During this subacute stage apply alternate hot and cold treatment. Use a hot damp tea towel applied for three minutes followed by a cold towel for two minutes. This helps to reestablish a healthy blood supply.

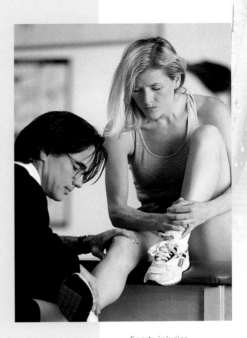

Sports injuries should be dealt with immediately to avoid problems later. Alternating cold and heat reduces swelling, and rest is essential, however much you love exercise.

COMPLEMENTARY THERAPIES

HOMEOPATHY

From the onset of the injury take Arnica 6C and Hamamelis 6C by mouth three times a day. A cream made from Hamamelis and Calendula can be very helpful in the early stages of an injury.

HERBAL MEDICINE

One of the classic herbal treatments for tissue damage is the application of Arnica cream. This soothes the pain and helps to reduce the swelling and bruising (see p.224).

NUTRITIONAL THERAPY

For tissue injury take 1,000mg vitamin C and 15mg zinc daily. This will help boost immune defenses until the injury has healed.

Soluble vitamin C

135

GOLFER'S AND TENNIS ELBOW

I rrespective of their names, golfer's elbow and tennis elbow are not confined to these sports. They can occur in any situation where there is overuse of the forearm muscles.

Damage to the elbow caused by golf or tennis can sometimes be prevented by changing the size of racket or club or by altering your technique

Their technical names for this condition are medial and lateral epicondylitis, which mean inflammation of the elbow muscles and tendons.

Tennis elbow (lateral epicondylitis) involves inflammation of the outer side of the elbow at the point where the muscles that extend the wrist are attached. Golfer's elbow (medial epicondylitis) is an inflammation of the inner part of the elbow where the muscles that flex the wrist are attached.

These injuries are the result of an overload placed on the muscles accompanied by repeatedly bending and straightening the arm or twisting the arm while gripping something like a racket or golf club. This causes tiny tears to occur.

The onset of this overuse injury can occur suddenly with pain ranging from a slight twinge in the elbow to a continuous severe pain which radiates up and down the arm. Power in the arm becomes greatly reduced so try to avoid pressure on the affected area for a few days.

THE CONVENTIONAL APPROACH

The inflammation will usually fade after a few days' rest but for more severe cases, if physical treatments have not helped, a steroid injection is often offered. This may help to settle down the inflammation and reduce pain and stiffness.

COMPLEMENTARY THERAPIES

HYDROTHERAPY

Ice packs need to be applied as soon as the pain is felt to reduce the degree of inflammation.

Applying an ice pack to the affected area reduces swelling. In the longer term, physiotherapy, ultrasound, exercises, and stretching are helpful treatments.

OSTEOPATHY

Along with general advice, such as when it will be safe to return to the sport or to work, an osteopath will recommend exercises and treat the muscles and tendons using specific stretching and strengthening exercises (see p.233).

HOMEOPATHY

Try taking the remedy Rhus. Tox. 6C to reduce the inflammation and tenderness.

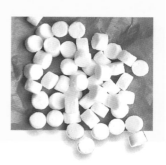

CARPAL TUNNEL SYNDROME

*T*his painful and aggravating condition is caused by compression of the median nerve as it passes through the tunnel formed by the carpal (wrist) bone. Symptoms have been described of burning, aching, and pins and needles in the palm, thumb, first, and second fingers.

Carpal bones

Ligaments
Median nerve

CAUSES

ARTHRITIS OF THE WRIST/
RHEUMATOID ARTHRITIS

•

FLUID RETENTION

•

PREGNANCY

•

WRIST FRACTURE

•

DIABETES

•

THYROID DISEASE

•

MENOPAUSE

Pains felt at night are a classic symptom of carpal tunnel syndrome since the inactivity of sleep allows fluids to accumulate and compress the nerve. During the day clumsiness or dropping things due to the altered sensations felt in the fingers is not uncommon.

Carpal tunnel syndrome has become more common with the increased use of computers and the keyboard activities that are associated with modern office work. The wrist posture that is commonly adopted by those involved in computer-based work (wrist bent slightly back) causes the tunnel to narrow and the ligament that forms the roof of the tunnel to thicken. It's not unusual for carpal tunnel syndrome to form part of the repetitive strain syndrome that frequently plagues computer users.

Widespread use of keyboards has led to an increase in so-called repetitive strain injury (RSI). Carpal tunnel syndrome often accompanies RSI.

The meridian nerve passes into the hand over a gap—the carpal tunnel—and under a ligament at the front of the wrist. Pressure on the nerve causes sensory disturbance.

THE CONVENTIONAL APPROACH

Medical approaches include immobilizing the area with wrist braces or splints, physiotherapy and anti-inflammatory drugs. Surgery may be necessary.

COMPLEMENTARY THERAPIES

NUTRITION

There is evidence to suggest that vitamin B_6 (pyridoxine) is beneficial but results may take up to six months to become evident. When taking B_6 it's important not to overdose because there is a slight risk of developing side effects similar to the symptoms of carpal tunnel syndrome—pins and needles in the hands. A dose of 100mg daily is adequate, plus 500mg of magnesium daily. Reducing protein in your diet is advisable.

HERBAL MEDICINE

Quercetin and Bromelain have shown great potential in the treatment of carpal tunnel syndrome. Take 125mg of both twice daily on an empty stomach.

ACUPUNCTURE

Acupuncture can be beneficial for carpal tunnel syndrome (see p.230).

ACUPRESSURE

Carpal tunnel syndrome affects the median nerve that lies just below the traditional Chinese acupressure point called Daling or Pericardium 9 (P9). The point is easily found on the center of the wrist crease in the midline of the palm. Gentle rhythmic pressure over P9 can help disperse the fluid congestion around the nerve.

DIABETES

There are two types of sugar diabetes: type one is known as insulin-dependent diabetes and usually starts in childhood. It requires a regular intake of insulin in the form of injections. Type two, noninsulin-dependant or mature-onset diabetes begins later on in life and can be controlled by diet.

Diabetes mellitus is a condition in which the amount of glucose in the blood is too high due to the body being unable to utilize it properly.

Glucose comes from the digestion of starchy foods such as bread or potatoes and from sugar and other sweet foods. It also comes from the liver, which produces glucose and passes it into the bloodstream.

Insulin, a hormone produced by the pancreas, helps the glucose to enter the body's cells where it is used as fuel.

Diabetes is a lifelong condition that may be hereditary. The appropriate diet and medication can control symptoms.

TYPE ONE DIABETES

Insulin-dependant diabetes appears before 40 years of age and develops due to a severe lack of insulin because most of the cells that make it have been destroyed.

TYPE TWO DIABETES

Noninsulin-dependant diabetes usually occurs in people over the age of 40. It develops when the body can still make some insulin but not enough to balance the blood sugars accurately enough for health, or if the insulin receptors are not functional.

SYMPTOMS

INCREASED THIRST

•

INCREASED NEED TO PASS URINE

•

WEIGHT LOSS

•

FATIGUE

•

DRY MOUTH

•

A NEED TO PASS URINE AT NIGHT

•

IRRITATION AFFECTING THE GENITALS

THE CONVENTIONAL APPROACH

For type one diabetes, the only treatment is insulin injections. For type two diabetes, diet is the main treatment prescribed, with hypoglycemic drugs to lower blood glucose levels if needed.

Naturopaths recommend a diet that is high in complex carbohydrates and high-fiber foods such as whole-wheat bread, whole-wheat pasta, brown rice, chickpeas, and dried beans.

COMPLEMENTARY THERAPIES

DIET
A diet that is low in artificial sweeteners and additives is essential. Increase your intake of dietary fiber and try to eat more whole grains and legumes to provide a good source of slow-release sugar for the body (see p.165).

NUTRITION
A dose of the mineral chromium (100 to 200 mcg daily) assists in the natural balancing of blood sugar levels. Additional nutrients are needed to help prevent other tissues from being affected by the diabetes; these include vitamin E, C, B$_6$, and biotin with the minerals magnesium, zinc, selenium, chromium picolinate, and vanadium sulfate.

HERBAL MEDICINE
Blueberry (*Vaccinium australe*) or Bilberry (*Vaccinium myrtillus fructus*) extract and *Gymnena sylvestre* extract give extra stability to blood glucose levels. In addition to these, Fenugreek seed extract (*Trigonella foenum-graecum*) and Bitter melon (*Momordica charantia*) can be helpful.

Navy beans

Kidney beans

Brown rice

MULTIPLE SCLEROSIS

Multiple sclerosis (MS) is a disease of the central nervous system. It attacks and gradually destroys the myelin sheath, which forms a covering over the nerves in the brain and spinal cord. Women are affected slightly more often than men. The onset of the disease usually occurs between the ages of 20 and 40.

The causes of MS are still unknown although a number of theories have been put forward. While there may be an inherited tendency to the disease there seems to be a strong link to a virus which triggers the immune system to attack the myelin sheath. Diet is also thought to play a role and studies have shown that there is a strong association between diets high in animal and dairy products and MS.

SYMPTOMS

The symptoms of MS can vary widely and patients can have periods of remission from their symptoms for many years.

THE CONVENTIONAL APPROACH

The latest medical approach to MS is the use of beta-interferon, which helps to normalize the immune system (see p.34) and prevent further degeneration of the nerve covering.

SYMPTOMS

PINS AND NEEDLES OR NUMBNESS IN A LIMB

•

SPEECH DIFFICULTIES

•

BLURRED VISION

•

FATIGUE

•

LOSS OF COORDINATION AND STAGGERING; DRAGGING ONE OR BOTH HEELS

•

INCONTINENCE

•

PSYCHOLOGICAL CHANGES SUCH AS MOOD SWINGS, APATHY

•

FACIAL NUMBNESS OR PAIN

•

IMPOTENCE IN MEN

Physiotherapy and very gentle exercises can help to strengthen the muscles and improve or maintain coordination.

COMPLEMENTARY THERAPIES

ACUPUNCTURE

A combination of points on the stomach, kidney, liver, and spleen meridians are used. Treatment may also involve the use of electrical stimulation of the needles known as electroacupuncture. Ear acupuncture is also used and is generally more effective than body acupuncture for treating the sufferer of MS (see p.230).

DIET

It is generally advised that MS patients avoid milk and dairy products and red meat (see p.165). Your diet should be low in fat and include plenty of antioxidants.

Cheese

Milk

NUTRITIONAL THERAPY

A purified extract from the cell walls of yeast has shown great promise as an immune system balancing agent especially in treating MS. The extract is known as Beta-1,3-glucan and should be taken as a 50mg dose twice each day between meals, along with a high potency dose of evening primrose oil.

High doses of evening primrose oil may help to fortify the immune system.

CANCER

ancer can be defined as benign, which is not life-threatening, as very rarely spreading, or as malignant. Malignant cancers can spread throughout the body infiltrating healthy tissue with the seeds of a new cancer. This new cancer may be slow-growing or aggressive, depending on the tissue involved.

Cancer can be viewed as an end point to many years of toxic overload. The body's ability to cope finally succumbs, cellular chemistry changes, and cells mutate; a cancer is born. A cancer is more likely to develop in those individuals who smoke, are exposed to toxic chemicals, excessive pollution and radiation and, in the case of colon cancer, those whose diet is nutritionally poor.

Smoking is classically associated with lung cancer but cancer of the throat, larynx, mouth, and tongue can also be associated with smoking. It is the small tar particles that are responsible for the cellular changes, not the nicotine. A recent study into the metabolic effects of smoking suggests that it adversely affects the thyroid gland, reducing its secretion of thyroid hormones. It would be impossible for the body to regain health with an under-functioning thyroid gland so stopping smoking is a prerequisite for improving health and reducing your risk of cancer (see p.172).

When considering cancer, much attention has been focused on the incidence of breast, colon, prostate, uterus, and ovary cancer, and the intake of saturated animal fats that are found in meats and dairy products. Other fats such as polyunsaturated fats tend to form more free radicals within the body, which attack the genes associated with cell division. This can cause cell changes to initiate cancer-cell formation.

Toxic chemicals are all around us, at work, in and on foods, in the water we drink and the air we breathe. Many people believe that these are contributory causes. Being aware of them helps us keep our exposure to a minimum (see p.153).

Many practitioners of complementary medicine believe that high levels of stress may increase vulnerability to cancer. It is important to learn to manage stress and to adopt a calmer attitude toward life.

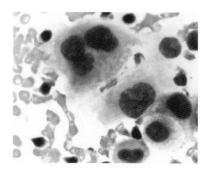

Here breast cancer cells (stained dark blue at center) are dividing in an uncontrolled manner and will spread throughout the neighboring body unless treated.

THE CONVENTIONAL APPROACH

Cancer treatment is complicated and depends on the type of cancer present and its stage of growth and development. The main therapies offered are chemotherapy, which aims to kill the cancer cells using specific cell toxins (cytotoxic agents) and radiotherapy, which directs radiation into the cancer, killing the cells by radiation exposure. Surgical removal of cancers is commonly carried out, followed up by radiotherapy or chemotherapy.

ACCEPTANCE

When cancer is diagnosed, it is not uncommon to deny or even dispute the findings. Such news often evokes similar reactions to that of the death of a close friend or family member; grief can overwhelm the person. This process was described in 1969 by the Swiss-born psychiatrist Elisabeth Kübler-Ross. The process is characterized by five specific stages: denial, anger, bargaining, depression, and acceptance. It is very important that all phases are experienced for the process leading to acceptance to be reached. During these phases, expressing your feelings to your family and friends, or in a support group makes the journey from denial to acceptance easier.

LIFESTYLE POINTS

Cut down on your total dietary fat intake, use monounsaturated oils such as extra virgin olive oil and reduce your meat intake in favor of fish, especially the oily types.

Lower your alcohol intake because an excessive intake will leach your body of protective vitamins and minerals as well as overstress your liver.

• Take a good multivitamin and mineral supplement. This can never replace a good diet and cannot be considered to rebalance a poor one, but it will ensure that your body receives all the protective nutrients daily. Check that your daily formula contains;

beta carotene	15,000 iu
vitamin E	200 iu
vitamin C	300mg
selenium	200mcg

Other nutrients such as potassium, iodine, the B group vitamins, zinc, copper, and vitamin K are also essential factors and should be present in your multiple formula.

• Increase your intake of high fiber foods, such as whole grains, fruits and vegetables.

• Include a daily serving of vegetables such as cauliflower, broccoli, and cabbage.

• Reduce your intake of smoked and salt-cured foods.

• Stop smoking. Use a nicotine patch, gum, or nasal spray to help wean yourself off the habit. These will help you to conquer the chemical addiction but you will need to find something else to do with your hands.

• A natural alternative to the nicotine patch is a homeopathic combination of tabacum, lobelia, and nux vomica. Tabacum can help control the trembling hands and craving for tobacco, Lobelia staves off the nicotine addiction, while Nux vomica helps with the irritable mood changes.

• Keep your weight within sensible limits.

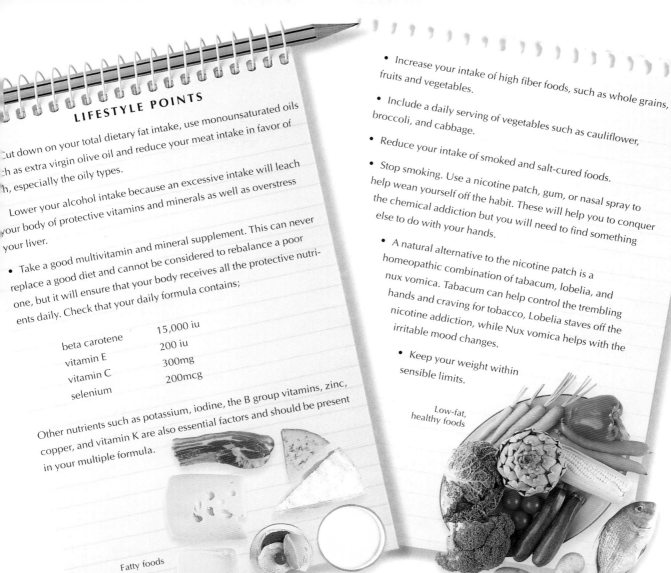

Low-fat, healthy foods

Fatty foods

COMPLEMENTARY THERAPIES

IP6 THERAPY

New research has discovered that a natural component of grains such as rice, wheat, and corn can reduce the rate of cancer cell multiplication and help shrink tumors.

The natural purified extract IP6 (inositol hexaphosphate) can be taken as a supplement.

BETA 1-3,1-6, GLUCAN THERAPY

The actions of the immune system have been the focus of much attention in natural medicines' fight against cancer. An extract from the cell walls of yeast known as beta 1-3,1-6, glucan has been shown to stimulate the activity of white blood cells and support the effective immune response.

HERBAL MEDICINE

An herb grown on the dry slopes of Nepal, *Coleus forskohlii*, has shown potential in reducing the risk of cancers spreading. Studies have shown that the active agent (forskolin) is a potent inhibitor of cancer metastasis (secondary spread).

VISUALIZATION

This method of focusing the mind is thought to have powerful effects on the immune response (see p.239).

Visualization aims to encourage the patient to relax and confront the process of the cancer by visualizing the site and destruction of cancerous cells.

AIDS

*T*he term AIDS is used to describe a specific stage of infection with HIV (human immunodeficiency virus) which involves a progression of symptoms or a decrease in the number of immune cells known as T-helper cells. Certain groups of people are more at risk from AIDS and these include male homosexuals and bisexuals with multiple partners, drug users who share needles and their sexual partners.

Diet should be tailored toward boosting the immune system. Wholegrains, cereals, and leafy green vegetables provide B vitamins. Live yogurt contains valuable bacteria; check labels to ensure that the yogurt has viable cultures.

HIV is an organism that can be acquired by contact with blood or body fluids from an infected person. Like all viruses it enters the cells of the body where it takes over the controls and reproduces at an alarming rate. After between one to six months, the body starts to make antibodies to HIV and it is when these antibodies can be detected that someone is said to be HIV positive. Although they are HIV positive for life, it does not mean they are guaranteed to develop AIDS.

HIV is often characterized by weight loss and muscle wasting with loss of nutritional health and status. However, it is not as simple as just eating more as many other factors such as poor absorption, diarrhea, poor use of nutrients and the ongoing battle against the HIV virus places a continual nutritional drain on the body's reserves.

HIV sufferers are prone to infections and antibiotics may prevent an opportunistic infection from getting out of control. Unfortunately many antibiotics are non-specific and kill off quantities of good gut bacteria along with the bad ones causing infections like thrush, herpes simplex, and shingles.

THE CONVENTIONAL APPROACH

AIDS research is a busy area in medicine but to date treatment has been aimed at the immune system and inhibiting viral activity. The drug Azidothymidine (AZT) is the most used but different cocktails of drugs are always being suggested and tested. For those with HIV infection no treatment is offered because the virus is present but not active.

NUTRITION
THE FOLLOWING NUTRIENTS ARE ESSENTIAL IN THE NATURAL TREATMENT OF HIV:

VITAMIN B1 (THIAMINE)
Good sources of B1 come from yeast extract and fortified breakfast cereals.

VITAMIN B2 (RIBOFLAVIN)
Riboflavin is involved in the metabolic processes of the body and is needed to convert dietary vitamin B6 into its active form. You can obtain vitamin B2 from many different foods, especially good sources are yeast extract, lambs' liver, pigs' kidney, fortified breakfast cereals and wheat germ.

VITAMIN B6 (PYRIDOXINE)
In general the main source of vitamin B6 in the diet comes from potatoes and vegetables, milk and meat but other good sources include wheat germ and white fish.

VITAMIN B12 (COBALAMIN)
Vitamin B12 is especially important in treating HIV because of its role in the healthy function of the nervous system and spinal cord.

Milk

Cereal

Potatoes

Cab

Lettuce

Brocc

COMPLEMENTARY THERAPIES

NATUROPATHY

Diet and lifestyle feature highly in the naturopathic approach to AIDS. Try using the beneficial bacteria *lactobacillus acidophilus* with *bifidobacterium bifidum*, both of these protect the body from disease and rebalance colon health. Live yogurt is a good food source of these "friendly" bacteria or they can be taken as a supplement, either a capsule (the preferred form) or as a powder.

Live yogurt and fruit

CHINESE MEDICINE

For well over 3,000 years the Shiitake mushroom has been used by Chinese doctors to treat all manner of immune-based illness. As a natural source of immune stimulating chemicals (beta glucan) the Shiitake mushroom is being used to support the body's fight against HIV and AIDS.

Shiitake mushrooms

LICORICE

The humble licorice root is being investigated as a potential treatment for HIV-related diseases including AIDS. After licorice has been eaten the active agent, known as glycyrrhizin, has been shown to increase the total number of specialized white cells called T-lymphocytes and helper T cells. These findings were noticed after a daily dose was taken for over 8 weeks.

HERBAL MEDICINE

A concentrated extract of olive leaves contains natural protease inhibiting substances that are known to be potent HIV and AIDS fighting agents. Olive leaf extracts taken over 15 weeks have been shown to benefit the immune system and to reduce the viral activity. The olive leaf extract can be taken as a concentrated tablet or as a natural infusion and drunk like a tea.

Herbal infusion

GLANDULAR THERAPY

The thymus gland (found sitting on the heart and important in the development of T-lymphocytes) helps regulate the immune system by releasing numerous hormones such as thymosin. Low thymus hormone levels are associated with low immune activity. Taking thymus extracts can boost this gland's function by supplying all the thymus-specific nutrients required for its optimal function.

Trained counselors offer practical help and advice for people with AIDS or who are HIV positive.

COUNSELING

Counseling sessions offer people who may be waiting for the results of tests, or who already know they are HIV positive, the opportunity to express, and deal with, very deep emotions.

AGING PROBLEMS

As tissues age, cells slow down their metabolic and division rates. This means that tissues take longer to heal and regenerate. In addition, toxic accumulations occur that may have damaging effects on the DNA structure of the cell itself. Conditions of advancing age are often degenerative by nature, for example, arthritis, cataracts, diabetes, heart disease, atherosclerosis, cancer, and nerve degeneration.

Free radicals are chemicals that are normally produced by cell metabolism. However, they have potentially dangerous effects on the cell's internal structure, since they attack the genes that regulate cell division. Normally the body has an adequate supply of nutrients to neutralize these attacking substances, but if the diet is deficient or extra free radicals are present (from cigarette smoke, pollution, and junk food) the natural neutralization process can be swamped and hindered. When this occurs tissue damage and degeneration takes place and the diseases of older age become apparent.

Adopting a positive attitude toward life and keeping your mind and body as fit and active as possible are constructive ways of dealing with aging.

In the past older people have been advised to take extra iron supplements in order to help keep themselves healthy. Excessive iron intake can have harmful side effects and may actually generate more free radicals.

As people get older,

CONSEQUENCES OF PROLONGED IRON OVERLOAD

LIVER DAMAGE

•

DIABETES (SEE P.138)

•

HEART DAMAGE

•

JOINT INFLAMMATION

•

LIVER CANCER

diet tends to change and intake may exceed need. A lower calorie diet may be beneficial with advancing years together with adequate exercise. On the other hand, many older people do not eat enough, so a physician's advice should be sought.

THE CONVENTIONAL APPROACH

Unfortunately there is no medical treatment for aging—at least yet!

COMPLEMENTARY THERAPIES

OSTEOPATHY

Keeping your body's framework in good order allows you to keep active. Exercise improves circulation of blood and fluids as well as keeping the heart fit and the lungs well ventilated. It also benefits the immune system. Osteopathy can keep the joints and muscles free and mobile (see p.233).

HOMEOPATHY

The remedy called Galium 6C is a strong detoxification agent and can help rid the body of unwanted by-products of metabolism. If the joints and muscles ache try using Urtica 6C, and for prostate swellings use Clematis 6C. If memory proves a problem taking Argentum 6C could help. To improve the circulation Aurum 6C is recommended.

NUTRITIONAL THERAPY

The antioxidant nutrients vitamin A, C, E, and selenium help mop up and neutralize free radicals causing the onset of degenerative age-related diseases. Melatonin, the hormone of the pineal gland, has been shown to delay aging in mice. It should only be taken under medical supervision.

CATARACTS

When the lens of the eye loses its normal clear appearance and becomes cloudy and dull a cataract is likely to be present. For a long time the exact cause was unknown but recent research now suggests that free radicals (see p.144) play an important role in damaging the tissue and causing degenerative changes.

Symptoms of cataracts can vary greatly depending on how extensive the clouding of the lens is and whether it occurs in one or both eyes. Cataracts become more common over the age of 50 with up to 65% of the 50–59 age group having some degree of lens degeneration present on medical examination.

When a cataract occurs in one eye the individual may not be aware of it until they can see the difference when the good eye is covered.

Cataracts are most common in people over 50 or those with diabetes. Injury, the use of steroids, and genetic factors may also cause cataracts.

COMMON SYMPTOMS

DIFFICULTY IN READING

•

DIFFICULTY IN RECOGNIZING FACES

•

DIFFICULTY IN WATCHING TELEVISION

•

DIFFICULTY IN SEEING IN BRIGHT LIGHT

•

DIFFICULTY IN DRIVING

LIFESTYLE ADVICE

It's wise to avoid strong light. Using ultraviolet coated sunglasses can be very helpful when outdoors. Increasing the fruit and vegetable content of the your diet will provide you with a good source of antioxidant nutrients and plant-based chemicals needed for optimal eye health. It's also important to drink about 3–4 pints (1.5–2 liters) of water daily for good hydration of the body tissues.

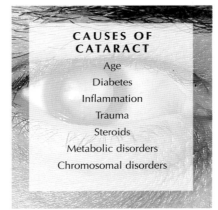

CAUSES OF CATARACT

Age

Diabetes

Inflammation

Trauma

Steroids

Metabolic disorders

Chromosomal disorders

COMPLEMENTARY THERAPIES

NUTRITIONAL THERAPY

The fact that free radicals are strongly implicated in cataracts suggests that the antioxidant nutrients are helpful. Taking vitamins A, C, E, and the trace elements selenium and magnesium should underpin any natural treatment for cataracts.

HERBAL MEDICINE

Chemical coloring agents in bilberries, known as anthocyanidines, can give significant protection against developing cataracts. Another powerful plant substance, pycogenol, extracted from pine bark, has strong antioxidant actions similar to vitamins C and E.

THE CONVENTIONAL APPROACH

Apart from correcting the underlying disease the only medical answer to cataracts is regular checkups and, when needed, surgical removal of the cataract itself.

Anthocyanidines, the chemicals in bilberries, and the antioxidant pycogenol in pine bark, can offer protection against cataracts.

Bilberries

Pine bark

ARTHRITIS

Unfortunately most people work in a repetitive way, often with a poor posture, which places damaging forces on the articular surfaces slowly resulting in wear and tear or osteoarthritis (OA). According to figures from the Arthritis and Rheumatism Council over 1.5 million people in the UK currently suffer from the symptoms of OA but over eight million have early X ray signs of the problem. Our framework comprises 206 individual bones, most of which have a smooth covering of cartilage known as the articular surface. Cartilage can withstand enormous forces and mechanical stress when the posture is good and the work varied.

Modern pharmaceuticals can be vital in the treatment of arthritis, and sometimes life saving in certain conditions but in the long-term management of osteoarthritis they have a questionable part to play. The prescription for arthritis is the drug ibuprofen, which helps to control the pain and inflammation in rheumatic disease and other muscle and joint problems, however, its long-term use is associated with a number of side effects, such as skin rashes and digestive upsets. Ibuprofen is one member of a large drug family known as nonsteroidal anti-inflammatory drugs (NSAIDs for short), all of which have similar side effects although some have more than others.

Yoga offers gentle stretching exercises that help to strengthen muscles and therefore give protection to joints.

THE FIVE CLASSIC EARLY WARNING SIGNS OF OSTEOARTHRITIS

If you can tick three or more of the following there's a good chance that your joints are showing the early signs of excessive wear and tear.

- ❏ Early morning stiffness in the joints that eases with movement.
- ❏ Bony swelling around the joint and a reduced range of movement.
- ❏ Pain and/or tenderness around the joint.
- ❏ Crunching or grinding sounds from within the joints on movement.
- ❏ Joint pain affected by a change in the weather.

COMMON SIDE EFFECTS OF NSAIDS

STOMACH PAIN/INDIGESTION

•

NAUSEA

•

DIARRHEA

•

STOMACH ULCERATION

•

STOMACH/GUT BLEEDING

•

ASTHMA ATTACKS IN SOME ASTHMATICS SENSITIVE TO IBUPROFEN

OCCASIONAL SIDE EFFECTS OF NSAIDS

HEADACHE

•

DIZZINESS

•

VERTIGO

•

HEARING DISTURBANCES SUCH AS TINNITUS

•

BLOOD IN THE URINE (HEMATURIA)

•

BLOOD DISORDERS

•

FLUID RETENTION

•

KIDNEY AND LIVER DAMAGE

THE CONVENTIONAL APPROACH

Treatment for arthritis will vary according to the severity of the problem. Conventional medicine can offer powerful drugs to combat the pain and swelling associated with degenerative arthritis (osteoarthritis), however they can have serious side effects when taken over a long period of time. The side effects usually include nausea, diarrhea, and stomach complaints (such as indigestion, ulcers, and stomach bleeding). Most patients with osteoarthritis only need simple pain killers such as acetaminophen (paracetamol) but some progress onto the nonsteroidal anti-inflammatory drugs (NSAIDs), for example, ibuprofen.

Your physician will be able to diagnose the severity of arthritis from an X ray or an analysis of fluid from the affected joint.

COMPLEMENTARY THERAPIES

NUTRITION

In view of the problems associated with the NSAID approach to controlling the pain and stiffness of OA the discovery of glucosamine (a natural joint nutrient) has been intensively studied. The results of numerous investigations show that it appears to normalize cartilage metabolism, preventing further degeneration. Glucosamine also stimulates production of chemicals called proteoglyans so that articular function is partially restored.

For an effective treatment it's recommended that 1,000mg is taken twice daily for the first month reducing to 500mg twice daily for the next two months. There's no guarantee that glucosamine will help all OA sufferers and it will take a good three months to work.

HERBAL MEDICINE

Of the many herbs available a few continue to provide special help. Devil's claw *(Harpagophytum procumbens)* can be used for a variety of painful muscle and joint problems.

The extract taken from Willow bark *(Salix album)* was first used as far back as the 1800s when the active agent salicin was shown to reduce the fevers, joint pains, and swellings associated with rheumatic fever. Licorice *(Glycyrrhiza glabra)* has shown some quite remarkable results in some joint conditions. It appears to have cortisonelike actions on soft tissue inflammation.

ACUPUNCTURE

Acupuncture can be very beneficial in OA of any joint (see p.230).

OSTEOPATHY

Regular therapy can be of great benefit to OA sufferers. Manipulation and mobilization of stiff joints can restore movement and relieve pain effectively (see p.233).

Osteopathy can be used to relieve stiffness and encourage mobility. However, gentle massage and reflexology are preferable in the acute stages.

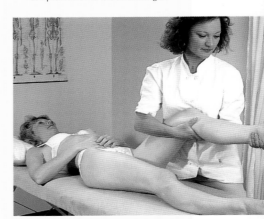

maintaining

WELL-BEING

contents

Introduction

I n the West we tend to take health for granted. We very rarely see or hear of deaths resulting from starvation or poverty, and our systems of healthcare can offer miraculous results and treatments, from driving out killer diseases by mass vaccination programs, to patching up damaged body parts and restarting hearts that have stopped beating. However, directly related to the way we live in the West today we are now witnessing a growth in the so-called diseases of affluence, and many of us suffer from a variety of ill-defined conditions that affect our vitality.

In many parts of the world food is still produced by traditional methods; diets may be simple but they are nutritious. By contrast, Western supermarkets overflow with convenience foods, many lacking in nutrients.

HIDDEN DANGERS

Despite a plentiful supply of food and access to medical fix-me-ups, it seems that Western populations have forgotten how to live healthily. Our food is often laced with preservatives and many other synthetic ingredients, and is high in fat, salt, and sugar. The combination of poor diet and unnatural working hours with the overuse of the automobile and underuse of our feet results in an overfed, underexercised, and overstressed Westerner with many avoidable health problems. Much of our food today provides calories in plenty but it is not nutritionally balanced. There is evidence that a diet based on convenience foods can be so lacking in essential vitamins and minerals in proportion to the other nutritional elements it overprovides that a state of "negative nutrition" can exist even in an apparently well-fed individual. Low-nutrient foods require vitamins and minerals in order to be digested and metabolized, which they themselves do not supply. Therefore, many an otherwise "overfed" and overweight person suffers from marginal nutritional deficiencies.

Because what you eat is responsible for making and maintaining every cell in your body, the first step in keeping your health is to consider what you are putting into your body—your daily diet. But diet is just one part of maintaining good health. Getting regular exercise is vital to keep the muscles and joints in good condition, and to maintain a healthy circulatory system so that blood can do its job of nourishing the body and helping to eliminate waste products. Finally, taking time for relaxation and reflection is essential for the emotional aspects of health, as well as having direct physiological effects.

HELPING YOURSELF

In this section we concentrate on diet, food and nutrition, and exercise. Being underweight or obese are both major avoidable threats to health. It would be impossible to plan a healthy maintenance program for yourself without understanding the fundamentals of nutrition. To enable you to get your eating habits and food choices in balance, this section offers a simple self-assessment that enables you to check your weight for height and energy (calorie) needs. Also included is an easy-to-follow guide to each vitamin and key mineral. The benefits of supplements are discussed in relation to health and those with special needs. Special dietary programs are described, especially the vegetarian and macrobiotic approaches, offering a complete outline of the basics of nutrition and health.

Putting health back into your life may sometimes mean taking a long, hard and critical look at your lifestyle.

Unfortunately there are many hidden factors complicating a healthy eating program. Food additives in the form of preservatives, flavorings, and colorings are so common that an appreciation of their potential impact on well-being is needed. Many of the worst offenders are described in this section allowing you to purchase your food with an informed choice in mind.

This section also includes advice on alcohol, coffee, and tobacco and the importance of food storage and hygiene. To finish off, an exercise and body fitness plan is outlined to make the best of your body and optimize general well-being.

FOOD SAFETY

Bacteria grow well in meat and poultry, fish and shellfish, dairy products (especially soft cheese), and cooked rice. Food poisoning causes stomach upsets in the fit and can be deadly in the unfit, the very young, and the elderly.

Food poisoning in the home is on the increase. In 1996, in Britain alone, there were 90,000 reported cases, and figures are rising. All fresh food must be covered or stored in a refrigerator.

Bacteria in food can double their number in half an hour. Raw meat and poultry contain potentially harmful bacteria such as salmonella, which is why they must be cooked carefully to kill all germs. For further safety, don't let foods that will be cooked come into contact with foods that will not. For example, make sure that meat is kept separately from cheese or butter, and that it doesn't drip onto them in the refrigerator. Don't use the same knife without washing it to cut raw meat and other foods; bacteria can be transferred this way. Keep a separate chopping board for preparing raw meat.

BACTERIA AND THEIR HAUNTS

- **SALMONELLA** particularly affects poultry, including hens' eggs, and duck eggs. It can be destroyed by thorough cooking.
- **CLOSTRIDIA** affects food that has been contaminated by dirt or flies.
- **SHIGELLA AND E COLI** inhabit the human body and are transferred to food by poor hygiene (not washing after using the toilet).
- **STAPHYLOCOCCI** can be transferred to food from boils or cuts.
- **BACILLUS CEREUS** develops on cooked rice that is kept warm and survives further cooking.

Salmonella thrives in all undercooked poultry and raw eggs. If not destroyed by cooking, it causes severe stomach pains and can be fatal in children and the elderly.

Hens' eggs

Quail eggs

USING THE FREEZER

FREEZE FOODS WHEN THEY ARE FRESH AND AT THEIR BEST

•

IF YOU ARE DEFROSTING FROZEN FOODS IN YOUR REFRIGERATOR MAKE SURE THEY CAN'T DRIP ONTO OTHER FOOD

•

DEFROST FROZEN FOOD THOROUGHLY BEFORE COOKING IT

HYGIENE

To keep harmful bacteria safely under control:
- Keep all kitchen surfaces, and the inside of the refrigerator, clean.
- Make sure that your refrigerator is cooled to 41°F (5°C) because most germs multiply more slowly in cool conditions.
- Store meat in the coldest part of the refrigerator.
- Don't let cats or other pets walk across kitchen surfaces.
- Wash your hands before preparing or eating food.
- Put food in the refrigerator as soon as you unpack it.
- Protect food from flies by using a cover.
- Change kitchen cloths and towels frequently.
- Don't buy cans with dented seams (bacteria could enter).
- Don't buy food with visible mold.
- Keep dried foods in clean, sealed containers.

ENVIRONMENTAL HEALTH

*T*here are so many poisons in our environment that just thinking about them is enough to harm our health. Some are beyond our control. Even so, it is wise to take every precaution to protect your health by avoiding exposure to harmful substances whenever possible. Keeping yourself healthy and strong will also help you fight off external threats to your physical well-being. A good diet, rest, and exercise will help maintain a strong immune system (see p.34).

Toxins can be inhaled from the air, ingested with food and drink, and absorbed through the skin by contact. They may cause allergic reactions such as rashes, puffy skin, vomiting, digestive problems, headaches, and general feelings of fatigue or light-headedness (see p.215). Toxins can affect us acutely with an immediate reaction, but regular small doses can build up and cause adverse reactions long after initial exposure.

FORMALDEHYDE

Many modern materials give off harmful formaldehyde gases. Laminated board, blockboard, plywood, and other home renovation materials, foams, rubbers, and some textiles all contain formaldehyde. Plastics, especially soft plastics and those with a strong smell, are also culprits.

COMMON TOXINS INCLUDE

INGESTED

- alcohol
- caffeine
- ingredients in medically prescribed drugs
- antibiotics in meat and fish
- residual pesticides in foods
- food additives
- traces of metals and plastics from cooking utensils
- fungal and bacterial infections in foods
- heavy metals, pesticide residues, nitrates in food
- aluminum and other metals, pesticides, nitrates, and pvc traces in water

INHALED

- tobacco smoke
- gasoline and diesel fumes
- airborne heavy metals (such as lead in gasoline)
- solvents and other substances from home renovation and household materials
- formaldehyde released from plastics and other materials
- perfume from soaps, cosmetics, and cleaning materials

SKIN CONTACT

- enzymes from laundry detergent residue on clothes
- irritants in cosmetics and cleaning materials
- substances in home renovation materials
- a range of materials used at work

SELF PROTECTION
Avoid inhaling:

- gasoline
- diesel fuel
- cigarette smoke
- solvents

- cleaning fluids
- garden pesticides and herbicides
- formaldehyde

- **GARAGE** Make sure the garage is well-sealed from the house.
- **RENOVATION MATERIALS** Don't store paints, solvents, or glues; they can leak fumes. Don't dispose of home renovation materials or plastics by burning. Use all such materials in a well-ventilated space.
- **TOXIC MATERIALS** Don't stay in the house if it's being sprayed for woodworm. Don't handle treated timber with bare hands. Use low-toxicity sprays, water-based paints, and other similar materials.
- **GARDEN** Follow instructions carefully if you use garden pesticides and fungicides.
- **CLEANING MATERIALS** Use low-perfume or eco-friendly soaps and household products. Avoid enzyme laundry detergents or rinse clothes thoroughly if you do use them.
- **NATURAL MATERIALS** Use natural materials for carpets, curtains, and clothes wherever possible.
- **PURE WATER** Consider using a water filter to filter out nitrates, pesticides, and metal traces.
- **CLEAN AIR** Consider using an air filter or an ionizer
- **ALUMINUM** Don't use aluminum pans, teapots (tea dissolves this metal), or coffee creamers (they contain aluminum).

ENERGY AND EXERCISE

*E*xercise and energy go together. Unless you are ill or completely physically exhausted, the best thing you can do to revive yourself when you feel tired after working at a sedentary indoor job is to get some brisk exercise.

BENEFITS OF EXERCISE

Swimming is one of the best exercises around—it tones almost every muscle in the body and is ideal for all ages.

Exercise has everything going for it. It protects the heart, and it helps you to lose weight. Regular exercise makes the metabolism more active, so calories are burned more quickly even when you are not exercising. It also stimulates the production of natural mind-calming chemicals in the blood. Most people find that exercise improves their mental powers and gives them more energy, and helps them to solve or put problems into perspective.

HOW MUCH EXERCISE DO YOU NEED?

If you are not used to exercise, start off with something gentle, such as t'ai chi, Qi gong, or yoga, which strengthens the muscles but is not physically demanding.

Medical researchers generally agree that getting three 20-minute bouts of exercise every week has a measurable physiological effect. The exercise should be one that makes the heart beat faster so that oxygen is delivered more quickly a round the body. The ideal to aim for is thirty minutes a day.

WHAT KIND OF EXERCISE?

Muscles that don't get used become weak and wasted and every kind of exercise is good for them. However, dynamic exercise that demands sustained, energetic effort, makes you run out of breath, and requires and develops stamina has the greatest physical benefits. Examples are running, swimming, dancing, fast cycling, and very brisk walking. These are aerobic exercises that use oxygen. Less dynamic forms of exercise, such as slow gardening, gentle walking, golf, yoga, stretching exercises, and most types of weight training, are also aerobic and will help you keep toned and supple. Choose one or two kinds of exercise that suit you temperamentally and fit into your timetable.

BENEFITS OF REGULAR EXERCISE

STRENGTHENS THE HEART AND LUNGS
•
KEEPS THE VEINS AND ARTERIES IN GOOD CONDITION
•
IMPROVES CIRCULATION, DELIVERING OXYGEN AROUND THE BODY AND REMOVING TOXINS
•
REGULATES BLOOD PRESSURE
•
STRENGTHENS MUSCLES AND TENDONS
•
KEEPS THE JOINTS SUPPLE
•
LEADS TO LOWER LEVELS OF HARMFUL FATS IN THE BLOOD
•
HELPS CONTROL BLOOD-SUGAR LEVEL
•
ASSISTS THE DIGESTIVE PROCESS
•
MAKES YOU SLEEP BETTER
•
MAKES YOU FEEL ALERT AND ENERGETIC
•
ENHANCES CONCENTRATION
•
KEEPS YOU SLIM AND IN SHAPE
•
INCREASES STAMINA
•
MAKES YOU FEEL HAPPY
•
KEEPS THE SKIN FIRM AND HEALTHY
•
CAN HELP TO PREVENT THE EFFECTS OF AGING

AEROBIC EXERCISE

Aerobics has come to mean a particular type of demanding exercise routine done to loud music. It sounds like something special, but in fact aerobic exercise is any kind of movement in which the activity of the muscles involves the use of oxygen to break down glucose in the blood. This is the way we normally use our muscles. By contrast, in anaerobic activity energy is produced in a way which involves a different kind of molecular activity that does not depend on oxygen. This happens when we make sudden spurts, as in many active sports and athletic feats where a quick burst of energy is required. This is why athletes train regularly and always warm up before taking part in their sport.

Prolonged aerobic exercise such as mountain climbing and hiking builds muscle strength and increases stamina.

ANAEROBIC EXERCISE

Anaerobic exercise has a less dramatic effect on the circulatory system and burns calories far more slowly than dynamic aerobic exercise. You need to train your body into fitness through normal exercise before pushing yourself in more demanding ways. This type of exercise is for trained athletes only.

During anaerobic exercise the body calls on emergency reserves of glycogen required when the body is pushed to the limit.

DAY-TO-DAY ACTIVITY

DON'T USE A CAR FOR SHORT JOURNEYS, WALK OR CYCLE INSTEAD

•

USE PUBLIC TRANSPORTATION WHENEVER YOU CAN AND WALK TO THE BUS STOP OR STATION

•

GET OFF THE BUS A STOP EARLY AND WALK THE REST OF THE WAY

•

JOIN A HEALTH CLUB, VISIT A GYM REGULARLY, OR JOIN A KEEP-FIT, EXERCISE, OR SPORTS GROUP

EXERCISE IS GOOD FOR

ASTHMA

•

BRONCHITIS

•

POSTURE

•

TENSION HEADACHES

STARTING AN EXERCISE PROGRAM

If you are underweight, overweight, recovering from illness, if you suffer from high blood pressure or any form of heart disease, are aged over 40 and inactive, or if you have any reason to be worried about your health, consult your physician before starting. It is important to build up gradually by starting with the level of exercise with which you feel comfortable. Always warm up before doing vigorous exercise. Don't overdo it—stop if you are in pain or dizzy.

HEALTHY EATING

I n the affluent developed world there's an overwhelming variety of convenience foods, luxury foods, and novelty foods, and a shortage of time—for menu planning, selective shopping, food preparation, and even relaxed eating. The result is diets that are far too high in fats and carbohydrates and low in fiber and vitamins.

Rice, corn, and other cereal grains are a valuable source of carbohydrate and are staple foods for many of the world's people.

No single food or food category is the key to healthy eating: what we need most is balance and variety in our daily diet. Unfortunately, the Western diet places heavy emphasis on meat and animal fats and very little on the staple fare of traditional diets—wheat, rice, corn, oats, barley, and other cereals. Despite having access to fruit and vegetables from all over the world, most of us eat far too little of these delicious and wholesome foods.

RECOMMENDATIONS FOR HEALTHY EATING

• Eat at least five portions of fruit/vegetables a day (total 14–28oz/400–800g).

• Make sure that "bulk" foods such as whole-wheat bread, pasta, and cereals form at least a third of your diet (total 21–28oz/600–800g a day).

• Eat fish instead of meat once or twice a week.

• Eat a vegetarian dish as your main meal at least once a week.

• Think Oriental: make meat just one part of the dish, not the main ingredient.

• Eat three good meals a day, and you're unlikely to want snacks.

• If you do want a snack choose fruit or a raw carrot, not cookies, potato chips, or chocolate.

• Eat four to six slices of whole-wheat bread a day.

• Base one meal a day on raw food such as salads rather than cooked food.

• Drink plenty of water (up to 4 pints/2 liters a day), but don't drink sweetened, carbonated drinks.

• Eat less red meat—you should have no more than 2¾oz/80g a day.

• Cut down on saturated fats and sugar

• Use less salt (maximum of 0.2oz/6g a day).

• Restrict your intake of tea and coffee to a maximum of 2–3 cups a day.

• Reduce your alcohol intake to the advised maximum (see p.170).

A well-balanced diet should include plenty of water, daily portions of fruit and vegetables, bulk foods such as pasta and rice, and fish or lean meat.

Fish and lean meat

Water

Whole-wheat pasta and brown rice

Fresh fruit and vegetables

HEALTH FOODS

In the wake of fears about BSE (bovine spongiform encephalopathy), and the effects of pesticides and artificial fertilizers, more people now prefer organically produced food. This includes fruit and vegetables produced by traditional methods relying on crop rotation, hand weeding, and natural, organic manures; and meat and animal products from animals reared without growth hormones and antibiotics, and fed on a natural diet. Unfortunately, organic food tends to be more expensive because it is much more labor-intensive to produce, but increased demand is encouraging prices to fall.

Are these foods better for us? Some experts claim that there is no clear scientific evidence for nutritional superiority of organically produced food, but anyone who compares the taste of lettuces or carrots produced by the two methods or does a blindfold comparison of free-range and battery-reared chicken finds this hard to believe. And it is generally agreed that fruit and vegetables grown for intensive agricultural production are often less nutritious than the tough old-fashioned varieties that have been grown organically.

WHOLEFOODS

Wholefoods are foods that have not been refined or processed, particularly grains such as brown rice and whole wheat. Grains consist of three parts: the outer layer (bran); the inner, starchy part (endosperm); and the heart of the grain (germ). During the refining process, the bran outer layer is removed in order to make a smoother, whiter product and the germ may be removed because the oil that it contains can go rancid, thus shortening the shelf life. A large proportion of the nutrients are lost in this process, such as vitamin E, potassium, iron, zinc, folic acid, and magnesium. Some nutrients are replaced synthetically but the end result is a less nutritious product that lacks fiber. All nutritionists recommend using wholefoods and wholefood products in preference to refined and processed food.

Easily digested when ripe, bananas are extraordinarily nutritious. They are packed full of potassium, vitamin B6, folic acid, and other minerals and vitamins.

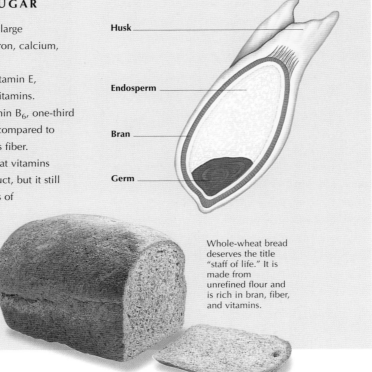

STARCHES AND SUGAR

BRAN provides fiber and contains a large proportion of the grain's vitamins: iron, calcium, and protein.

THE GERM contains essential fats, vitamin E, thiamine and some of the other B vitamins.

WHITE RICE has under half the vitamin B_6, one-third vitamin B_3, and one-fifth thiamine compared to brown rice, and has lost much of its fiber.

WHITE FLOUR is so impoverished that vitamins and calcium are added to the product, but it still has only about 85% of the nutrients of whole-wheat flour.

SUGAR is not (or should not be) an important part of our diet, but refining (which produces white sugar) removes the mineral traces that are present in unrefined sugar.

Husk

Endosperm

Bran

Germ

Whole-wheat bread deserves the title "staff of life." It is made from unrefined flour and is rich in bran, fiber, and vitamins.

Wheat is a nutritious unrefined wholefood. The grain consists of three layers: bran, endosperm, and germ, or heart, of the grain. When refined, the outer layers are removed, resulting in a less nutritious food.

DAILY DIETARY REQUIREMENTS

Adults need food for energy, body repair, cell replacement, and efficient functioning and maintenance. Children additionally need food for growth and development. The main elements of the human diet, which are known as macronutrients, are carbohydrates, protein, and fats. Vitamins, minerals, and trace elements are known as micronutrients (see p.162–p.163).

COMPLEX CARBOHYDRATES

These provide energy and are supplied by starchy foods such as rice, pasta, potatoes and other root vegetables, and cereal grains and their products (such as bread). Unrefined forms also provide essential dietary fiber or roughage, and most contain some vitamins and minerals. The other source of carbohydrates, sometimes known as "empty" carbohydrates, is sugar, which is pure energy.

Carbohydrate-rich foods such as whole-wheat pasta and brown rice provide the energy you need for your daily tasks.

PROTEIN

Proteins form the main building blocks of our muscles and tissues. They also produce hormones and enzymes necessary to control body functioning. Any excess protein is converted into energy or stored as fat. In most Western diets the principal sources of protein are meat, fish, and dairy products but proteins can also be obtained from cereals, legumes, and nuts.

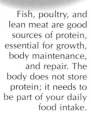

Fish, poultry, and lean meat are good sources of protein, essential for growth, body maintenance, and repair. The body does not store protein; it needs to be part of your daily food intake.

FATS

Fat is stored in the body, where it cushions the bones and vital organs and provides insulation against the cold, as well as being a reserve energy supply. Fats are also essential for nerve functioning, transporting vitamins and lubricating skin and hair. Compared to carbohydrates, much smaller quantities of fats are needed for energy, but in the West we obtain up to 50% of our energy from this source. For optimum health you should cut down on fat and consider cakes, heavy desserts, and chocolate as occasional treats. (See also p.119 and p.160.)

DIETARY FATS AND ENERGY

Fats and oils provide about 9.3Kcal of energy per gram, while carbohydrates supply about 4.2Kcal per gram. So 50g of breakfast cereal, which fills you up and helps your digestion, is much less fattening than 50g of fat, which you could eat in ice cream without even noticing it. Most people who want to lose weight find that by reducing their intake of fats (including fatty meat) and eating more cereals, lean meat, fish, and vegetables, they do so without hunger pangs. Dairy fats are also associated with high cholesterol (see p.119 and p.160), as well as being the main cause of obesity.

Butter

Cheese

VEGETABLE PROTEIN

Proteins are made up of more than 20 amino acids, which all have to be present together. Animal proteins contain all the amino acids but proteins from vegetable sources each contribute different groups. Therefore vegetable proteins need to be combined to provide the full complement. Food proteins are broken down in the digestive process, and the amino acids are reassembled to make the body's own protein. We need balanced protein in our diet, because unlike herbivores, we cannot produce the full range of amino acids in our body.

DAILY DIET

The amount of any of the macronutrients needed depends on your age, size, and occupation. For example a child of 13 needs as much protein as a grown man, and a person with a sedentary job needs less than two-thirds of the carbohydrates required by a person with a demanding manual job. The average daily requirements for a sedentary man are 2,500 calories. Women generally require fewer calories than men and a sedentary woman needs only 2,000, except when pregnant or breast-feeding, when the requirement goes up to 2,750.

AMINO ACID COMBINATIONS

Some amino acids may not combine well with prescribed medication or should be avoided in certain health conditions.

AMINO ACID	DON'T COMBINE WITH
Phenylalanine	MAO drugs (Monoamine oxidase inhibitors)
	Medication for high blood pressure
	Pregnancy & lactation
Tyrosine	MAO drugs (Monoamine oxidase inhibitors)
	Patients with myeloma
Tryptophan	MAO drugs (Monoamine oxidase inhibitors)
	Pregnancy & lactation
Cyateine	Patients with diabetes
	Patients who are prone to kidney stones
Arginine	Patients with schizophrenia
	Patients with active or recurrent herpes infection
Histidine	Patients with schizophrenia
	Patients suffering manic depressive states
Ornithine	Patients with schizophrenia
	Patients with recurrent herpes infection
Methionine	Patients with elevated blood homocystein levels

What you do tends to determine your calorie needs. Active people need more calories than sedentary ones. But because of differences in size, an active woman may need fewer calories than an active man.

UNDERNOURISHMENT AND OVEREATING

Too little fiber is linked to:
• allergies
• cancer of the large intestine
• cancer of the colon
• constipation
• hemorrhoids (piles)
• diabetes
• diverticular disease
• irritable bowel syndrome
• being overweight

Too much sugar is linked to:
• allergies
• diabetes
• gall-bladder disease
• breast cancer

Too much fat is linked to:
• allergies
• breast cancer
• other forms of cancer
• diabetes
• gall-bladder problems
• heart disease
• high blood pressure
• strokes

Too much protein can:
• affect the body's mineral balance
• put a strain on the liver and kidneys
• make you overweight

A GUIDE TO DAILY REQUIREMENTS

As a rough guide, our daily diet should consist of one-third carbohydrates and one-third fruit and vegetables. Following these guidelines will provide a balanced diet with plenty of fiber, minerals, and vitamins. Wherever possible, choose wholefoods in preference to processed or refined foods. To reduce animal fats, select low-fat dairy products and vegetable oils for cooking and salads.

bread/ cereal grains/ potatoes	4–5 portions	provides energy + fiber, vitamins
lean meat/white meat/fish/ vegetable protein	2 portions	provides protein + minerals, vitamins, energy, fiber
fresh fruit/vegetables	5 or 6 portions	provides vitamins, fiber + sweet fruit provide energy from fructose
milk/cheese/yogurt	2 portions	provides protein, fat, calcium, vitamins

FATS AND CHOLESTEROL

*F*ats make food taste good, and some provide essential nutrients. The body can handle fats in moderation. Like carbohydrates, fats give us energy and make us overweight if we eat more than we need. But weight for weight, fats are much more fattening.

There are two types of dietary fat: saturated and nonsaturated, the latter being subdivided into polyunsaturated and monounsaturated fats. Animal fats, which are linked to the so-called "diseases of affluence" such as heart disease, are high in saturated fats, while most vegetable oils, particularly monounsaturated ones, such as olive or canola oil, are low in them and better for us.

FATS AND CHOLESTEROL

Cholesterol is a vital lipid—a fat-like substance required by the body but harmful in excess. It is made by the body and found in some foods. Essential fatty acids (EFAs) help cholesterol work and can help control cholesterol levels. The best source of EFAs is polyunsaturated oils. High cholesterol levels, a factor in heart disease and arterial disease (see p.16–p.17), can be reduced by losing weight, cutting down on high-cholesterol foods, and, instead of saturated fats, using polyunsaturated and monounsaturated oils—particularly olive oil since it protects the high-density lipoproteins that prevent the deposit of cholesterol on artery walls.

Milk, cheese and other dairy products are high in saturated fats, which the body converts into cholesterol. They are best avoided.

IMPROVING YOUR DIET

You can start reducing fat in your diet by cutting obvious fat off meat. Cut down on sausages, burgers, and other foods that contain "hidden" fat. Eat more fish and substitute plant protein for meat. Replace fats with carbohydrates for your energy needs. Switch to lowfat dairy products and replace butter and lard with vegetable oils. Use less butter, not more margarine, and eat very little cream. Finally, check the fat content of all packaged foods.

SATURATED FATS

(linked to high cholesterol—limit intake severely)

MEAT FAT

lamb	52
beef	41
pork	35
chicken	30
duck	29

COOKING FATS

butter	68
suet	41
lard	44
hard margarine	39
low-fat spreads	17–30

VEGETABLE OILS

coconut	89
peanut	15
olive oil	14
soybean	14
corn	13
sunflower	12
walnut	8
rapeseed (canola)	4

OILS IN FISH

salmon	27
herring	22
mackerel	20
sardine	20
tuna	19

AVOID	FAVOR
Meat fat (all types)	Nut oils
Butter	Seed oils
Cream	Olive oil
Suet	Corn oil
Lard	Oils in/derived from
Hard margarine	fish
Coconut oil	Low-fat spreads

WEIGHT

*B*eing overweight can put a significant strain on your health. The heavier you are, the greater the long-term health risk. But being overweight is not the only risk to health and being seriously underweight can be even more harmful.

Being 10% or more over the ideal weight counts as being overweight, and more than 20% over the ideal counts as obesity. It's estimated that 50% of American adults are obese, with other Western countries catching up. The simple way to lose weight is to get most of your calories from carbohydrates instead of fats. Carbohydrates (except for sugar) fill you up, so that you don't even want to eat more than you should.

ANOREXIA NERVOSA

Many people—often young women—wrongly believe themselves to be overweight and take up obsessive and unnecessary dieting (anorexia nervosa). Being seriously underweight is a more immediate threat to health than being overweight. It's thought that zinc, found in shellfish and wheat germ (see p.163), may help stimulate appetite. Anorexia nervosa can permanently damage the digestive system and be fatal. It usually requires specialized medical treatment (see p.111).

HEALTH RISKS OF BEING OVERWEIGHT

Being overweight is a contributory factor in:

• diabetes
• heart disease
• hardening and narrowing of arteries (arteriosclerosis)
• high blood pressure
• poor blood supply to internal organs
• stroke
• kidney disease

ASSESSING YOURSELF

Your ideal weight will depend on whether you have a small, medium, or large frame. Make an honest appraisal of your body. Look at yourself naked in a full-length mirror. Your frame should be covered with a layer of firm flesh. If your bones show when you are standing still you are underweight. Flabby areas, spare tires, and ripples of flesh are all implications that you're overweight.

FATTENING FOODS

Fats make up at least half the daily diet of Western people. Fats need carbohydrates for combustion, so the more fats, the more the carbohydrate intake—a very fattening combination. Most diets also include huge amounts of sugar in the form of cookies, canned food, ice cream, sweet drinks, and so on. Besides being high in calories, refined sugar is believed to have an adverse effect on fat disposal in the body.

Obesity is a major problem in the West due largely to sedentary lives and overconsumption of sugars and fats.

GUIDE TO IDEAL WEIGHT

WOMEN	
5ft—5ft 2in	107—113lb
5ft 3in—5ft 5in	116—123lb
5ft 6in—5ft 8in	128—136lb
5ft 9in—5ft 11in	140—148lb
MEN	
5ft 2in—5ft 4in	123—130lb
5ft 5in—5ft 7in	133—140lb
5ft 8in—5ft 10in	145—153lb
5ft 11in—6ft 1in	158—166lb

Obsession with weight is common among young Western women, many of whom follow stringent, and unhealthy diets.

VITAMINS AND MINERALS

Vitamins and some minerals are essential to health but are needed in relatively small amounts. Anyone who has a varied diet, which contains plenty of fresh fruit and vegetables, as well as meat and fish, dairy products, bread, whole grains, and some nuts, seeds, and vegetable oils, is unlikely to suffer from a deficiency.

Vitamins and minerals are essential for vitality and health. But we only need them in small quantities; a balanced diet should provide for all our needs.

The roles of the various vitamins are still being studied. With few exceptions (vitamin D from sunlight, vitamin A from carotene in carrots, and vitamin K, produced in the gut) the body cannot make its own vitamins, so they have to come from the food we eat. Although most foods supply several different vitamins, some foods are particularly high in certain vitamins.

VITAMINS, THEIR VALUE AND SOURCES

VITAMIN	IMPORTANCE	SOURCE
A (retinol*)	growth, vision; an antioxidant so prevents damage to cells and premature aging	liver, oily fish, dairy products, carrots
B_1 (thiamine+)	brain, nerve, and muscle function	cereal grains, pork, beans, and peas
B_2 (riboflavin)	energy production from food	dairy products, offal
B_3 (niacin/nicotinic acid)	energy production, essential for growth, helps maintain healthy skin	poultry, meat, fish
biotin	energy production from food	liver, egg yolks, legumes, nuts
B_5 (pantothenic acid)	energy production from food	most foods, including meat and offal, grains, nuts, eggs
B_6 (pyridoxine)	energy production from food, essential for absorption of vitamin B_{12}	most foods, including offal, molasses, eggs
B_{12} (cyanocobalamin)	involved in production of red blood cells, essential for health of nerves (is stored efficiently in the body)	dairy products, liver, and all meat
B complex folic acid	involved in production of red blood cells; deficiency in mother may cause spina bifida in unborn child	leafy green vegetables, offal, legumes, oranges, bananas
C+ (ascorbic acid)	aids growth, tissue repair, iron absorption	fresh fruit and vegetables, especially oranges, tomatoes, blackcurrants, potatoes, parsley
D* (calciferol)	essential for bone development and maintenance	oily fish, butter, eggs, synthesized in the body from sunlight
E* (tocopherol)	maintains healthy cells, fights free radicals	most foods, especially cereal grains, nuts, vegetable oils, eggs
K* (phytomenadione)	required for blood to clot	leafy green vegetables, pork liver, also produced in the gut

Most vitamins are water soluble, which means that they dissolve in cooking water, and cannot be stored in the body in significant amounts. Some of these (marked $^+$ in the table) are easily destroyed in cooking. The fat-soluble vitamins (marked * in the table) are stored in the body tissues and so it isn't necessary to replenish them from food sources every day. Vitamin E has only a short storage time and is also destroyed by heating to high temperatures. Vitamin C is lost in food storage.

MINERALS AND TRACE ELEMENTS

Our bodies need some minerals in substantial amounts, while others, known as the trace elements, are required only in very minute quantities and the exact role of many of them is still being researched. Although the importance of minerals such as iron and calcium is well understood, the exact role of many of the trace elements is still being studied. Most nutritionists agree that a balanced diet provides all we need (see p.158). Some experts believe that a lack of trace elements such as zinc can be a factor in various physical and mental problems. However, it is always inadvisable to try to diagnose your own dietary deficiencies.

SOURCES OF MINERALS

The erosion of rocks over millions of years creates soils with different mineral contents in the form of minute particles known as mineral salts. These become part of our diet through the food chain. Microbes active in the soil ingest the salts and transfer them to plants. If we eat meat we also obtain minerals in our diet by eating animals, and some are obtained directly (e.g. table salt).

Spinach (especially raw) is rich in carotenoids and folic acid, which offer protection against cancer.

MINERALS: THEIR VALUE AND SOURCES

MINERAL	IMPORTANCE	SOURCE
Calcium	essential for healthy bones, teeth, and muscles	dairy products, leafy green vegetables, tofu, canned sardines, and salmon
Iodine	essential for proper functioning of the thyroid gland	seafood, seaweed, fortified table salt
Iron	essential for formation of hemoglobin in the red blood corpuscles and muscle protein	offal, cereal grains, dried fruits
Potassium	vital in regulation of body fluid (functions in conjunction with sodium)	fresh fruit and vegetables, especially celery, bananas, potatoes
Magnesium	involved in all biochemical processes	cereal grains, soybeans, nuts, legumes
Phosphorus	important for healthy bones and teeth, involved in energy production	dairy products, cereals, nuts
Sodium chloride	vital in regulation of body fluid	table salt, salty food (most of us have too much)
Sulfur	essential for healthy bones and body protein	meat, dairy products, legumes
Zinc	involved in enzyme activity and sperm production, aids healing of wounds	meat, cereal grains, legumes, nuts, shellfish
Manganese	needed for energy production, healthy nerves, lactation	cereals, nuts, leafy green vegetables
Copper	involved in production of healthy blood, essential for manufacture of melanin	liver, cereal grains, seafood, legumes
Selenium	antioxidant, involved in enzyme production	meat, seafood, cereal grains

Studies show that good nutrition aids memory and concentration. Busy students will benefit from including zinc and vitamins B_1 and B_2 in their diet.

SUPPLEMENTS

*L*ooking at vitamin and mineral supplements in health food stores, we can be tempted into believing that they will make us feel wonderful, restore our vitality, and make up for skipped meals, bad eating habits, and busy but sedentary lives. Unfortunately, they are unlikely to do so. The answer usually lies in ourselves, and we can quite easily save the money spent on bottles of pills. In fact it's inadvisable to take dietary supplements except on the advice of a medical practitioner or professional nutritionist.

During pregnancy a woman needs more folic acid, vitamins B and C, calcium, zinc and magnesium. But supplements must only be taken on the advice of a physician.

WHO NEEDS SUPPLEMENTS?

Generally you will get all the nutrients you need from a good mixed diet. But supplements may be helpful or even medically necessary in a few cases:

- **VEGETARIANS**, especially vegans, may need vitamin B_{12}—see p.166—and occasionally iron.
- **ELDERLY PEOPLE**, especially those living on their own, may have inadequate diets and may need multivitamin and mineral supplements.
- **PEOPLE WHO ARE ILL** or recovering from illness may need vitamin C for tissue repair, B complex for tonic effect, multivitamin and mineral supplements. Proprietary powdered "meals" for balanced nutrients are also available.
- **PREGNANT WOMEN** need folic acid, and may need calcium, iron, vitamins A, B_2, C, and D, or multivitamin and mineral supplements.
- **WOMEN WHO ARE BREAST-FEEDING** may need multivitamin and mineral supplements.
- **PEOPLE WHO DRINK TOO MUCH** alcohol may need vitamin C and B complex.
- **PEOPLE ON A CRASH DIET**, (not a good idea for anyone) may need a multivitamin and mineral supplement.
- **WOMEN WHO HAVE HEAVY PERIODS** may need iron supplements.
- **WOMEN WHO SUFFER PMS** may be prescribed up to 150mg daily of vitamin B_6.
- **PEOPLE WITH DIAGNOSED UNDERACTIVE THYROID** may benefit from iodine.
  - **IN HOT WEATHER OR AFTER HEAVY EXERCISE** there may be a need for extra salt.

EFFECTS OF EXCESS

Soluble vitamins are excreted in the urine if the body contains too much—unless the excess is extreme. Vitamins A and D are stored in the body and can build up to toxic levels.

EXCESS OF	CAUSES
VITAMIN A	dry skin, hair loss, vomiting, poor appetite, headache, irritability, poor growth in children, liver enlargement
B VITAMINS (GENERAL)	malfunctioning of nervous system
VITAMIN B_3	hepatitis, vision defects
VITAMIN B_6	depression, fatigue
VITAMIN C (VERY HIGH AMOUNTS)	increase in blood estrogen, nausea, kidney stones
VITAMIN D	faulty metabolism of calcium, with abdominal pain and kidney stones
VITAMIN E	nausea, bloating, diarrhea, headache, visual disturbance
IRON	liver damage
FLUORIDE	mottling of teeth
ROYAL JELLY	aggravation of asthma symptoms

WHEN TO SEE A PROFESSIONAL

Certain supplements may help various conditions, including infertility, CFS, eczema, tinnitus, and rheumatism. Always consult a qualified practitioner.

VALUABLE EXCEPTION

Cod-liver oil is a much-used supplement that has been tested clinically. Medical evidence shows that a daily 10ml supplement can improve joint stiffness and rheumatism (see p.30–p.31).

SPECIAL DIETS

To most of us "diet" means cutting back on food to lose weight, but a balanced, nutritious diet, with wholefoods, fresh fruit and vegetables, and protein from vegetable, meat, and dairy sources, will not be fattening and will make you feel healthy and energetic. Crash diets leave you malnourished and hungry, and don't help break bad eating habits. But sometimes special diets are needed for well-being.

There can be medical reasons for going on a restrictive diet. Common reasons are allergies (see p.215), congenital illnesses such as celiac disease (wheat intolerance), and conditions such as diabetes, which affects the body's metabolism of glucose (see p.138), or hypoglycemia (low blood sugar). Special diets are prescribed for people with kidney disease, where diet has to minimize waste products that the kidneys are unable to deal with, and people with heart disease, who are prescribed a low-salt, low-cholesterol diet. In these cases the diet often has to be followed for life.

Some diets (such as a macrobiotic diet) may be promoted as being more healthy than others and may also be connected with a particular philosophical system or approach to life. Many forms of complementary therapies, being holistic in their outlook, include dietary advice. In naturopathy diet, of course, is seen as being paramount.

Other reasons for following a special diet include illness, regaining weight after illness, and moral or ethical reasons such as opposition to eating meat as in vegetarianism.

NATUROPATHY

Naturopathy means treatment of disease using natural methods. Naturopaths assist the body in self healing by stimulating the powers of detoxification and elimination while building up the body's nutritional status and inner strength. Working with diet therapy and nutritional or herbal supplements, naturopaths offer treatments that are normally free of adverse side effects and based on traditional teachings (see also p.223).

Eggplants, potatoes, and tomatoes belong to the Solanacea family of plants, which also includes deadly nightshade. They can cause an allergic reaction in some people. Naturopaths can help you isolate foods that are unsuitable for your body.

Dietary needs change at different life stages. Young children, for instance, need to eat protein-rich foods while growing.

DIET FOR CELIAC DISEASE

Celiac disease occurs in people who have an allergy to the wheat protein known as gluten. The bowel inflammation that occurs can be controlled simply by avoiding all foods containing gluten, namely: wheat, rye, barley, and oats. Only gluten-free flour may be used in breadmaking, and great care must be taken when shopping to avoid foods with hidden gluten.

Cookies
Wheatflakes
Cake
Pasta
Bread

DIETARY ADVICE FOR SPECIAL CASES

- **AFTER ILLNESS** or loss of blood the body will benefit from a high-protein diet.
- **GROWING CHILDREN** require more protein, especially during growth spurts. Protein is essential for the growth and repair of cells.
- **ATHLETES** may need a high-protein diet to help build muscle tissue.

VEGETARIANISM

Most people who adopt a nonmeat or vegetarian diet do so because they dislike the idea of animals being slaughtered to provide food, when we can survive perfectly well without meat. There's a sliding scale of vegetarianism, with some people eating fish, and vegans eating only plant products, and refusing cheese and dairy foods.

For many people vegetarianism is a positive choice made on health or moral grounds. But it is important to substitute meat with a healthy, balanced diet that meets all nutritional needs.

Meat is the major provider of protein in many diets, and animal proteins provide a complete range of the amino acids for all our needs (see p.158). If, however, you decide not to eat any meat or fish, you must be careful to include enough protein in your diet.

It's not a good idea to rely too heavily on dairy products, because cheese is very high in saturated fats and calories, and too many eggs could add more cholesterol than you need.

A mixed diet that includes plenty of vegetable protein from a variety of sources, eaten in one sitting, should provide all the nutrients you need. It's generally found that vegetarians who follow this sort of diet are slimmer and more physically fit than most meat-eaters.

ADOPTING A VEGETARIAN OR VEGAN DIET

Switching to a vegetarian or vegan diet involves a great deal more than simply leaving out meat. What you include is as important as what you leave out. It is vital to plan your diet carefully to ensure that you get all the proteins, vitamins, iron, and other minerals that meat supplies. Legumes, cereal grains, soy products and, for vegetarians, dairy products are all good meat substitutes.

Seek advice if you decide to follow a vegan diet, removing all dairy products as well as meat. You may need vitamin and mineral supplements.

OVERCOMING POSSIBLE DEFICIENCIES

IF YOU ARE A VEGAN and do not eat milk products, your diet may be low in calcium. Vegans can obtain calcium from beans, peas, onions, green leafy vegetables, lemons, rhubarb, figs, almonds and Brazil nuts, soy (beans and flour), whole-wheat breads and pastas, molasses, and cocoa.

TO OBTAIN SUFFICIENT PROTEINS, you will need to eat a variety of cereals (grains), legumes (peas and beans), lentils, nuts, and seeds.

IRON DEFICIENCY IS RARE among both vegans and vegetarians, provided the diet includes plenty of fresh vegetables.

The body absorbs iron more readily from meat than plants, but vitamin C contained in vegetables aids iron absorption.

IF YOU DO NOT EAT DAIRY PRODUCTS, your diet will almost certainly be deficient in vitamin B_{12} and it is advisable to take a supplement.

CAREFUL EXPOSURE TO SUNLIGHT will enable your body to manufacture its own vitamin D. Do not overexpose yourself to the sun, especially when it's at its hottest, and do not sunbathe without using a sunscreen. Supplements may be needed during the winter, when there are fewer hours of sunlight.

VEGETARIAN CHILDREN

Vegetarian parents usually want to raise their children as vegetarians too. Generally, there's no problem in bringing children up on a vegetarian diet as long as parents ensure that the children have adequate energy sources, protein, calcium, iron, and vitamin D.

Children will thrive on a vegetarian diet, provided it contains all the proteins, fats, vitamins, and minerals they need. Ideally, children should decide themselves whether to be vegetarian.

DID YOU KNOW?

Soybeans offer the most complete form of protein possible for vegans, as well as being the staple of many vegetarians' diets. They also provide essential vitamins and minerals. Many people are concerned about the genetically engineered soybeans now being sold and used in the manufacture of vegetarian and nonvegetarian food products and feel that these products should be banned, or at the very least clearly labeled for those who wish to avoid them.

Soybeans

MACROBIOTIC DIET

The macrobiotic diet originated in Japan. It consists mainly of cereals and miso (a fermented rice, soy, and sea-salt product), and some cooked vegetables, and it allows no raw food and very little liquid. Absolutely no animal products are permitted. It may be harmless (or even beneficial in certain cases) to follow a macrobiotic diet for a very short time but it is harmful in the long term, because it is nutritionally inadequate. It would be very unwise to adopt such a diet unless under the supervision of a trained physician or nutritionist.

Macrobiotics believe that foods may be yin or yang and that some, such as brown rice, are a perfect balance. A macrobiotic diet tends to be low in protein and can, ultimately, be unhealthy.

VEGETARIAN CHEESE

Cheese is normally made by adding rennet (from a cow's stomach) to milk, but it is possible to buy "vegetarian" cheese which is made without relying on slaughtered animals in any way.

Vegetarian cheeses

HIDDEN ANIMAL PRODUCTS

Care needs to be taken when selecting suitable food, drink, and even dietary supplements if a strict vegetarian diet is to be followed. Animal by-products such as rennet and gelatin are often incorporated into foods as gelling agents. Gelatin is often used in the outer capsule of vitamin supplements. Wine, especially red wine and port, may have made using meat by-products. It is advisable for vegetarians and vegans to read all labels very carefully to be sure.

ADDITIVES

Additives are substances added to packaged food in the form of colors, preservatives and antioxidants, emulsifiers, stabilizers, and flavorings. A few additives are unmodified substances from completely natural sources, but most are either completely synthetic or chemically modified versions of natural substances.

Salt, vinegar, and sugar have long been used as preservatives and sugar, honey, herbs, or flowers as flavorings; even ingredients such as turmeric have been added as a coloring. With the exception of sugar, these are all tried and tested natural substances in their natural state. But during the 20th century, as competitive supermarkets have aimed to prolong the shelf life of food and reduce the price, literally thousands of additional ingredients have been added to those traditionally used.

Humans have preserved food for hundreds of years using natural products such as salt, honey, or vinegar. Only recently have we begun to use synthetic preservatives.

Many people would argue that it's only thanks to preservatives and stabilizers that Westerners have access to as much food as they need, which is palatable and reasonably priced. But while some additives do the arguably useful job of preventing spoilage and delaying decomposition in food, many more of the 6,000-plus that are now permitted are used solely to give "eye appeal" or to enhance the flavor of food which, if it's really worth eating, should taste good in its own right.

ARE ADDITIVES HARMFUL?

It is estimated that each of us in the Western world consume an average of 8–10lb of additives a year. Before any substance is allowed to be used in food it has to be rigorously tested and approved by a panel of experts. Occasionally substances that receive approval are later withdrawn from use on suspicion or hard evidence that they are not safe after all. As with all new drugs, however well the ingredients may have been tested, over time problems can still show up.

WHAT ARE E NUMBERS?

When an additive has been authorized for use by the European Community (EC), it is given an E number. These numbers are allocated according to type. Colors are E100 to E180; preservatives and antioxidants are E200 to E322; sweeteners E420 to E421, and other E400 numbers are for emulsifiers, stabilizers, and thickeners. Flavorings, of which there are several thousand, generally are not given E numbers. Some additives that are permitted for use in the UK are not allowed in other EC countries and these therefore have no E numbers.

HOW TO DETECT ADDITIVES

All additives used as ingredients (excluding those used in the manufacturing process, for instance to stop a product from sticking to the mixer) have to be listed on the label. Some manufacturers have begun to give the ingredients their full names instead of numbers, believing this is less off-putting.

FAMOUS "BADDIES"

Some E numbers are widely implicated in adverse reactions in susceptible people and thought by many experts to be linked to such problems as hyperactivity in children and asthma (see p.99 and p.121). It's only fair to point out that some people have violent allergic reactions to perfectly natural foods such as eggs or strawberries.

TARTRAZINE (E102) (yellow coloring) has been so frequently implicated in children's hyperactivity and rashes that it's now seldom used.

THE SWEETENER CYCLAMATE has been linked to cancer and is now banned in the UK.

NITRATES AND NITRITES have also been linked to cancer if consumed in large amounts.

COLORINGS

Colorings are completely unnecessary on any practical score, but without them much bought food would be gray. Colors probably have the highest appeal to children and are used a great deal in candy, soft drinks, and ice popsicles, even though they are linked to adverse reactions in children.

NONSUSPECT

- Riboflavins—vitamin B$_2$ (E101 and E101a)
- Chlorophyll—makes plants green (E140)
- Betanin—extracted from beets (E162)
- Carotenes—gives carrots their color (E160 and E160a)

* not permitted in the USA

COLORS TO PARTICULARLY AVOID

- Sunset yellow FCF (E110)
- Brilliant red FCF (E113)
- Yellow 2G* (E107)
- Amaranth* (E123)
- Red 2G* (E128)
- Brown FK* (E154)
- Caramel (E150). Production methods have not been fully tested, and it's consumed in high quantities since it's so widely used.
- Brown HT* (E155)

Bright colorings used in candy and soft drinks have been linked to hyperactivity in children.

Candy

Ice popsicle

PRESERVATIVES AND ANTIOXIDANTS

NONSUSPECT

- Ascorbic acid (vitamin C) and its salts (E300–304)
- Tocopherols—vitamin E (E306–309)
- Citric acid (E330)

* not permitted in the USA

TREAT WITH CAUTION

- Benzoates* (E210–219)—E212 permitted in the USA to treat malt
- Sulfur dioxide, sulfites (E220–23)
- Sodium nitrite (E250)
- Sodium nitrate (E251)
- Potassium nitrite (E249)

Dried apricots

Dried apricots may contain sulfur and should be treated with caution.

EMULSIFIERS AND STABILIZERS

NONSUSPECT

- Lecithin—from egg yolk and soybeans (E322)
- Pectin (E440)
- Natural plant gums (E406–415)

SLIGHTLY SUSPECT

- Carageenan (E407). Though based on Irish moss, there is a suggested link with cancer in animals.

Carageenan

FLAVORINGS AND FLAVOR ENHANCERS

The following are associated with migraines and other unpleasant reactions if overused and also implicated in hyperactivity.

Monosodium glutamate (E621)

Monopotassium glutamate (E622)

Calcium glutamate* (E623)

* not permitted in the USA

Potato chips

Potato chips may contain monosodium glutamate, linked with migraines and hyperactivity.

ALCOHOL AND CAFFEINE

*W*hile a small amount of alcohol may be beneficial, it is important for our physical and mental well-being alike to keep a careful watch on the amount we consume. In fact alcohol is a depressant and an addictive drug: tolerance to it builds up and increased consumption is damaging (see p.112).

All things in moderation is a well-known cliché; in the case of alcohol and coffee it's wise advice.

Alcohol is a depressant, affecting the central nervous system and every cell in the body, including the brain cells. It is the third most common killer in many Western countries. One-fifth of men admitted to hospitals as acute cases drink too much, a third of people admitted to emergency units are above the legal alcohol limit, and between a quarter and one-fifth of accidents are related to alcohol.

REASONS FOR CUTTING DOWN

Alcohol can cause considerable damage to the body as well as making it vulnerable to disease. Although alcohol contains sufficient calories for the body's needs, it contains no nutrients; it's fattening but not nourishing and can lead to malnutrition. Too much alcohol can also cause serious vitamin and mineral deficiencies. Alcohol prevents the absorption of folic acid and vitamins B_1 and B_{12}, while to break down alcohol, the liver uses vitamins needed for other functions, leading to vitamin B and C deficiencies. Alcohol also makes the body pass more urine, so water-soluble minerals such as zinc, potassium, and magnesium are lost.

ALCOHOL ABSORPTION

The higher the concentration of alcohol in a drink, the more quickly the body absorbs it. Carbonated drinks such as champagne or gin and tonic aid absorption, although alcohol is less quickly absorbed from sweet drinks.

SAFE DRINKING LEVELS

Many doctors advise that the safe limit is 9–14 units a week for women and 18–21 units a week for men. This should be spread throughout the week with no "binge" drinking.

High alcohol consumption increases the risk of heart and circulatory disorders including hypertension, or high blood pressure.

THE EFFECTS OF EXCESS ALCOHOL

While moderate alcohol consumption is linked to slightly lower risk of arterial disease and heart attacks, excess consumption is linked to:

- liver disease
- stomach ulcers and digestive disorders
- malnutrition
- heart disease
- kidney disease
- cancers (including cancer of the esophagus)
- brain damage
- neuritis (nerve damage)
- hormonal imbalance and infertility in women
- loss of libido, impotence, and infertility in men
- accidents
- impaired memory
- depression
- marital breakdown
- high blood pressure

ARE YOU AT RISK?

If your alcohol intake is over these maximum safe limits you begin to encounter health risks. Anyone who drinks more than a moderate amount of alcohol is increasingly susceptible to liver damage and strokes and the higher you go in the "definite risk" area the more likely it is that your judgment, mental alacrity, and emotional balance will suffer too. Anyone who drinks alcohol at the "serious risk" level in the long term is set to suffer serious mental or physical damage, some of which is irreversible or may be fatal.

REDUCING ALCOHOL INTAKE

Do not attempt to cut down your intake to the recommended level at once; reduce your intake by five drinks a week (or ten a week if you are drinking over 50 a week until you have reached this level, and five thereafter). Write down your aims and keep a record of how much you actually drink and, if possible, avoid situations in which you normally drink. Instead of your usual drink after work or evening drink at home find an alternative activity, such as going the gym, jogging, or going to night school to keep your mind occupied.

Don't be afraid to join a support group, such as Alcoholics Anonymous, where you can talk and share experiences with other people in the same situation. If you suffer withdrawal symptoms or find it impossible to cut down, seek your doctor's advice. Medical help may be needed.

CAFFEINE

Caffeine (found in coffee, tea, and chocolate) is a stimulant that dilates the blood vessels, stimulates the heart, and increases the flow of urine. It wakes you up if you're drowsy and compared to alcohol it is relatively harmless. However, it is generally not advisable to drink more than two to three cups of coffee or tea a day.

Without realizing it, you may be a caffeine addict. If you are, cutting down may cause headaches or other withdrawal symptoms (these are a sign of how dependent you were) but they will soon disappear.

WHAT IS A UNIT?
One unit is 10g of alcohol.
This is roughly the amount contained in

 ½ PINT OF BEER, OR

 A MEASURE OF SPIRITS, OR

 125ML GLASS OF TABLE WINE, OR

A SMALL PORT OR SHERRY.

At definite risk
men 35–50
units a week
women 21–35
units a week

At serious risk
men over 50
units a week
women over
35 units a week

PREGNANCY AND BREAST-FEEDING
Alcohol in the mother's blood passes into the fetus's bloodstream, and also enters breast milk. Current medical advice is to drink no more than one unit a day if you are pregnant or breast-feeding. There is also evidence that a high level of alcohol in the blood can cause abnormalities in the unborn child. If you are hoping to become pregnant, you and your partner are advised to drink no more than one or two units, once or twice a week.

HARMFUL EFFECTS OF CAFFEINE

IRRITATES THE LINING OF THE DIGESTIVE TRACT

•

INTERRUPTS SLEEP PATTERNS

•

CAUSES PALPITATIONS

•

IN LARGE AMOUNTS, CAUSES NERVOUSNESS AND ANXIETY

•

OVERCONSUMPTION IS LINKED TO INCREASED AMOUNT OF HARMFUL FREE RADICALS (SEE P.144) IN THE BODY

•

OVERCONSUMPTION LEACHES VITAL VITAMINS AND MINERALS FROM THE BODY

DRUGS AND SMOKING

Not all drugs are illegal. While there are worrying reports of schoolchildren being introduced to drugs such as cannabis, some of their parents are more hooked than they realize on the social drug alcohol or on drugs prescribed for anxiety or insomnia. Tobacco is sold in supermarkets and gas stations, and more children than ever are lighting up in the schoolyard, despite all the warnings about the health risks.

Tobacco kills more people than all other forms of drugs. Yet it remains legal and can be bought over the counter.

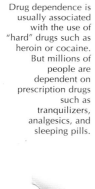

Drug dependence is usually associated with the use of "hard" drugs such as heroin or cocaine. But millions of people are dependent on prescription drugs such as tranquilizers, analgesics, and sleeping pills.

ILLEGAL DRUGS

Recent studies suggest that cannabis is less harmful, and less addictive than tobacco and some people feel that consumption should be legal. The fact that it is currently against the law is one good reason for not taking the drug and trying to prevent your children from taking it. Other illegal drugs, such as Ecstasy or LSD, may be implicated in permanent adverse mood changes. The use of the drug Ecstasy has also been the cause of death in several cases.

Drug-taking can lead to changes in behavior, poor performance at school, and involvement in a drug culture that may lead to more and more harmful drugs and drug dependence. If you suspect your child is taking drugs, arrange for him or her to talk to an independent expert counselor as soon as you can. Your own influence is important but it is unlikely to be enough.

PRESCRIBED DRUGS

Tranquilizers, sleeping pills, or beta-blockers may be prescribed by a doctor for reasons that are perfectly valid at the time. Beta-blockers are not thought to be habit forming, but long-term use of tranquilizers and sleeping pills can cause permanent absent-mindedness, speech slurring, double vision, and psychological and physiological dependence. No drug solves the underlying problem that causes its use. There are many ways of helping yourself come to terms with such problems, including counseling, relaxation techniques, psychotherapy, hypnotherapy, and biofeedback, and complementary therapies such as acupuncture, aromatherapy, and the Alexander technique. Some of these may be available through your doctor. Any of them may be able to offer you more help than drugs in dealing with anxiety, stress, or going through a crisis. And never forget the value of exercise, which can transform your mood and restore you to good health.

SMOKING

We all know smoking damages health and affects those who have to breathe other people's smoke, especially children. Asthma and bronchitis in children are often directly related to their parents' smoking. Smoking while pregnant can damage the health of the unborn child. There's no safe level of smoking, but the more you smoke and the longer you smoke, the more dangerous it is. Give it up. Ask your doctor for advice and consider getting help from one of the therapies mentioned previously. Acupuncture and hypnotherapy can be particularly helpful (see p. 230 and p. 238).

GIVING UP SMOKING

DON'T ATTEMPT TO STOP SMOKING ALL AT ONCE. Cut down by five cigarettes a day (or ten a day if you are smoking over 50 a day, and five thereafter).

DECIDE ON A TARGET FOR EACH WEEK AND FOR EACH DAY OF THE WEEK. Write down your aims and keep a record of how much you actually smoke.

AVOID SITUATIONS IN WHICH YOU NORMALLY SMOKE. Find a displacement activity for your drink at the bar or after-dinner cigarette (go swimming, go for a walk, do something you have been putting off).

HAVE AN EXCUSE READY FOR NOT SMOKING IN SOCIAL SITUATIONS ("Doctor's orders") to make it easier to say no when you are offered a cigarette.

DENTAL CARE

Strong, healthy teeth are essential to well-being and a bonus to good looks. But teeth are only as strong as the gums they live in. Gum diseases are a major cause of tooth loss and need to be guarded against as much as tooth decay. To make sure that your teeth last as long as you do, you should see your dentist once every six months unless you're advised otherwise.

Effective toothbrushing will clean particles from between the teeth, remove plaque, and stimulate the gums. Brush your teeth for at least three minutes morning and evening, and ideally after every meal. Brush vigorously up and down on both sides, then brush back and forth across the gums. Use floss to clean food particles and bacterial deposits from between the teeth.

PLAQUE AND PERIODONTAL DISEASE

We all have a multitude of bacteria inhabiting our bodies. In the mouth, bacteria at work leave a debris on the teeth that gathers around the gums in particular. Plaque is the buildup of this debris. If it's not removed by daily brushing and flossing, it forms a hard substance known as tartar, which causes inflammation of the gums (gingivitis). Untreated, this will lead to sore, bleeding gums, bad breath, and loose teeth.

There is evidence to suggest that people who have unbalanced diets, and especially diets lacking in vitamin C, are more prone to gum infections.

Smoking also contributes to plaque buildup. Some people find that plaque builds up no matter how scrupulously they brush their teeth, and they need to make a special effort to see their dentist regularly.

DIET

To help prevent your saliva from being too acidic, make sure that your diet includes plenty of fresh fruit and vegetables. This also provides the vitamin C vital to the maintenance of healthy tissue and tissue repair, and so helps to keep the gums healthy. Calcium is essential for good teeth (especially as they are being formed). In soft water areas in particular, calcium may be lacking in the diet and supplements may be needed. Fluoride helps to keep the tooth enamel strong and is an important factor in preventing tooth decay. Almost all water supplies now contain fluoride, however, and supplements are not considered necessary. Too much fluoride can permanently stain the teeth.

Good dental hygiene and avoidance of sweet foods can enable you to keep your own teeth well into old age.

Plaque is the cause of most dental problems. A daily routine of brushing and flossing prevents plaque from building up.

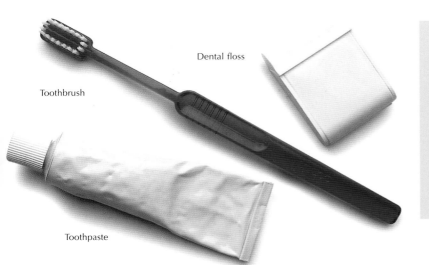

Dental floss

Toothbrush

Toothpaste

SUGAR

Sugar is a major cause of tooth decay.

Don't eat sugary or starchy foods without cleaning your teeth afterward.

Don't drink sugary drinks.

Don't give sweet foods and drinks to children. Drinking sweet drinks through a straw is particularly bad for their teeth as it keeps the sugar in contact with teeth.

SECTION SEVEN

lifestyles

AND WELL-BEING

contents

Introduction

This section looks at ways of maintaining and improving your well-being through taking a different and more positive approach to yourself and your life. Most of us today have very stressful lifestyles, but taking a positive approach can be much more helpful than giving in to negativity.

The following pages describe different stressful situations and the ways in which they can affect our lives. The section looks at how you can recognize stress in yourself and explores various ways in which you can alleviate stress both personally and at work, as well as offering ways of managing stressful situations.

Overstressed and overworked Westerners can learn a great deal from many Eastern cultures' relaxed approach to life in order to achieve balance of mind, body, and spirit.

IMPROVING SKILLS

Improving your communication skills, honing your decision-making abilities, and improving your memory and thought processes all help to manage stress. Other techniques are also useful, and this section contains some positive hints and tips to help you relax and learn better breathing.

Lifelong health comes from keeping a positive outlook and a joy in life, friends, and family.

DID YOU KNOW?

According to Dr. Susan Everson of the American Public Health Institute in Berkeley, California, middle-aged people who give up hope and consider themselves to be failures are at greater risk of dying of heart disease. She claims that giving up hope has the same effect on the arteries of a middle-aged person as smoking 20 cigarettes a day. She reached her conclusions after a four-year study into 942 people whose attitudes to life were followed and whose arteries were studied with ultrasound scans. She said that her findings showed feeling hopeless could upset the balance of hormones in the body, putting people at greater risk of heart disease and strokes.

By improving these skills, and with positive thinking, you can control the feelings of hopelessness that are a common feature of today's stressful society, as well as learning how to control and manage stress.

A BROADER SOCIETY

Societies are constantly changing and reaching out to meet and embrace other cultures. As we encounter other societies, we can take the best from different cultures and incorporate their principles into our lifestyle in order to enhance well-being. For instance, you could learn t'ai chi, a form of exercise and health awareness from China; or practice yoga, originally from India. Enhance your diet by understanding the principles of macrobiotics, or learn how to rid yourself of harmful stress by using encounter groups, relaxation techniques, and meditation drawn from different cultures around the world. Today we can use whatever principles and practical support we need to change and adapt our lifestyle to make it more positive and health enhancing.

We are living in a very privileged time in the history of the world. On the whole we tend to enjoy good health, suffer little physical hardship, and live the longest compared to our predecessors. However, we still strive for longer lives and even better health. This drive for perfection makes us human and has spurred mankind on to develop methods of improving health since the earliest recorded evidence of medical practice existed.

Traditional folk methods have stood the test of time, and some have quite correctly stated that they represent the longest-running clinical trials known to us. With this knowledge we can reassure ourselves that many of the traditional teachings carry with them a great deal of truth. Traditional methods can, therefore, form the foundations for profound lifestyle improvements that require little more than dietary adjustment and the commitment to structured mental and physical exercise.

The following pages will provide many useful ways of doing just that.

We have more access than ever before to different cultures. Embracing and incorporating different aspects of these cultures, such as t'ai chi, can enhance our daily lives.

STRESS

*S*ince *our earliest evolutionary history, we've had a built-in technique for dealing with stress: the fight or flight response. When we lived in caves we had only two ways of dealing with a threat—we could stand and fight, or we could flee. In both cases our bodies underwent some radical changes to ensure our survival. There was an increase in oxygen, raised heart rate, increased muscular tension, and a huge surge of epinephrine.*

The body's response to stress—the fight or flight response—evolved early in prehistory, possibly as a coping mechanism when attacked by wild animals.

We still have the fight or flight response. Even though the dangers we face today are different, the same physiological changes occur. Stress happens when we fail to deal with these changes properly.

BURN-OUT

Stress itself is not harmful—but our inability to deal with our bodies' responses to it can be. If you can learn to cope with the changes, or change your responses, you can handle any of life's stresses. Those who can't cope, and suffer prolonged stress,

are said to suffer from burn-out. Burn-out affects people in all occupations and usually follows three stages. First, energy reserves and work demands become unbalanced—more time is spent at work and less with family and friends; there are frequent minor illnesses and sleep disturbances. In the second stage there may be angry outbursts, irritability, anxiety about health, and persistent fatigue. Finally the person may become derogatory about colleagues, family, and friends and take an overly rigid approach to their work, accompanied by a loss of self-esteem.

LOCUS OF CONTROL

Stress-management consultants often use a questionnaire to determine how much stress a person is under and how well they are coping with it. This questionnaire is called the locus of control. What it does is identify which of two main types of person we predominantly tend to be. Most of us will fit somewhere in the middle; some will fall at either end of the spectrum. These two ends are known as A and B, and the types of people who tend toward each end are known as A or B types. Each has their own way of dealing with stress.

An A type person is liable to be aggressive and impatient and to react to stress with anger and confrontation.

A TYPES—impatient, aggressive, ambitious, hasty, rushing, quick, stressed, demanding, difficult, loud, creative, leading, rousing, dynamic, confident, decisive. They tend to vocalize their stress in anger.

A person in the B category is likely to be indecisive and rather nervous and to bottle up or retreat from stress.

B TYPES—patient, defensive, relaxed, considerate, cautious, careful, following, receptive, caring, nervous, questioning, indecisive, quiet, philosophical, thorough. They tend to bottle up their stress.

MANAGING STRESS

A TYPES should learn to slow down, make more time for themselves, take up more leisure activities, stop seeing everything as a competition, take up a relaxation technique such as meditation or yoga, deal with one thing at a time, and learn to explore and vocalize their feelings more.

B TYPES should practice assertiveness training, learn to say "no" more often, be more adventurous, open to challenges and new experiences, be more decisive, stop putting other people's needs and desires ahead of their own, think of themselves more, work on improving their self-esteem, and generally express their wants and needs more forcefully.

A types tend to be prone to heart attacks, while B types are prone to carcinogenic disorders. Hopefully we all fit neatly in the middle of these categories without too much of any one type being dominant. If this isn't the case, however, it's worth thinking about some forms of stress management (see p.183).

Taking up a challenging activity such as rock climbing may encourage a B type person to be more decisive and assertive.

MONITORING STRESS LEVELS

Another good way to check your stress levels is to rate your emotional responses. There are some emotions that can be detrimental if experienced on a long-term basis. If you experience them only infrequently they'll have no lasting effect on your health. Check the following emotions to find out which you experience occasionally and which you experience frequently. If you are experiencing over half of them constantly then you need to take action. Rate them for frequency and also, on a scale of one to 10, intensity. Any that you experience at a level of more than five should be taken as indicative of high stress levels.

- ❏ Anxiety
- ❏ Panic
- ❏ Restlessness
- ❏ Helplessness
- ❏ Desperation
- ❏ Hopelessness
- ❏ Guilt
- ❏ Depression
- ❏ Self-consciousness
- ❏ Irritation
- ❏ Anger
- ❏ Rage
- ❏ Frustration
- ❏ Trapped
- ❏ Unloved
- ❏ Lonely

These are not arranged in any particular order. You should check this list periodically, asking yourself how you have felt in the past, how you are feeling right now—and also how you expect to feel in the not-too-distant future, say over the next six months.

COMPLEMENTARY THERAPIES

CHINESE MEDICINE

Thorowax root, schizandra fruit, and peony root will be prescribed to alleviate stress and anxiety (see p.225).

ACUPUNCTURE

The underlying causes would be investigated, but acupuncture is a very effective treatment for stress-related disorders (see p.230).

AUTOGENIC TRAINING

These self-help exercises are excellent for helping train the mind and body to relax (see p.242).

RELAXATION AND VISUALIZATION

Deep relaxation for at least 15–20 minutes twice a day is one of the best therapies for stress (see p.239).

PERSONAL STRESS

The body reacts stressful situations, such as an argument, by producing stress hormones, such as epenephrine. Tension also builds up in neck and back.

*C*heck your lifestyle for signs of personal stress and stress-related problems using the 20 statements in the checklist below. You should respond to each statement with the word true or false. If you respond to at least eight of them as false, then stress may well be affecting you to some extent. If you answer false to more than eight, then stress could be affecting you severely, and prompt action should be taken.

If you're lucky enough to be able to answer true to all of the statements, then chances are you're enjoying a fairly stress-free life. If, on the other hand, you responded to all of the statements as false, then your stress levels are likely to be extremely high.

This should be seen as a cause for immediate concern. You need to do something right away to reduce the overall stress in your life before your health is affected in the long term, or there is a serious chance that you will at some stage suffer from one or more stress-related illnesses. Once you have completed the questionnaire, refer to the box on the next page for advice on how to control and relieve the symptoms of stress.

Talking freely with a friend, sharing anxieties and tensions, can help to alleviate stress. However, being offered unasked for advice, can itself be stressful.

PERSONAL STRESS CHECKLIST

- ❏ I have enough income to meet my basic requirements
- ❏ My general health is good
- ❏ I am experiencing love in my life
- ❏ I weigh about what I should for my height and build
- ❏ I am able to express my feelings freely
- ❏ I take part in social activities on a regular basis
- ❏ My intake of caffeine drinks is three or less a day
- ❏ I eat at least one well-balanced meal a day
- ❏ I do something just for pleasure at least once a week
- ❏ There is at least one relative to whom I can turn in crisis who lives within a reasonable traveling distance
- ❏ I have some time to myself every day
- ❏ I get seven or eight hours sleep a night
- ❏ I have some religious convictions that give me strength
- ❏ I exercise at least twice a week
- ❏ I have at least one good close friend to whom I can turn
- ❏ I have a good network of friends and acquaintances
- ❏ I can discuss family problems freely with my family
- ❏ I feel I can organize my time well
- ❏ I smoke less than 10 cigarettes a day
- ❏ I take less than five alcoholic drinks a week

STRESS-RELIEVING TIPS

Here are a few tips and hints for relieving stress, using a four point plan for self-awareness, control, communication, and expressing yourself.

SELF-AWARENESS

- Be aware of your body. Notice if stress or tension is building up in any area. This is a useful tip if you perform any routine tasks that are likely to lead to RSI (repetitive strain injury). Try to avoid bad postural habits.
- Be aware that sometimes you may experience more than one emotion at a time and that sometimes these emotions may conflict.
- Notice that your emotions affect your actions and that your actions affect other people's emotions.
- Accept that you have emotions. You are allowed to have them and to express them freely.

COMMUNICATE

- If you have trouble expressing how you feel, you're allowed to rehearse. Practice when you are by yourself. Take the time to find the right words to describe how you feel. This will make it easier when you need to do it for real.
- Be assertive. If you feel uncomfortable or annoyed or undervalued by someone, then tell them—they may not have realized and can then do something about it.
- Remember to communicate and share when you're feeling fine and happy too. Sharing your emotions and feelings doesn't mean you have to focus on just the bad ones.
- Get someone to listen. When you need to get something off your chest, ask a friend to merely listen. They don't have to say anything or offer any advice.
- Be prepared to listen to others without offering advice. Let others around you tell you about themselves and how they feel without making judgments—just listen.

CONTROL

- It's important to learn to control your breathing, either through breathing techniques or some form of meditation. Overbreathing or hyperventilation can lead to bodily tension and ill health.
- Concentrate on what's positive around you— even in stressful situations, it is always possible to see something positive.
- You have control over situations. If they are causing you stress, then leave. If you choose to stay, then that's your choice, and that acceptance alone can alleviate your stress.
- You have the right to say no. Be assertive in stressful situations. Exercising control can alleviate stress.

EXPRESSING YOURSELF

- Learn to let off steam without hurting anyone. Bash a pillow, smash some dishes (old stuff and in private), shout in an empty room, sing in the car very loudly, or scream in a place where you won't be overheard or frighten anyone.
- Take up a physical exercise just for the fun of it. Try ballroom dancing, canoeing, rollerblading, trampolining, or a martial art.
- Take up something creative and allow yourself to be not very good at it—water-color painting, sculpture in papier mâché, origami, weaving, or poetry.

Communication is not just about sharing anxieties and problems. It also means having fun together and sharing the good times.

Instead of letting angry feelings out onto a person, try punching a cushion or a punching bag. The release of emotion is enormous.

COMPLEMENTARY THERAPIES

HYPNOTHERAPY

Hypnotherapy can also be helpful
(see p.238).

COUNSELING

For thorough treatment, see a psychotherapist or a counselor trained to deal with stress
(see p.243).

STRESS AT WORK

*O*nce you've isolated your problem areas you can do something about them. Here are some tips to help you eliminate stress from your work and be more relaxed about it. Be clear about what is work and what is not. Separate your work from your home life. Don't take work home with you, and don't take your home problems to work with you.

Typically, a stressed person cannot leave his or her work behind but keeps worrying about it, even when the working day is over.

Getting away from your desk and taking a walk or having a swim at lunchtime helps to relieve stress and lets you return to work refreshed.

- **GET SUPPORT** If you need to retrain, develop new skills, get help, or just talk about work problems, you are entitled to support from senior staff.
- **WORK TO LIVE, NOT THE OTHER WAY AROUND** It's only a job. Your health, happiness, and welfare come first.
- **TAKE BREAKS** You need to get away from your work every so often, whether it's every few hours, days, weeks, or months.
- **HAVE A LIFE** Don't spend all your free time thinking and talking about work. Have some interests and social activities outside your work area.
- **DON'T TAKE ON TOO MUCH** Learn to say no to too much work. If you can, delegate.
- **HAVE A FIXED WORKING DAY**—and stick to it. Go home when you are supposed to.
- **EAT SENSIBLY** Don't binge on high-calorie snacks. Limit your caffeine intake. Watch your smoking. Be aware of your drinking habits.
- **BE ASSERTIVE** If you feel under stress, then say so. Express your feelings openly and honestly at work.
- **BE FOCUSED AT WORK** You are there to do a task, so do it. You are not there for the social life, the company car, or the view from the office window.
- **BE ORGANIZED** Plan your workload, your desk, your calendar, your day. Don't put things off.

- **BE COMFORTABLE** Make sure your office chair is right for you. Make sure your working environment is the right temperature. Make sure you're comfortable enough to do the job properly, but not so comfortable that you fall asleep.
- **BE SAFE** Make sure your work environment is suitable. Check your Health and Safety regulations.
- **BE COMMITTED** If you have chosen to do the job then do it. If you find you can't, then change jobs.
- **HAVE GOALS** Make sure your job furthers your personal life goals, and that you aren't just filling in the time until something better comes along.
- **BE HEALTHY** Make sure the job is adding to your health, not detracting from it. This applies to your moral and emotional health as much as your physical health. If your job conflicts with your personal views and beliefs, you will suffer stress.

DID YOU KNOW?

Drinking coffee has already been shown to raise anxiety levels and blood pressure, but it may also make you lose your temper, says Marc Parmentier of the Institute for Interdisciplinary Research in Brussels. Caffeine, he explains, blocks a "receptor" chemical in the brain that induces a calming effect on our minds. Male mice genetically engineered to simulate the effects of regular coffee drinking were found to be unusually aggressive.

MANAGING STRESS

I f you do nothing about your stress, it will not go away of its own accord—it will only get worse. It's vital to take immediate and practical steps to relieve the stress. The first thing to do is identify the cause—relationships, work, health, social life—and then do something to alleviate the symptoms.

It is vitally important to find a balance between work and a home or social life. Examine your working patterns critically and ask whether working into the night is really productive.

There is no evidence to suggest that stress can kill healthy people, although it may act as a trigger in people already suffering from heart disease. Hard workers may be too busy to notice the warning signs and so fail to seek medical advice, but that doesn't means stress caused the problem in the first place.

Poor breathing—breathing restricted to the upper chest area—is one of the most common causes of stress-related disorders. It can lead to a variety of problems because it causes the body to eliminate too much carbon dioxide, which, in turn, causes the blood to become too alkaline. This causes the blood vessels in the brain to constrict, slowing the circulation of oxygen in the brain and causing palpitations, dizziness, and faintness. These can create panic attacks, causing poor breathing and hyperventilation—which will prolong the panic attack.

To recover, you must stop the hyperventilation at once before it has a chance to set off this cycle.

KEY WAYS OF MANAGING STRESS

- make sure you relax regularly using a positive technique such as meditation, a breathing exercise, visualization, autogenic training, or yoga.
- enjoy a social life.
- Get regular exercise.
- don't make too many important changes in your life at the same time.
- take responsibility—change what you can change and let go of the rest.
- express your emotions—don't bottle things up.
- deal with one problem at a time.
- prioritize your time.
- have a belief system to support you during crises.

RESPONSES TO HYPERVENTILATION

STOP IT BEFORE IT GETS WORSE
Check your breathing during the day, especially if you are prone to hyperventilation or panic attacks.

RECOGNIZE THE SIGNS
Watch out for your breathing rate increasing, your breathing becoming more shallow, or sighing.

TAKE IMMEDIATE ACTION
If you find any of the above signs, then sit down and concentrate on your stomach breathing. Cup your hands over your mouth and nose and take four or five breaths (slowly and calmly) and rebreathe your exhaled air (see also p.191).

At the first signs of a panic attack, cup your hands, breathe in slowly and exhale, either into your hands or a paper bag.

OVERCOMING HYPERVENTILATION

Hyperventilation, and the possible subsequent panic attacks, create the same effects as severe shock and need to be treated accordingly;

- rest
- take a little warm sweet liquid such as a cup of tea
- avoid alcohol
- breathe calmly and slowly
- allow yourself to be emotional
- allow yourself to be comforted
- talk to a sympathetic person who has medical training and can help
- take steps to prevent a recurring attack
- adjust your lifestyle to avoid stress

STRESS AND HEALTH

To counteract the effects of stress, we have to recognize the signs. These may include insomnia, panic attacks, weight loss, trembling, unfounded anxieties and phobias, irritable bowel syndrome, palpitations, irritability, hyperventilation, muscular tension, headaches, addiction problems, high blood pressure, and a rapid pulse. Some of these symptoms are obviously more serious than others and will, to a certain degree, indicate your ability to channel and process stress.

Religious celebrations, such as Christmas, with its financial and emotional demands, can be a surprisingly stressful experience.

Bereavement and divorce rank high on the list of stressful events. But even happier situations, such as weddings, bring their own stresses and anxieties.

Once we have recognized the signs and realized that we too are suffering from the badly processed response to stress, we need to identify the causes of stress in our lives. Most stress-management consultants work with a general list of around 45 principal life events that are known to cause some degree of stress. These range from the death of a spouse (rated at 100), to a change in one's relationship with a partner (rated at 36), down to a minor breaking of the law (rated at 15). If you clock up a score of more than 150 in a year, the chances are that you'll experience some sort of problem with your health. A score of anything over 300 in one year will almost certainly lead to major health problems unless action is taken.

This list can help you reduce stress in your life. Once you know which life events are on the list and how high each item normally scores, you can try to plan in advance how many of the major changes you'll make in one year. Of course, some events are beyond anybody's control—but at least you can keep the stressful occasions that are within your control to a minimum.

The rating of stress levels on this list may seem arbitrary or subjective, but that is because it takes into account the long-term effects of various events. For example to some people the stress of Christmas may seem higher than its rating here. But while Christmas is over relatively quickly, the death of a close family member or a prison sentence may take years to adjust to, grieve over, or come to terms with.

EXAMPLES OF STRESSFUL LIFE EVENTS

Event	Score
Death of a child or spouse	100
Divorce	75
Marital separation	65
Prison sentence	65
Death of someone close in the family	65
Serious injury or illness	55
Getting married	50
Redundancy or dismissal	48
Marital reconciliation	45
Retirement	44
Illness affecting close family member	44
Pregnancy	40
Sexual difficulties	40
New baby	39
Change in business	38
Change in financial affairs	38
Death of close friend	38
Change in work	37
Change in relationship with partner	36
Mortgage rate rise/renegotiating mortgage	31
Loss of mortgage	30
New boss	28
Children leaving home	27
Problems with in-laws	26
Winning award	26
Partner changing type of work	25
Beginning or stopping study course	23
Change in living conditions	23
Change in personal habits	22
Argument with boss	21
Change in working conditions	20
Moving house	20
Children changing schools	19
Change in social activities	18
Change in religious activities	18
Taking out loan	17
Altered sleeping habits	17
Change in family location	16
Dieting	15
Vacations	15
Christmas	15
Minor law-breaking	15

THE EFFECTS OF STRESS

We can't avoid stress in our lives. Stress is an integral part of being a human and we're designed to cope with it as part of everyday life. Without stress to challenge us and keep us active and alert we would atrophy and never progress. The way that we cope with stress and stress overload determines whether the stress could be regarded as positive or negative. Stress in itself is neither good nor bad, right nor wrong. In order to ascertain whether we need to manage our stress more effectively we must be aware of any warning signs in our behavior that might indicate a need to take action.

There are a number of things you can do to help relieve the symptoms and control the stress levels. First you have to identify the stress. It may be coming from more than one area such as work, home, your relationship, or even your social life. Identify the worst areas and deal with them first.

There are general symptoms and warning signs of stress that you can watch out for. You may find that you are experiencing sleep problems and consequently feel constantly tired or lethargic, more irritable, and impatient. This in turn will lead to an inability to concentrate or make decisions, and short-term memory lapses. Symptoms of stress may also manifest themselves in muscle aches, joint pains, and loss of libido. People who are unable to cope with stress are quick to lose their temper and tend to neglect their health by excessive drinking and smoking.

As well as general symptoms, there may be other symptoms of a more medical nature (see box opposite).

It is important to recognize the symptoms of stress and seek help before your health is seriously affected.

MEDICAL SYMPTOMS OF STRESS

- Eczema, psoriasis, or other skin eruptions.
- Asthma.
- Sudden hair loss.
- Depression, nervous breakdown.
- Recurrent headaches and migraines.
- Impotence or premature ejaculation.
- Problems with the digestive system including IBS, ulcers, and gastritis.
- Infections and reduction in the efficiency of the immune system.
- Increase in blood pressure.

If you suffer from any of the above you must seek medical help.

COMPLEMENTARY THERAPIES

HERBAL MEDICINE

Herbal teas for relaxation can be made with valerian, hops, passion flowers or chamomile. To help restore nerves after a period of stress, take teas made with skullcap or ginseng which provide relaxants too.

YOGA

Yoga can be very effective in the development of long-term stress management skills through relaxation, better posture, and improved breathing (see p. 244).

MASSAGE

An effective way of relieving physical discomfort due to stress.

MEDITATION

For clearing the mind.

HOMEOPATHY

For symptoms of stress due to overwork or general exhaustion try Nux vomica 40. Ac. Phos. is prescribed for stress due to depression and Ignatia 30 for stress due to sudden shocks or trauma (see p.226).

T'AI CHI

"Meditation in motion" is very good for learning long term relaxation control and balancing the harmony of mind, body, and spirit (see p.245).

The measured movements of t'ai chi or similar exercises will relax the mind and body.

Herbal tea

185

COMMUNICATION

We're not islands. We need to communicate with our fellow human beings or we lose our sense of well-being. Good communication offers a way of expressing hopes and fears, dreams, emotions, troubles, and worries in an honest and considerate way. If you can achieve this you will open up channels for others to communicate better with you.

LISTENING AND RESPONDING

Here are some basic ground rules for good communication.

DON'T BE JUDGMENTAL Listen to the other person in an objective way.

BE TOLERANT of what the speaker is saying. Respect the speaker's views and don't put him or her down verbally.

BE CARING and don't dismiss the speaker's worries and concerns.

DON'T INTERRUPT Let the speaker finish what he or she is saying.

ASK OPEN QUESTIONS such as "How do you feel about...." rather than closed questions that beg a simple "Yes" or "No."

LISTEN CAREFULLY and make certain the speaker knows you are listening. Repeat back some of the speaker's words as proof that you are listening and not just waiting to speak.

ENCOURAGE THE SPEAKER by using body language that shows you are attentive, and using encouraging words such as "really" or "go on then."

MAINTAIN EYE CONTACT by keeping visible facial contact rather than staring intensely.

BE DISCRIMINATING and ensure that you communicate at the right time.

BE BRIEF and say what you have to say simply and precisely.

EXPRESS HOW YOU FEEL, not what you think the other person makes you feel. Say "I feel angry," not "You make me angry."

Our ability to communicate verbally separates us from other animals in many ways. Communication via speech enables us to pass on learned information to future generations, while written communication allows us to document our findings.

Human communication is, therefore, a very powerful tool. Good communication is the key to sharing ideas and wishes with others, and maybe even winning them over to our point of view. This type of communication skill is at the heart of successful negotiation which occurs in the business world as well as in personal relationships.

Learn to listen to the person who is talking to you. Maintain eye contact and show with your body language that you are hearing what he or she is saying.

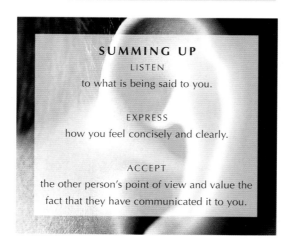

SUMMING UP

LISTEN
to what is being said to you.

EXPRESS
how you feel concisely and clearly.

ACCEPT
the other person's point of view and value the fact that they have communicated it to you.

POSITIVE THINKING

W e learn thinking from our parents—or whoever it is that brings us up—and teachers. If we are given good role models, our thinking will be free, easy, logical, and sharp. If our role models are vague, cluttered, illogical, and ponderous thinkers, there's a good chance we will pick up their thinking patterns and habits.

In order to enjoy the benefits of positive thinking, you have to determine whether or not you have good thinking habits first. This is easy to do—next time you have a conversation, simply make an effort to listen to yourself. There are some key phrases that indicate "closed" thinking and if you hear yourself using them a lot, it's a good indication that you may be suffering from a stunted or closed thinking process.

Every time you hear yourself use the words *should*, *have to*, *must*, *got to*, *ought to*, stop and think. Take a moment to ask yourself why *should* you?,

why do you *have to*?, who said you *must*?, why have you *got to*?, whose rule is it that you *ought to*? This sort of questioning obviously also applies to the opposites of these phrases—*shouldn't*, *can't*, *mustn't*, *oughtn't*.

Questioning where we get all these rules and regulations from will help our thinking. Who decides what we *should, ought, must,* and *have to* do? We are the only ones who can decide those things. We can only be positive when we know we are thinking for ourselves, not following predetermined patterns that may no longer apply.

Train yourself to think about the positive aspects of life: the beauty of nature, the support you have from family and friends.

STEPS TO POSITIVE THINKING

FIND OUT AS MUCH AS YOU CAN
Without sufficient information it's difficult to make decisions or be positive enough in our thinking. Ask questions—you may not like the answers, but at least you will know. Having information changes our thinking. The more we have, the less fear, uncertainty, and hesitation we suffer.

BE AWARE OF YOUR MOODS When we are tired, stressed, or bad-tempered our thinking becomes much less positive. When we are relaxed, happy, and rested our thinking is much more positive and we are better able to make decisions, make plans, and be realistic.

BE EXPERIENCED We all have fears of the unknown. We believe we can't because we have never tried. When we have experience of things we are better able to cope. Only by knowing can we understand. It's good to try— even if we fail—just to expand our horizons and add to our experience.

WE ARE ALL THE SAME
Remember that everyone around you suffers from negative thinking just as much as you do—it's helpful to keep this in mind and make allowances. Don't be too harsh with others, or with yourself.

Laughter and positive activities are literally beneficial to your health and well-being. Laughter eases muscle tension, improves the body's circulation, and stimulates antibodies. The more optimistic and positive you are, the healthier you will be.

MAKING DECISIONS

I f we feel that we can't make decisions, we become vague and afraid of the future. When we have a definite and focused attitude, decisions are easy to make and we feel free to get on with our lives in a positive way.

If you find it difficult to make decisions, then you need to start by knowing why: are you in possession of all the facts? Are you frightened of the results of your decisions? Knowing what steps can stop you from making decisions is a step toward becoming more decisive.

The ability to be decisive not only makes life easier in general, but it also improves your general level of confidence. Confidence in yourself soon spills over into others gaining more confidence in you and your ability to handle important situations. From a work aspect the rewards are often improved job prospects and promotion to a position that requires more responsibility. From a personal point of view, knowing that you are able to make the correct choice gives you a feeling of security and improved self-esteem.

GUIDELINES FOR EFFECTIVENESS

Here are some guidelines to enable you to both identify what stops you from making decisions and help you to make them quickly and effectively.

- **WRITE EVERYTHING DOWN** Draw up an action plan. Next to each item, list what you need to make your decisions and what you expect from that decision.

- **BRAINSTORM** Ask your partner/close friends/family to help you. Write down anything and everything you can think of around your decision, no matter how wild or silly it seems.

- **BE REALISTIC** Don't make plans or attempt goals that you know you simply can't achieve. Allow space for your own personality into every decision.

- **PRIORITIZE** Check your decision on what's most important to you and put it at the top of your list.

- **DO NOT ALLOW CONFLICTS** Make sure your plans and decisions don't conflict with each other.

- **BE CLEAR** What exactly is it you want? Be very clear about the detail of your decision.

- **RESEARCH YOUR DECISION** This may sound like a lot of work, but the more we know, the easier our decision becomes.

- **REWARD YOURSELF** As each step of your decision comes to fruition, you can reward yourself. Plan these rewards in advance.

- **KNOW THE RESULTS** Be clear about what you think the results of your decisions will be.

- **BE PREPARED TO CHANGE PLANS** Write an element of contingency for both change and failure into your decisions.

We are all faced by decisions— students have to choose courses, or decide on a career—and it can be an excruciating process. Listing and prioritizing options and researching implications help to focus the mind.

IMPROVING MEMORY

*P*eople with good memories have a more enhanced sense of well-being because they do not feel helpless or threatened by their environment. Poor memory causes a loss of well-being because we flounder in a world of uncertainty. It's generally found that memory deteriorates when it isn't used enough. Those who have good memories have been found to be consistent and regular users of their memory. Good memory is a skill which can be learned.

A retentive memory is not something we have to be born with. It is a skill that can be acquired. There are recognized techniques that,

with some practice and application, can help anyone sharpen their ability to remember. However, recurrent memory lapses may be a symptom of illness and medical help should be sought.

One helpful tip for retaining information is to be selective about what you are trying to remember. Choosing only the information you need is more efficient than trying to fit everything in.

HOW TO IMPROVE YOUR MEMORY

NEEDS AND WANTS Before you can improve, you have to differentiate between what you need to remember and what you want to remember. On a very basic level, you need to remember who you are, but you don't need to remember the entire contents of an encyclopedia.

SORTING INFORMATION Once you know what you need and want you can begin by sorting the information you want to remember. Poor memory is often caused by trying to remember information in chunks that are simply too large. Break things down into manageable pieces. Write things down. Keep notes. Make lists.

ACCESSING INFORMATION If you don't encode the information at the time, you will have no means of

recalling it later. If you meet someone new and want to remember his or her name later, then mentally create an image of them using their name as a code. For instance if they have a wide mouth and their name is Powell you could remember them as the person with the powerful smile.

BE RELAXED The more relaxed you are when the information goes in the more likely you will be to remember it later.

ASSOCIATE If you want to remember lists of things, associate each of them by linking them together with jokes, visual puns, or any sort of mental nonsense that actually works for you.

Using someone's name at first meeting and repeating it occasionally during conversation will avoid embarrassing memory lapses later.

Chinese herbs are used to stimulate the kidney, believed to be associated with memory.

COMPLEMENTARY THERAPIES

ACUPUNCTURE

Memory loss is considered a kidney weakness; acupuncture seeks to improve this by balancing the chi (see p.230).

HERBAL MEDICINE

Ginkgo biloba can help strengthen memory.

CHINESE MEDICINE

Again, to strengthen the kidney, essence of mulberry fruit, dodder seed, eucommia bark, and wolfberry seed are prescribed (see p.225).

Mulberry fruit

Dodder seed

Wolfberry seed

Eucommia bark

189

RELAXATION AND BREATHING

*T*o relax properly you need to take some positive action; just slumping in a chair may seem relaxing, but it won't really do any good. It's important to actually do some form of muscle relaxing exercises.

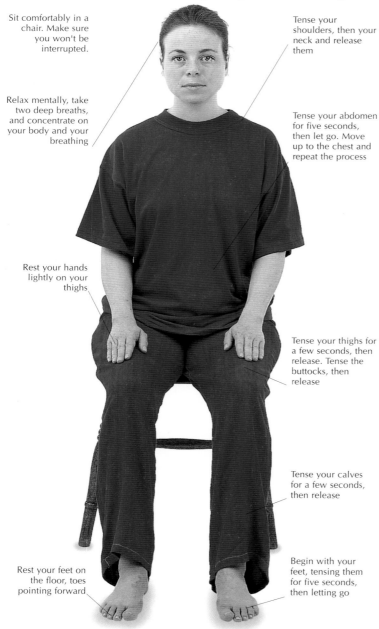

Sit comfortably in a chair. Make sure you won't be interrupted.

Relax mentally, take two deep breaths, and concentrate on your body and your breathing

Rest your hands lightly on your thighs

Rest your feet on the floor, toes pointing forward

Tense your shoulders, then your neck and release them

Tense your abdomen for five seconds, then let go. Move up to the chest and repeat the process

Tense your thighs for a few seconds, then release. Tense the buttocks, then release

Tense your calves for a few seconds, then release

Begin with your feet, tensing them for five seconds, then letting go

Find a quiet place for the following relaxation exercise, and make sure that you won't be interrupted for about 20 minutes. It's a good idea to take the phone off the hook, or switch on the answering machine.

Choose a comfortable chair to sit in, where you can be fairly upright. Rest your hands lightly on your thighs. Keep your legs together and your feet pointing forward flat on the floor.

Prepare by allowing yourself to relax mentally so you can enjoy this exercise. Try to empty your mind of any pressing thoughts or worries.

When you feel that you have stopped thinking about work or your troubles, take a couple of deep breaths. Now you are ready to begin concentrating on your body. Without actually tensing anything, try to sense where in your body you are holding any tension.

Begin relaxing your body by tensing your feet. Scrunch up your toes as tightly as possible for about five seconds, then let them go. Do this for each part of your entire body in the following order. Tense for each part for just five seconds, hold it, and then let go.

1 Push your feet down firmly, then let go.
2 Tighten your ankles, calves, and knees, tightening them while pressing your feet hard against the floor, then relax.
3 Push your thighs hard against the seat of the chair, hold, then relax.
4 Clench your hands into fists, hold them, and then relax them.
5 Tense your arms by tightening your biceps, hold them, and then relax.
6 Clench your buttocks, hold them, and then relax.
7 Push out your lower abdomen, hold, and relax.

MORE TENSION RELIEVERS

If you work sitting down a lot, you can try hunching your shoulders and letting go to relieve any tension you may be accumulating. Or you could try tensing and relaxing your leg muscles while sitting watching television.
You might like to try this exercise in bed last thing at night. It's especially useful for people who have trouble getting to sleep because it relaxes the whole body.

1 Hands: clench the hands tightly into fists.

2 Then let go and relax the hands. Your can follow the same procedure for the arms: tighten the biceps and then let go.

3 Jaw: clench your teeth together as hard as possible and then let go. Eyes: screw up your eyes as tight as possible and let go.

4 Face: scrunch up your face as much as possible (imagine you are eating a lemon) and let go.

5 Forehead: frown as deeply as possible and then let go.

6 Shoulders: hunch your shoulders up towards your ears as far as possible and then let go suddenly.

BREATHING EXERCISE

Once your muscles are relaxed, you might also like to practice breathing exercises. They'll enhance the work you've already done and help you maintain good and adequate breath.
Once again, it's important to find somewhere quiet to sit down where you won't be disturbed.

Put one hand on your chest and one hand on your stomach to see where you are breathing. Listen to your breathing. Breathe in and out through your nose only. If you can hear your breathing, you are doing it too heavily.

Concentrate on breathing with your diaphragm. Breathe in through your nose and out through your mouth slowly and calmly. Make sure your chest doesn't rise and fall. Look straight ahead and keep your eyes open. Make sure that each breathing movement in your body is forward and back rather than up and down.

Allow a pause between each in and out breath. You can silently mouth the word "relax" or "calm" to help you take the pause. Allow your body to relax naturally, and let all tension go.

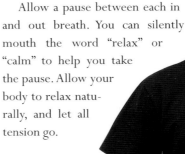 

Learning to relax is not always easy and may involve spending a few sessions with a practitioner. The essential thing to learn is abdominal breathing.

191

SECTION EIGHT

well-being

MIND, BODY, AND SPIRIT

contents

Introduction

To achieve complete well-being we may need to turn the clock back and re-examine our true values in life.

W hy do we find life more difficult than we did in the 50s? In material terms, says the clinical psychologist Oliver James, we are vastly better off than we were in 1950, when Britain was "a world of unheated winters, rationed food, and very limited pleasures." But we're much less happy than we were then. However this trend in dissatisfaction appears to be a problem affecting all developed countries including the consumer-dominated USA.

For instance, 25-year-olds are between three and 10 times more likely to suffer from depression. Violent crime has mushroomed. Many kinds of compulsive behavior, including eating disorders, "are at epidemic levels." At least 20% of us will now suffer from some form of mental illness during our lives.

Dissatisfaction and envy are endemic in the modern world. Learning to place greater value on what you have—yourself and your relationships—is one way of overcoming them.

The real villain of the piece, according to James, is modern capitalism, which stokes our sense of dissatisfaction and "makes money out of disappointment." To put it succinctly: "Envy is at the root of modern misery."

This next section investigates ways of tackling this modern misery and enhancing your life through improving confidence and sleep patterns, and by investigating ways of getting the most out of work, leisure time, hobbies, and interests. This section also provides some useful and helpful tips on self care, financial well-being, dealing with grief, bereavement, divorce and separation, and living with illness. There are some useful techniques for enhancing relationships, your spiritual health and well-being, improving your friendships, and coping with a midlife crisis.

When you have sorted out your personal well-being you're likely to be a little less inclined to envy the possessions, wealth, or health of others. Once you feel secure, confident, healthy, well-adjusted, and focused you can branch out with ease and assurance. Always remember to keep aware that your being is made up of three parts, mind, body, and spirit. You need to look after all three aspects if you're to achieve a complete and overall sense of well-being.

THE BODY

For your body's well-being, you need to keep physically fit, monitor your body for health problems, maintain a healthy weight, eat nutritious, balanced meals, and remain active and supple.

A healthy body brings confidence, happiness, and physical well-being. Looking after your body is a must.

THE MIND

For mental well-being, you should think clearly and logically, improve and maintain your memory, remain mentally active and alert, stay open to new ideas, and keep mentally supple by making sure your brain is challenged and exercised. You should learn to think positively and cultivate an optimistic view of life.

Keep your mind alert and active. Learning is a lifelong process

In today's consumer society, the spiritual side of life is often forgotten. Take time alone to enhance and listen to your inner self.

THE SPIRIT

For spiritual well-being, you need to find a personal belief system that you can trust and have faith in. Devoting time to such a belief system can help you find your niche in life and will help sustain you in times of crisis. You also need to learn to look within yourself for strength and sustenance. Spending time alone to seek guidance from your own "inner voice" will help you discover what is really meaningful and important to your life, and teach you to jettison the things you don't need to do.

EMOTIONAL HEALTH

*H*appiness is a state of mind. The way we approach our emotional well-being is through a positive and enhanced mental outlook on life. There's nothing you can buy and no amount of money that can give you long-term emotional health. Likewise there is no new love affair that is going to do so, either. It's only your own approach to life that counts, and that depends on several things.

Happy people tend to live longer and more contented lives. This is supported by numerous studies into the connection between the emotions, the nervous system, and the immune system. Only a few years ago this mind-body connection was not taken seriously by medical science, but the new science of psycho-neuro-immunology has changed that. Hard scientific proof now confirms the importance of emotional health.

Happy thoughts make for a healthy, well-functioning immune system, while depressed people tend to get sick more often. The irrefutable connection between mental health and physical health should be enough to motivate some positive emotional housekeeping.

Having a goal, whether learning skydiving or a new language, gives incentive and personal direction, vital for emotional well-being. Making the most of every opportunity and valuing the moment as it happens is a far healthier way to live than regretting the past.

Avoid aggressive confrontations. Learn to express your feelings honestly, directly, and without inappropriate rage or blame.

YOUR OUTLOOK

- Are you able to take responsibility for your own emotional well-being? If you blame others, you can't improve or change for the better. When you take responsibility, you take control. Those in control are better equipped to deal with life.
- Are you flexible in your thinking? If your thought processes are very rigid and full of "should" and "must" and "have to," then you will be unable to adapt quickly and readily to new challenges.
- Do you enjoy the moment? If you spend your life yearning for what has gone and longing for what will be, then you will miss the best part—what is happening now. Now is the only reality we have, and if we don't enjoy it, it slips away.
- Do you accept and love yourself? If you don't, then no one else can. Learn to live with all your foibles, faults, and fallibility—they are what make you the wonderful, unique human being you are.
- What are your goals and dreams? If you have nothing to work toward then you will have no direction and may find yourself being tossed aimlessly on the sea of life.
- Are you managing your time well? If you don't, you will always be in a hurry to be somewhere else doing something else. Learn proper time management.
- Can you express your feelings freely? The key to healthy emotional well-being is expressing your feelings in an appropriate manner at the appropriate time and then moving on, leaving behind your resentment, guilt, and anger.

GROUPS AND FRIENDS

Having friends and belonging to various social groups teaches us a lot, especially how to be in touch with our emotions. Becoming emotionally literate is beneficial to overall well-being and enhances lifestyle and health.

People who are in touch with their emotions take responsibility for their actions and feelings and don't blame others. They recognize their own emotional patterns and try to correct any negative or unhelpful ones. They can see clearly the most appropriate behavior in certain circumstances and act accordingly.

Such people can be discriminating about their own negative and positive qualities. They are more in touch with their bodies and can see how their emotional responses affect their bodily functions, language, and responses. They can express themselves in a much wider range of emotions than those who are detached from their emotions, and are likely to know what they want out of life and how to get it. They can also be more helpful in dealing with other people who are in crisis and are skilled in communicating their emotional needs to others.

Good friends are a valuable asset. Cherish those who are most compatible, and perhaps move away from those with whom you have less in common.

RELATIONSHIP GUIDELINES

There are some techniques you and your partner might like to try to improve your relationship, which will undoubtedly improve your well-being.

BE ALLOWED TO TALK Ask for time to talk over any problems. It's not healthy to bottle up your true feelings if there's something you need to get off your chest but you may have to "make an appointment" to take time to talk in a calm environment. Your partner doesn't need to reply afterward—this is the time to express something important.

BE FRIENDS Sometimes we treat our partner in ways we wouldn't treat our friends. Endeavor to be at least as nice to each other as you would be to your friends.

BE SURPRISING Try to surprise each other by breaking your routines or habits so that you don't become predictable and staid.

BE KIND TO EACH OTHER Treat each other occasionally to meals out, flowers, breakfast in bed, a massage with oils, sleeping in late, a little gift, or cooking a special meal.

SPEND TIME TOGETHER Not just doing chores, bringing up the children, or watching TV, but real quality time. Go for a walk and hold hands. Book a weekend in a hotel together. Special time together shouldn't be spent "doing things"—just being together.

APPRECIATE EACH OTHER You both have a role and a function, but that doesn't mean you should go unappreciated. Praise each other for the little tasks you take for granted. Be courteous with each other and say "please" and "thank you" and "I appreciated it when you did …" and "it was really nice of you to…"

APPRECIATE WHY YOU ARE TOGETHER Make time to talk about how you met, how you fell in love, why you are together, where you are going together, how you feel about each other, and what makes you feel good about each other. Be positive.

TO IMPROVE YOUR CIRCLE OF FRIENDS, YOU MIGHT LIKE TO:

MAKE A LIST OF ALL YOUR REGULAR SOCIAL CONTACTS, FRIENDS, AND ACQUAINTANCES

•

LIST NEXT TO THEM THE QUALITIES THEY BRING TO YOUR LIFE

•

LIST HOW YOU FEEL ABOUT THEM

•

DECIDE IF YOU HAVE THE TIME AND EMOTIONAL CAPACITY FOR THEM

•

DECIDE IF YOU NEED TO PRUNE ANY OF THEM FROM YOUR LIFE

An unexpected bunch of flowers is a lovely gift and a good way of showing appreciation of your partner.

Confidence and well-being stem from self-esteem and a recognition of one's own self-worth.

SELF-ESTEEM

When we feel happy and confident our internal view of ourselves is good. We have positive self-esteem and can cope with the world. If for any reason our internal view of ourselves is less than what it might be, we suffer low self-esteem.

People who suffer from low self-esteem are underconfident, fearful, and reluctant to venture forth or make changes. Being apprehensive of new situations and new challenges means low self-esteem is seriously affecting your outlook on life and your well-being; however, there are effective ways of improving self-esteem.

By all means try the following techniques, but don't expect instant results. Low self-esteem is invariably the result of many years of negative programing. It took a long time to develop, so it will almost certainly take a while to overcome. Be patient with yourself. Take things slowly at first and gradually build up your self-confidence step by step. Even small steps forward represent progress, so be sure you remember to congratulate and reward yourself along the way.

IMPROVING SELF-ESTEEM

WATCH YOUR BODY LANGUAGE If you are hunched and slumped you will feel low. This is also true in reverse. If you put your head up and shoulders back you will feel happier. This is because your body posture affects your breathing. If you are slumped you are probably using upper chest breathing (see p.191). Sitting up and back makes you use your diaphragm to breathe, which makes you feel better.

BE NICE TO YOURSELF Treat yourself. Even in your worst moments, be aware that you are still a valuable, unique, wonderful human being with special talents and skills, and you need to be rewarded. If no one else does it—do it for yourself.

BE ASSERTIVE What you want is important. Learn to approve of your needs and expect them to be met.

PLAN YOUR STRATEGY Rehearse first. Plan how you will conquer a small fear and then go and do it. Visualize how the triumph will feel and then go and achieve it.

USE OTHERS That's what they're there for. Express your feelings. Talk to people about how they can help you feel better. Value your importance and be prepared to tell others.

DRESS THE PART Confident people wear confident clothing and have well-groomed hair. If you dress scruffily and don't take care of your personal hygiene and appearance, you will feel worse than if you do.

REHEARSE THE PART Practice in front of a mirror. Stand up straight and look confident. See what your body does. Practice speaking in a confident way until it becomes easier to do it for real.

AVOID FRIENDS WHO DRAIN YOU Socialize with high-energy friends. Stay with positive people who appreciate you and make you feel good.

Low self-esteem is debilitating and particularly common among women. Lack of confidence, withdrawal and possibly alcoholism may result.

ASSERTIVENESS

Being assertive is not being aggressive or pushy. Being assertive is knowing what we want and how to get it without being discouraged. It is knowing how to say "no" to what we don't want. There may be many factors that stop us from having the confidence to be assertive.

Being assertive is all about standing up for yourself, for your own needs and wishes, and for your beliefs and opinions. Standing up for yourself is a key ingredient toward attaining self-esteem, and the more you are able to do it, the higher your self-esteem will be. Here are some common difficulties that many people have with assertiveness, and what you can do about them.

COMMON ASSERTIVENESS DIFFICULTIES

If you believe that any of these is true for you then you may want to work on your assertiveness.

- If you say "no" people will think less of you or stop liking you.
- If you say what you mean you run the risk of offending people.
- Other people should instinctively know what you want without you having to voice it.
- You shouldn't be a burden to other people, and other people don't care about your concerns.
- It's wrong to change your mind or be indecisive.
- People shouldn't discuss their feelings.
- It's selfish to voice what you want.

Standing, rather than sitting, using direct eye contact, and refusing to be deflected from the matter at hand, are useful assertiveness techniques for this female employee.

ASSERTIVENESS GUIDELINES

You may want to try:

- Learning to voice your opinions, wants, cares, worries, and feelings in a clear, precise, and simple way so that you are understood.
- Learning to say "no" and meaning it, and learning to stick to it.
- Making sure you complain if someone's behavior is unacceptable to you.
- Acknowledging compliments and/or criticism openly and objectively.
- Expressing your feelings in an appropriate way and acknowledging when you don't.
- Knowing the difference between being passive, assertive, and aggressive.
- Apologizing when your behavior has been inappropriate or misdirected.

Assertiveness is the art of honest, clear and direct communication. Dressing well can help to achieve it.

LIFE SKILLS

As we grow older we learn more about how to deal with life. When we are young we learn as we go along. Sometimes, however, we fail to learn as well as we should, and that can have a negative effect on our well-being.

There are a number of "natural" rules that can help all of us to manage life, with all its excitement, stresses, and trauma. If you haven't automatically learned all of these natural rules, it might be worth looking at these basic ground rules and practicing the ones that you need help with.

Studies show that people with a good sense of humor experience less tiredness, anger, and stress than those without it.

Life is made up of good and bad events. It is important not to personalize bad events, but accept them as just part of everyday living.

SOME BASIC GROUND RULES

DON'T TAKE LIFE PERSONALLY All of life is a mixture of good and bad. When bad things happen to you, accept them as part of the bigger picture.

EVERYTHING CHANGES No matter what your situation is now, it will change. There's nothing you can do, so accept that change is inescapable.

STOP TRYING TO BE PERFECT Accept that we're human beings, full of faults and foibles.

TAKE RESPONSIBILITY It's no one's fault that you're the way you are. If you take responsibility, you can take positive steps to change anything you consider needs changing and get on with your life.

STOP DEMANDING Allow life to work around you rather than trying to bludgeon it into submission.

WHERE ARE YOU RUSHING TO GET TO? Life is not a destination, it's a journey. The more you rush through it, the sooner you get to the end of it! Take time to enjoy it when you can.

CHECK THE MECHANICS Without proper sleep, food, and exercise you will deteriorate. Looking after your body well isn't selfish or vain—it's common sense.

STOP BANGING YOUR HEAD AGAINST THE WALL If you habitually encounter situations where you feel frustrated and unable to change anything, it might be helpful to avoid them or alter your response.

LEARN TO LAUGH MORE Research has shown that laughter can help you recover quicker from illness, allow you to cope better with life's dramas, and generally improve your health.

EXPRESS YOUR FEELINGS You are allowed to express them. Learn to talk more about how you feel.

KNOW WHAT YOU WANT Look ahead and plan where you want to be and what you want to be doing. Give your life direction.

MANAGE YOUR RELATIONSHIPS Unless you put in some time and effort, relationships will decay and fall apart. You have to do some work (see p.197).

MANAGE YOUR TIME EFFECTIVELY Allow time for yourself, leisure interests, family, love, fun, work, travel, study, solitude, rest, and more fun.

LOOK FOR CHOICE There are always two ways (at least) of doing anything.

DEVELOP YOURSELF You are not a static being. Develop new interests and new friends. Study new things, improve your education. Read lots.

BE FLEXIBLE IN YOUR THINKING Don't get stuck in routines or habits. The more unconventional and unpredictable you are, the more you develop and grow mentally.

SET YOURSELF STANDARDS Strive for quality and improvement in your intellectual standards so that you remain interesting and vibrant.

BE AWARE OF WHAT YOU ARE You are a complex being made up of emotions, physical parts, mental processes, and a spiritual quality. We all need to devote some time to all three aspects of ourselves.

FINANCIAL WELL-BEING

*S*tress *and anxiety caused by continual worrying about money problems can seriously affect your well-being, although any problems relating to financial matters can be overcome if you have the determination.*

When money problems occur between partners you may need to sit down together and check that you're managing your finances the way you both want. The checkpoints below may help you to focus on possible problems.

CHECKING FINANCIAL WELL-BEING

JOINT ACCOUNTS Do you need joint accounts? What benefits are there in them? Could you keep your finances separate?

BILLS Who makes sure they are paid? Do you have any system for monitoring them?

HOUSEKEEPING Who is responsible for the housekeeping?

MORTGAGE Whose name is it in, and which of you is responsible for it?

SPENDING MONEY Who sets the level of spending money? Are you both happy with what the other spends?

WEEKLY MONEY This may be the children's allowances or the money one of you receives from your partner. Who decides at what level it should be set? Why is it that person?

PETTY CASH Do you have a petty cash system? Who pays for expenditures such as spontaneous charity donations?

BUDGETS Do you have them? Who sets them and checks if you stick to them? How could you improve them?

SAVINGS Do you have any? Do you both want them? What are you saving for? Do you both agree and set the goals for saving?

INVESTMENTS Who decides on them?

PERSONAL MONEY Do you have any? Is the level appropriate to both partners? Who sets the limits? Do you need to explain anything to the other partner?

OVERDRAFTS Who is responsible for them? Are you both happy with the levels set?

LOANS Whose are they? Are you both happy with what they are for?

DEBTS Whose are they and what caused them? Is there any resentment about them?

CREDITORS If one of you lends money are you both happy with that? Who owes you money?

CREDIT PLANS Do you have any? Are you both happy with what you bought on credit? Are you both happy with the levels set?

Money problems cause huge stress. Overcoming them means first confronting the situation then drawing up realistic budgets and plans.

JOB SATISFACTION

*P*erhaps you are lucky enough to have chosen a career that gives you satisfaction and are able to combine personal ambition with an income. If not there are some important steps you can take to remedy the situation.

Start by asking yourself what it is you want from your work. Does your current employment satisfy that want? What do you need from your job? Again, does your current employment meet that need? You may find that your wants and needs are quite separate, but both are important and must be considered. Your job may be fulfilling all your needs, but perhaps your wants are still unsatisfied. Look at your long-term goals. Ask yourself what it is that you want or expect from life. Where do you want to be, and what do you want to be doing, in

five years? What about in ten years from now? If you discover that your work isn't satisfying you, or helping you to achieve your life goals, then there are various options for change that you can consider. Thinking about change may seem a little unnerving at first, but if you examine your choices carefully change can be a less frightening choice than a lifetime of unfulfilled goals and desires.

Job satisfaction manifests itself in different ways according to personality. For some people being an architect offers a challenge to be creative. For others it may be of no interest.

Working with children as a nurse or pediatrician is hard, demanding work but offers enormous rewards in terms of satisfaction, although it may provide less money than other professions.

OPTIONS

CHANGE WITHIN YOUR ORGANIZATION—SPEAK TO SENIOR STAFF ABOUT NEW TASKS, SWITCHING DEPARTMENTS, OR ROLES.

•

CHANGE OUTSIDE OF YOUR ORGANIZATION—LOOK FOR A NEW JOB.

•

DOWNSHIFTING—SEEK A NEW DIRECTION ENTIRELY

•

STAY WHERE YOU ARE—KEEP YOUR CURRENT JOB BUT EMBARK ON A NEW COURSE OF STUDY SO THAT YOU HAVE THE OPPORTUNITY TO CHANGE JOBS AT A LATER DATE.

•

LOOK FOR THE REALIZATION OF YOUR DREAMS AND GOALS OUTSIDE WORK ALTOGETHER IF YOU CAN'T FIND THEM IN YOUR CAREER.

DID YOU KNOW?

Job dissatisfaction is bad for your health, according to Professor Cary Cooper of the University of Manchester Institute of Science and Technology in England. His study claims that 30 million working days are lost each year through stress. Dr James Lefanu agrees: male patients who answered negatively to enquiries about work were often found to be suffering from headaches, palpitations, or sleeping difficulties. "This distress poses a much more significant threat to the physical and mental well-being of young men than virtually everything else combined," he says.

WORK AND LEISURE

O bviously some people find their work intensely satisfying and that can spill over into their leisure activities. By socializing they improve their work contacts and can combine the two successfully. For most of us, however, there has to be a definite cut-off point between work and leisure and we mix the two at our peril.

Working extra hours at the office or taking work home to be done in the evenings or weekends could be bad for your stress levels and may also be unfair to your partner, children, and friends at times. They all expect to see you and to enjoy your company at regular intervals in order to sustain good relationships, and not just snatched moments with someone who is too exhausted by work to communicate properly or give them the care and attention they need.

If work demands that you do overtime or take work home, try to be assertive about your own needs. We are not machines and all of us have our cut-off point. Our loved ones also have their cut-off point, and we need to respect this in ourselves and in them (see p.182).

Work should challenge, stimulate, and reward you, and leisure activities should do likewise. A job should not dominate your life unless you want it to. Make sure that you have time for leisure activities in your life, Having an interest outside work will help broaden your horizons and prevent you from stagnating. You may get paid less, but you will certainly get a well-being bonus.

New technology means that increasing numbers of people are choosing to work from home, a good solution for those who combine parenting and earning. But it can be difficult to cut off from work.

It is extremely important to offset time at work with enjoyable leisure activities, whether horseback riding, working out at the gym, or walking.

FIVE KEY POINTS ABOUT WORK AND LEISURE

SEPARATE THE TWO AND KEEP THEM SEPARATE.

•

STOP WORK WHEN YOU ARE SUPPOSED TO AND ENJOY YOUR LEISURE TIME.

•

HAVE OTHER INTERESTS APART FROM WORK TO KEEP YOU VIBRANT AND INTERESTING

•

REALIZE THAT YOUR LEISURE ACTIVITIES ARE RECHARGING YOU FOR WORK EVEN IF THEY ARE STRENUOUS, SUCH AS SPORTS OR DANCING.

•

USE SOME OF YOUR HARD-EARNED WAGES TO ENJOY YOURSELF, NOT JUST FOR PAYING BILLS. WORK TO LIVE, DON'T LIVE TO WORK.

HOBBIES AND INTERESTS

Recent research has thrown up two interesting facts about hobbies and interests. First, people who were recovering from heart attacks made much better progress and were subsequently less likely to have a recurrence if they had a social support group of some kind. (Even enrolling in a night-school class was found to be beneficial.)

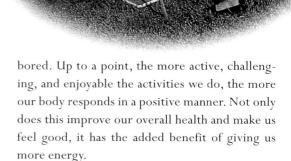

Taking up a hobby such as painting can have a very beneficial effect on your health, providing interest and perhaps realizing a long-held dream of creativity.

Second, a recent 10-year study into happiness and what causes it found that the best guarantee of long-term happiness was "serious leisure." This can mean any hobby or leisure interest that you find stimulating, challenging, interesting, absorbing, and—perhaps most important—fun.

The people who took part in the study reported that dancing was the most popular and probably one of the most effective serious leisure activities. Whether it be Latin-American, ballroom, or jazz, dancing is fun, a good way of meeting new friends, keeps you in shape, and it is an activity that could be enjoyed by just about anyone. Team sports, such as softball, basketball, and football, and religious activities came a close joint second.

The less that we do in our leisure time (watching television, which is a more passive activity, doesn't count) the more likely most of us are to become depressed, lethargic, unfit, overweight, and bored. Up to a point, the more active, challenging, and enjoyable the activities we do, the more our body responds in a positive manner. Not only does this improve our overall health and make us feel good, it has the added benefit of giving us more energy.

It's apparent, then, that for good health, well-being, happiness, and longevity, it's essential to keep up a variety of interests.

Joining a dance class provides interest and the chance to meet new people and learn a new skill.

GO FOR IT

If you want to stave off heart attacks and enjoy long-term happiness—join something today.

MAKE A LIST OF ALL THE LEISURE ACTIVITIES YOU USED TO DO THAT YOU DON'T DO ANY MORE BUT THAT YOU ENJOYED AND WOULDN'T MIND DOING AGAIN

•

MAKE A LIST OF ALL THE THINGS YOU'D LIKE TO DO IF ONLY YOU HAD MORE TIME, MONEY, ENERGY, ENTHUSIASM, OR MOTIVATION

•

PICK ONE FROM EACH LIST AND DO IT WITHIN THE NEXT MONTH. PROMISE YOURSELF YOU WON'T MAKE EXCUSES OR DELAY

TIME MANAGEMENT

With only a limited amount of time each day it's best to be very clear about what we will spend or squander that time on. Good time management means setting goals and being realistic about them.

The pace of modern life has never been so rapid. While the invention of fax machines, the Internet, and e-mail have revolutionized the working world, they have also brought many new problems with them. Work-related stress is a growing problem. For the human species to happily interact with the ever-growing hi-tech office, a close look at time management is a necessity. The pressure for us to react immediately to a request often means that we find ourselves in turmoil with the jobs in the in-tray growing by the hour. Time management will enable you to prioritize jobs while protecting your valuable health.

The practical aspects of life can easily get out of control. Setting up a filing system for important papers is one way of reducing stress.

TIME MANAGEMENT GUIDELINES

ONE TASK AT A TIME Finish each thing before you move onto the next. Have a clear picture of what you are doing. Knowing what the end should be is important. If you're working haphazardly you cannot be focused.

BE ORGANIZED Make lists. Keep a filing system for everything. Write down everything you need to know, remember, think about, plan, and resource.

SET DEADLINES Allot yourself realistic and attainable time to finish tasks.

DON'T PUT IT OFF Do it now—not tomorrow. Prioritize your time. Know how important or urgent each task is, and do the most urgent first.

DON'T DO IT ALL YOURSELF If you have a family, make sure they are pulling their weight. Establish household chore rotas.

KNOW WHEN YOU WORK BEST Perhaps first thing in the morning or last thing at night. Whenever it is, allot important or difficult tasks to that time.

SCHEDULE FAILURE Build time into each task for disappointment, failure, being let down, or having to delay.

PLAN TIME FOR YOURSELF Allow a little time each day for fun and enjoyment. This isn't laziness—it's healthy, therapeutic, and essential.

BE ASSERTIVE Learn to say "no" and mean it. Finish what you're doing before attending to the needs of others.

BUILD IN TIME OFF Into any plan, build in some time for vacations, days off, and breaks.

BE STRICT ABOUT WEEKENDS Weekends are for you and your loved ones.

BE STRICT ABOUT FINISHING TIMES Finish when you said you were going to.

KNOW YOUR TIME Allocate the proportion of your time you'd like and are able to spend working, resting, socializing, playing, and relaxing.

FIND WAYS TO SPEED THINGS UP Be on the lookout for ways to get things done quicker—especially routine tasks that take up a lot of time.

SELF CARE

You have your car serviced at regular intervals and think nothing of it. But how often do you carry out routine maintenance and servicing on yourself? Your car may get replaced every year, but you certainly won't.

Your body has to last an entire lifetime and with some preventive care it may last a little longer than you expect it to!

A well-maintained body is essential to doing one's best both at work and at play. Looking after yourself—taking care of your health, and paying attention to your body and your physical needs—is not a sign of being selfish or self-absorbed. On the contrary, taking good care of yourself is the least you can do for your family and friends. People who love you, and those who depend on you, want, and need you to be at your best.

Here are some things you can do for yourself.

Deciding to give time to keeping fit is one of the best investments you can make. A healthy, agile body is a lifetime asset.

SELF CARE GUIDELINE

MAINTAIN A HEALTHY DIET There's no one looking over your shoulder telling you what you and your family should and shouldn't eat. It's entirely your choice. But you wouldn't put junk in the fuel tank of your car because it simply wouldn't run well—nor do you on junk food (see p.156–p.157).

MAINTAIN FITNESS Get some exercise every week. You may not notice the difference the first week, but you will after the first month (see p.155).

BE THE RIGHT WEIGHT Check with your doctor if you are unsure (see p.161).

LOOK AFTER SKIN AND HAIR Your skin will reflect what you eat, drink, and smoke. Your hair lasts longer if you shampoo it regularly and treat it gently (see p.33).

LOOK AFTER YOUR FEET Keep nails short and cut across squarely to avoid in-grown toenails. Check between your toes and wash regularly to avoid fungal infections. Wear good, well-fitting shoes.

LOOK AFTER YOUR EYES Have them checked at least every two years, and if you are told you need to wear glasses then wear them (see p.26).

LOOK AFTER YOUR TEETH Check oral hygiene and the condition of your gums regularly. Clean teeth two or three times a day after eating and floss your teeth at the end of the day. Watch for any irregularities inside the mouth, especially if you smoke or drink a lot (see p.173).

STRESS Watch your stress levels (see p.183).

STIMULANTS AND DRUGS Don't smoke, don't drink too much, and don't take recreational drugs (see p.172).

It is probably impossible to estimate how many miles we walk during our lives. Looking after our feet should be a fundamental part of looking after ourselves.

ESSENTIAL CHECKS

PERFORM REGULAR CHECKS Men should regularly check their testicles, and women should check their breasts every month, for any lumps or changes. Women should have regular cervical smear tests (Pap tests) as recommended (every year in the US, every three years in the UK). Keep an eye on any moles or warts—watch for changes in size, color, or texture (see p.33, p.43 and p.58–p.59).

GET YOUR HEARING TESTED FROM TIME TO TIME Having your hearing tested is not a sign of advancing years—it's simply common sense. Hearing loss can be so gradual that you may not be aware of it without a test. Hearing tests should always be performed by a qualified medical practitioner (see p.25).

MAKE SURE YOUR INNOCULATIONS ARE UP TO DATE These may include tetanus, flu, tuberculosis, hepatitis (A or B if you are at risk), polio, and diphtheria if you didn't have immunization as a child.

GET YOUR EYES TESTED at least every two years, so that any potential eye defects can be spotted early and treated.

VISIT THE DENTIST EVERY SIX MONTHS As well as your routine of twice daily brushing and daily flossing, you should visit the dentist regularly for a checkup.

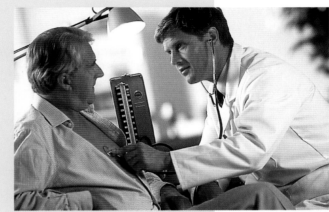

Regular health checks are an important part of preventive medicine and can either prevent problems or catch them before they become serious.

IF YOU NOTICE ANY OF THE FOLLOWING, SEEK MEDICAL ADVICE

BLOOD IN THE URINE
•
UNEXPLAINED WEIGHT LOSS
•
COUGHING UP BLOOD
•
PERSISTENT HEADACHES
•
RECURRENT HOARSENESS
•
TESTICULAR ABNORMALITIES
•
LUMPS IN THE BREAST
•
PERSISTENT DIFFICULTY SWALLOWING
•
RECURRENT ABDOMINAL PAIN
•
BRUISES WITHOUT INJURY
•
UNEXPLAINED CONSTIPATION OR DIARRHEA
•
SORES OR SCABS THAT FAIL TO HEAL

PERSISTENT WHITE
PATCH INSIDE THE MOUTH
•
RECTAL BLEEDING
•
BLOOD IN THE FECES

Caught up in everyday activities, it's easy to neglect your health. The arrival of a young family, however, may remind you of the need to care for yourself as well as them.

SLEEP

We always seem to need about five minutes more sleep than we actually get. Falling asleep is a problem we all encounter at some time in life and going without it can be extremely detrimental to our well-being. However, there are a number of ways to ensure a better night's rest.

Sleep, as well as time, is a great healer. A good night's sleep reduces stress and rejuvenates body and mind.

A warm milky drink before going to bed helps to encourage good sleep.

For a good sleeping position, try lying on your side, pillow tucked between neck and shoulder, legs slightly bent at the knees.

GETTING A GOOD NIGHT'S SLEEP

RELAX IN A WARM BATH before going to bed, and have a warm milky drink.

GO TO BED TO SLEEP, not to eat, watch television, or quarrel with your partner.

A QUIET BEDROOM aids sleep. Soundproof windows are useful, but make sure you have enough fresh air.

A COMFORTABLE BED is essential. Change your mattress if it is more than five years old.

LISTEN TO SOOTHING MUSIC as you fall asleep.

CARRY OUT the muscle-relaxing exercise on p.190 before sleep.

MEDITATE in bed before falling asleep.

IF YOU CAN'T SLEEP after half an hour, get up and do something relaxing like having a warm bath or reading. But read something soothing and relaxing. Avoid horror novels.

SIMPLE MENTAL EXERCISES also aid sleeplessness. For instance, choose two letters randomly, and think of all the books, films, or movie stars whose names begin with these letters. Try remembering the names of everyone you were at school with.

GENTLE PHYSICAL EXERCISE, particularly having sex, is a good way of encouraging sleep.

FOLLOW A NIGHTLY BEDTIME ROUTINE and always go to bed at the same time and in the same way.

SLEEPING POSITION

Make sure you adopt a good sleeping position. Lying on your back can cause you to snore; having too many pillows can place strain on your neck muscles; lying face down with your head turned to the side can cause cramp in the neck muscles, which can give you headaches. The best evidence seems to be that lying on your side is best with the pillow pulled into the angle between your neck and shoulder. Your legs should be slightly bent with one in front of the other.

If insomnia is a problem, don't lie there worrying about it. Switch on the light and read a relaxing novel until you feel sleepy.

CAUSES OF SLEEPLESSNESS

Check you're not doing anything to prevent a good night's sleep:

WORRYING ABOUT PROBLEMS WHILE TRYING TO GET TO SLEEP

•

GOING TO BED TOO LATE, WHEN YOU ARE OVERTIRED AND FRACTIOUS,
OR TOO EARLY, WHEN YOU ARE NOT TIRED ENOUGH

•

GETTING INTO BED BEFORE YOU HAVE HAD A CHANCE TO RELAX AND
UNWIND AFTER THE DAILY TASKS

•

DRINKING TOO MUCH BEFORE BEDTIME. MAKE SURE YOU
HAVE EMPTIED YOUR BLADDER BEFORE RETIRING

•

EATING A HEAVY OR SPICY MEAL WITHIN THREE
HOURS BEFORE GOING TO BED

•

DAYTIME NAPPING—AVOID THESE IF YOU HAVE
PROBLEMS FALLING ASLEEP AT NIGHT

•

THINKING ABOUT TOMORROW'S TASKS. IF YOU
CAN'T SWITCH OFF, MAKE A LIST OF WHAT YOU NEED
TO DO THE NEXT DAY, THEN GO TO BED.

Everybody's sleeping requirements are different. Younger children need up to ten or eleven hours a day but adults need only around six or seven hours.

DON'T

DRINK ALCOHOL JUST BEFORE GOING TO BED

DRINK COFFEE OR TEA BEFORE BED

EAT A SPICY MEAL WITHIN THREE HOURS OF BEDTIME

COMPLEMENTARY THERAPIES

ACUPUNCTURE

For low heart heat and weakness in the kidneys caused by fire and water being out of balance, resulting in restless shen (spirit) (see p.230).

NUTRITIONAL THERAPY

A snack of either turkey, milk, peanut butter, or a banana are foods rich in tryptophan, a nutrient that helps to induce feelings of calm by triggering the brain's "feel-good" neurotransmitter, serotonin.

HOMEOPATHY

Homeopathic practitioners might recommend a single dose of Sepia 1M or 10M, or the remedies Coffea, Nux Vomica, Aconite, or Ignatia, depending on the nature of the sleep problem.

There are many herbal remedies to cure insomnia.

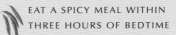

Herbal tea

Dried chamomile flowers

HERBAL MEDICINE

Try chamomile tea—infuse 1 tsp. of dried chamomile to 9 fl. oz./250ml of hot water before going to bed. Lime flowers or hop flowers can be used to reduce any depression. You can also try teas made with mullein flowers, passion flowers, and orange blossom.

For a very effective remedy for insomnia take a mixture of 2 parts skullcap, 2 parts passion flower, 1 part hops, 1 part valerian, and a tiny pinch of licorice. Make an infusion of 2 tsp. of the dried ingredients in 9 fl. oz./250ml of hot water. Take before bedtime and sip slowly. 100–500mg of kava kava can also be beneficial.

Licorice sticks

OVERCOMING TRAUMA

A ccidents can be minimized by doing things such as periodically checking your home for safety, not taking unnecessary risks, and making sure your car is roadworthy. But some things that happen that are beyond our control, such as a train crash or witnessing a car accident. Events like these may well cause us to suffer serious long-term effects. This is known as trauma.

People who see the world as relatively orderly and within their control may suffer more trauma than those of us who believe that things happen much more randomly and under the control of fate. Trauma needs to be dealt with effectively and the sufferer may need specialist treatment.

EFFECTS OF TRAUMA

If you suffer a trauma you may well encounter:

FEAR OF IT HAPPENING AGAIN

•

GUILT THAT YOU SURVIVED OR WERE UNINJURED

•

ANGER ABOUT WHAT HAPPENED

•

REGRET THAT YOU DIDN'T TAKE MORE APPROPRIATE ACTION

•

DISAPPOINTMENT THAT YOU NOW HAVE TO CHANGE YOUR PLANS OR LIFE

•

SHAME THAT YOU MAY HAVE PANICKED OR BEHAVED IRRATIONALLY OR EMOTIONALLY

OVERCOMING TRAUMA

To recover from trauma you may need to:

ACCEPT YOUR FEELINGS AND ALLOW TIME TO COME TO TERMS WITH THEM

•

ACCEPT SUPPORT FROM A PROFESSIONAL CARER OR COUNSELOR

•

ACCEPT THE REALITY AND DEAL WITH THE AFTERMATH, SUCH AS ATTENDING FUNERALS OR REVISITING THE SCENE OF THE ACCIDENT

•

KEEP BUSY TO HELP YOU GET OVER THE SHOCK; TALK ABOUT YOUR FEELINGS TO ENABLE YOU TO PROCESS THEM

•

ALLOW TIME AND SPACE FOR GRIEVING

COMPLEMENTARY THERAPIES

HERBAL MEDICINE

Hawthorn, dandelion root, dandelion leaf, and lime blossom.

CHINESE MEDICINE

Chinese angelica, ginseng, thorowax root, and white peony root to get the liver chi moving again.

Dandelion plant

COUNSELING OR PSYCHOTHERAPY

Usually recommended for post-traumatic stress disorder (see p.243).

A counseling session

ACUPUNCTURE

Treats trauma as a depression of the liver and a weakness of the spleen (see p.230).

CRANIOSACRAL THERAPY

It's claimed that corrective pressure to the spine and cranium may help unwind body memories of the event.

HOMEOPATHY

Belladonna, Calcarea, or Arnica are remedies can be used after accidents and trauma.

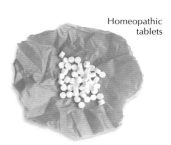

Homeopathic tablets

MIDLIFE TIME

*S*ome people during their late 30s and early 40s go through a midlife period of intense disruption. They may begin to feel that all they had previously believed in and been happy with no longer seems to serve them well.

Midlife crisis doesn't have to affect us all. Some people sail through their middle years with no major difficulties, and even feel that they are in the prime of their life and at the peak of their mental and physical powers. But if a midlife crisis does hit, you're bound to find that advice, help, support, and kindness will all be helpful in your questioning and reappraisal of your life.

The middle years can be a difficult time as you re-evaluate your life. Friends and family can be particularly helpful during this period.

CRISIS GUIDELINES

YOU ARE NOT ALONE Others have gone before you and survived. Seek support from wherever necessary. Have therapy, talk to friends, talk to your doctor, or talk to your partner. Read about the midlife crisis. Gather as much information in advance as you can so you're prepared (see p.46).

PUT SOMETHING BACK During midlife changes you may question the value of your life. One way to restore our self-esteem is to put something back. Often people have concentrated so much on work, career, and family that they've neglected the larger world. You could try charity work, passing on your experience to others, becoming involved in local politics, becoming involved in a pressure group that interests you, or taking up new interests.

HAVE A GOAL Plan your future and set goals for yourself. Look ahead with interest and enthusiasm and don't be negative in your thinking. There's still time to change careers, move abroad, write that book, start a garden, study a new subject, learn a language, take up a sport, get fit, lose weight, or learn to play a musical instrument.

FEEL YOUNG Nothing can make you feel younger or older than your mental attitude. Take care of your appearance, look after your physical needs, and don't neglect your health. Stay interested in the outside world. Keep abreast of fashion, politics, music, art, current thinking, modern technology, and don't let life slip past you.

TAKE THE INITIATIVE This may be a good time to change, reevaluate, and take stock. If you don't like what you see, then change it.

This is the time when many people decide to take up new interests or revisit hobbies and activities that have been abandoned.

SEPARATION AND DIVORCE

Relationships are meant to nurture, support, and provide us with stability, security, and emotional well-being. Through the process of courtship, romance, and wooing we are able to select our partner and they us. For a great many of us, things often work out as hoped and planned, and we marry and stay with the same person for all our lives.

Divorce has become part of our daily lives. Legal changes, people's greater independence, and perhaps higher expectations in general, mean that fewer people are prepared to stay in unhappy relationships.

Sometimes, however, we are not so lucky, and things go can go irredeemably wrong. Despite both partners best efforts, the relationship simply doesn't work any longer. When that happens, we have no choice but to accept the situation and take appropriate action.

If you have no option but to separate there are ways to help you through this difficult time.

Divorce or separation can be difficult experiences. But in some ways, they should also mark the start of a new life. Now may be the time to take up new activities and find new friends.

GUIDELINES FOR SEPARATION

UNDERSTANDING WHAT WENT WRONG You are both in the relationship 50/50, and it's impossible to apportion blame. You must both share the responsibility no matter what goes wrong. Even if a relationship ends badly there are no victims—you were both involved and at separation or divorce you are now both no longer involved.

YOU AREN'T ALONE This is an experience many people have been through before—and are going through—and they all manage to survive. Some even do better afterward than they would ever have thought possible.

DON'T TAKE IT PERSONALLY Just because your partner and you have split up doesn't devalue you as a person. You are still the person you were and your friends and family still love and need you.

ALLOW TIME TO GRIEVE If you are upset by separation and divorce, treat it as you would a bereavement and allow time to grieve properly.

BE NICE TO YOURSELF Pamper yourself and treat yourself to something you've always wanted. Keep up your proper diet, sleep patterns, and exercise. Don't let yourself go. Get out and make new friends, take up new interests, and start new projects.

RELAX Make sure you breathe properly and don't hyperventilate through tension. Study the plan for reducing panic attacks on page 191. Make sure you keep up any relaxation techniques that you know work for you.

KEEP BUSY Fill in the time you used to spend on your relationship by embarking on a course of study, a new project, renovating your entire home, travel, and, when you feel up to it, a new relationship.

BEREAVEMENT

*S*ometimes, when misfortune and tragedy come into our lives, we need to be sad. If we lose a close friend or relative we need to grieve, come to terms with our loss, and express our sadness. Losing a close partner or relative is a painfully emotional experience that may even be accompanied by physical pain.

GUIDELINES FOR BEREAVEMENT

TRY TO ACCEPT NATURE All things go in cycles—life and death, beginnings and endings. If we accept that things change and there are cycles to life, we can accept loss more easily. It may not be what we want, but it is the reality of life.

TIME HEALS It can take up to three years to grieve properly for someone really close who has died. But you will heal. Take it one day at a time.

LOOK AFTER YOURSELF You need proper sleep, food, rest, and time to get over your loss—now more so than ever. Don't neglect yourself.

GET SUPPORT If you are sad or grieving, then say so and ask for help and support. Seek professional help—it's what doctors, counselors, and therapists are there for.

TALK ABOUT IT Express how you feel—don't bottle it up. Don't think that others don't want to be burdened. What you feel is valid and genuine. If you feel angry, then express it. Don't feel guilty if your feelings seem inappropriate—they're not.

LET IT OUT If you need to cry or rage, then do so. If you want time and space, ask for it. If you feel the need to express your grief or sadness, then it's important that you let it all out. You need to recognize your pain and experience the emotions to be able to come to terms with them, deal with them, and get on with your life.

MOVE ON You still have to live. Moving on doesn't mean that you're forgetting your loved one or being heartless, it means that you've accepted your loss and are ready to pick up the pieces of your life.

The death of a family member or friend is deeply upsetting. It is vital to allow yourself as much time as you need to grieve. Seek support too if it is helpful.

COMPLEMENTARY THERAPIES

HOMEOPATHY
A homeopath would probably prescribe Arnica 30 for sudden loss and Ignatia 30 for someone who is hysterical with grief. For long-term help Natrum mur. 6 would be used, and Nux vomica to treat the accompanying anger. Pulsatilla would be used if the person remained weepy for some time.

MASSAGE
A massage is an effective way to treat the physical symptoms of grief if it is applied in a comforting way. In such cases, light stroking of the back and arms are the most beneficial (see p.231).

COUNSELING
There are various counselors and counseling organizations that specialize in bereavement (see p.243).

Grieving eventually comes to an end. A vacation, or visiting new places, may help you overcome feelings of loss.

LIVING WITH ILLNESS

If you suffer from constant or recurring illness then your sense of well-being will be considerably different from other people's. For some sufferers, merely having a day without pain might be considered bliss.

Anyone suffering from a long-term illness will have their own tried and tested methods for coping with pain and debilitation. You could try some of the following techniques, which may help you.

GUIDELINES FOR COPING WITH ILLNESS

KNOW YOUR ILLNESS Keep a record of when your illness is at its worst and best so you can monitor when your "good" periods are. Try to look for patterns in your illness diary so you may be able to isolate illness triggers. Try to be most active during your "good" periods.

SET YOURSELF GOALS Have a plan of action but be realistic. Try to set small goals so you will feel you are conquering a lot each time you reach one.

BE ACTIVE Don't allow yourself any time to sit around and focus on your illness. Try to distract yourself if you feel the onset of illness.

Learn to monitor your illness. Keep a diary and record good and bad times, so that you can plan your life around them.

VISUALIZATION Try to imagine the illness as something hot that you can visualize being cooled down—or something cold being heated, or heavy or wet or whatever suits you best.

BREATHE Try not to tense up when you are ill because it affects your breathing.

DON'T ALWAYS BE JOVIAL When people ask how you are doing, you don't always have to say that you are fine. You are allowed to express your illness when you need to.

DON'T BE A MARTYR Ask for help when you need it. Ask for support if you need it.

GO FOR IT Simply go for whatever it is that gets you through without worrying about what other people might think or say. It's your illness and how you manage it is up to you.

COMPLEMENTARY THERAPIES

An herbalist will advise on the most appropriate remedies.

AROMATHERAPY

For arthritis and intense muscular pain, use eucalyptus and juniper essential oils, which can also help reduce inflammation. Marjoram and lavender will help relieve headaches, including migraines, and chamomile and rosemary can be helpful with muscular cramps.

HERBAL MEDICINE

An herbalist may prescribe Jamaica dogwood (which should not be taken during pregnancy), aconite, and yellow jasmine (which should only be taken under professional supervision). Wild lettuce and Californian poppy may be safer and gentler alternatives, but professional advice is always recommended.

ACUPUNCTURE

Acupuncture is an effective treatment since it works by stimulating the release of endorphins and prostagladin-suppressing hormones. It also helps to relieve the anxiety and depression of long-term illness (see p.230).

Eucalyptus

ALLERGIES

*I*n medical terms an allergy is a condition where we are sensitive to a substance, called an allergen, which is usually a protein or chemical. An allergy is a reaction is caused by eating, breathing in, or touching an allergen.

There seems to be some evidence that the susceptibility to allergies may be hereditary, although the allergy itself may manifest quite differently in different people, even in members of the same family. For instance, you may have hay fever (allergic rhinitis) but your children may suffer from asthma. One of your parents might be allergic to certain foods such as eggs but you are allergic to animals.

There's a simple skin test that will highlight the substances you are allergic to and you can even have desensitizing treatments that slowly build up your tolerance. Or you may be treated with certain drugs, such as antihistamines or steroids. People who have allergies can take certain steps to alleviate their condition.

Hay fever is very common. Caused by pollen, it is usually worse during spring and summer.

AVOIDING TRIGGERS

AVOID THE SUBSTANCE IF AT ALL POSSIBLE. IF IT'S A KNOWN FOOD, ELIMINATE IT FROM YOUR DIET. IF IT'S HOUSE DUST OR MITES, THEN VACUUM MORE FREQUENTLY

•

AVOID SITUATIONS WHERE YOU KNOW YOU ARE MORE LIKELY TO GET A REACTION. IF YOU SUFFER FROM HAY FEVER TAKE YOUR VACATIONS ON A BEACH RATHER THAN IN THE COUNTRY. IF YOU SUFFER FROM ASTHMA, TRY TO AVOID CONGESTED STREETS WITH HEAVY EXHAUST FUMES

AVOID STRESS, WHICH SEEMS TO BE A CONTRIBUTING FACTOR IN TRIGGERING AN ALLERGIC REACTION OR IN SETTING OFF AN ATTACK

•

TELL DOCTORS IN ADVANCE OF ANY DRUGS SUCH AS PENICILLIN OR ASPIRIN THAT YOU KNOW YOU ARE ALLERGIC TO

•

AVOID CONTACT WITH ANY ALLERGENS THAT YOU KNOW TRIGGER A REACTION—WEAR GLOVES IF NECESSARY

An allergic reaction to penicillin is very severe. Avoid all penicillin-based medication.

COMPLEMENTARY THERAPIES

ACUPUNCTURE

Hay fever is seen as a wind-heat invasion of the lungs, and treatment would be carried out to open the lung chi to expel the wind heat.

CHINESE MEDICINE

A Chinese herbalist will prescribe mulberry leaves, Ephedra, magnolia flowers, chrysanthemum flowers, and cinnamon twigs.

HOMEOPATHY

Hay fever (allergic rhinitis) and other respiratory allergies can be treated with a number of remedies such as Allium cepa (homeopathic onion). Giving homeopathic potencies of Pollens also works (see p.226).

HERBAL MEDICINE

Treat with meadowsweet, golden seal, and eyebright to reduce phlegm. Lobelia and pill-bearing spurge (*Euphorbia hirta*) help reduce spasm and ease breathing in asthmatics.

Beech can be used to treat food intolerances.

BACH FLOWER REMEDIES

These have proved effective in treating many allergies: Mimulus for treating the fear of allergic reactions; Rescue Remedy for soothing allergic rashes; Beech for food intolerances; Impatiens for treating skin irritations, and Clematis for general oversensitivity (see p.227).

PRAYER AND MEDITATION

*R*ecent research in the United States into the recovery rate from heart attacks and their subsequent recurrence revealed that if the person recovering belonged to a social group of some kind, practiced some form of relaxation or meditation technique, and participated in some form of religious belief system, the rate of recovery was faster and the likelihood of subsequent attacks drastically reduced.

Caring for the spiritual element in ourselves is just as important as caring for the mind and body. Take time off to reflect and focus on your inner self.

Meditate where and when you will not be interrupted. Concentrate on your breathing and clear your mind of any distracting thoughts.

We're all made up of three parts—mind, body, and spirit. This third part needs just as much attention as the other three if we're to maintain good all-round levels of well-being.

In the American research, participating in a religious belief system did not necessarily mean belonging to a major organized religion. Having a belief system of one's own was sufficient. Those patients who didn't have a belief system (along with the other two factors) had an 80% chance of a subsequent heart attack. Obviously we cannot manufacture a belief in a higher power or faith in ourselves, but it is worth noting that the absence of one may be detrimental to our health and longevity.

Someone once said that if prayer was talking to God, then meditation was listening to the answer. A modern dictionary says that meditation is to "reflect deeply; to engage in contemplation; to consider deeply; deep thought." It has also been likened to turning off the mind and wiping the slate clean for a moment or two. Here are a few pointers for meditation and prayer.

BREATHING MEDITATION

FIND SOMEWHERE TO SIT COMFORTABLY WHERE YOU WON'T BE DISTURBED.

•

LET YOUR HANDS FALL NATURALLY INTO YOUR LAP AND CLOSE YOUR EYES.

•

ALLOW THE TENSION IN YOUR NECK AND SHOULDERS TO DROP AWAY. TRY SHRUGGING YOUR SHOULDERS UP TO YOUR EARS AND THEN LETTING THEM DROP.

•

CONCENTRATE ON YOUR BREATHING. BREATHE IN THROUGH YOUR NOSE AND OUT THROUGH YOUR MOUTH. WITH EACH IN-BREATH MENTALLY SAY THE WORD "WELL." WITH EACH OUT-BREATH MENTALLY SAY THE WORD "BEING." BREATHE LIKE THIS FOR ABOUT 10 MINUTES AND THEN SLOWLY RETURN TO NORMAL AND SEE HOW RELAXED YOU FEEL.

GUIDANCE FOR PRAYER AND MEDITATION

MEDITATION AND PRAYER SHOULD BE DONE SOMEWHERE SAFE BUT ACCESSIBLE.

•

BE AS COMFORTABLE AS YOU LIKE.

•

NOTHING ABOUT MEDITATION OR PRAYER SHOULD CONFRONT YOU OR CAUSE YOU TO CHANGE YOUR LIFESTYLE, DRESS, DIET, OR RELIGION.

•

PRACTICE FOR ONLY A FEW MINUTES EACH DAY AT FIRST AND BUILD UP SLOWLY.

•

IF YOU LIKE A TECHNIQUE AND IT WORKS, DO IT. IF YOU DON'T LIKE ONE OR IT DOESN'T SEEM TO WORK FOR YOU, DON'T DO IT.

•

THERE ARE NO RULES ABOUT MEDITATION OR PRAYER—WHATEVER WORKS FOR YOU IS FINE.

GUIDANCE FOR HAPPINESS

*I*f we look at research into statistics of depressed people or people who have had trouble coping with life, it would appear that happy people—those who seem to go through life easily and with little emotional trouble—live their life by certain fundamentals or principles.

If we adopt some or all of these principles it can certainly improve the quality of our lives and may make us one of those seemingly naturally lucky people. We cannot control all the circumstances of our lives, but there is much in our lives, and our reaction to life, that we can control. Recognizing this is one key to being happy.

Happiness is an almost indefinable state: it comes from within, encouraged by enjoyment in activity, pleasure in friends and an awareness of personal achievement.

HAPPINESS PRINCIPLES

These are not arranged in any particular order—they are all important in one way or another.

- Take responsibility for your own life.
- Let others take responsibility for their own lives.
- Make time to relax.
- Be with people you like and who make you happy.
- Eat healthily.
- Take your time—there's no point in rushing.
- Avoid things that hurt your body, such as excessive alcohol, tobacco, drugs, danger, and extremes of temperature.
- Give yourself plenty of treats and rewards.
- Be selfish when you need to be, without guilt.
- Take up leisure activities that please and satisfy you without them having to "have a point" to them.
- Make plans that you can look forward to.
- Be assertive.
- Constantly strive to improve your education and studying.
- Look after your appearance.
- Praise and approve of yourself.
- Exercise and stay in shape.
- Enjoy pleasurable activities and do some every day.
- Sleep properly and regularly.
- Express your emotions and talk to people about them.
- Allow others to get close to you.
- Be kind to yourself when you let yourself down.
- Have a spiritual dimension to your life.
- Avoid hurting others whenever possible.

therapeutic

WELL-BEING

contents

Introduction

Herbs played a central role in the treatment of illness well before the development of drug therapy.

Conventional cures for illnesses may offer relief, but not all medicines benefit the body, even though they alleviate symptoms. Take the case of a fever. The body's natural response to an infective organism is to mount an immune reaction and destroy the bug. To assist this process the temperature of the body increases. The combination of a raised body temperature and an effective immune response usually resolves the illness within 24 hours or so. Many prescriptions for simple fever and infections include drugs that reduce the temperature and thus impair the immune response. The thinking behind this approach is more concerned with symptom relief than promoting well-being or stimulating the healing powers of the body.

Complementary therapies differ from conventional medicine in that they take a holistic view, seeing the mind and body as being inextricably linked.

NATURAL HEALING

Holistic treatment is quite different. Fever is to be encouraged and promoted; it's seen as a very positive sign that should not be suppressed. So-called diaphoretics (substances that promote profuse sweating) are used to aid the elimination process and detoxify the body during the fever. Alongside this, immune-stimulating remedies are given to support the natural response that's already underway. Physical treatments using hydrotherapy methods may be employed to ease symptoms while not impairing the natural healing processes. The end result is natural eradication of the invading bug, effective elimination of related toxic by-products, and strengthening of

the body's natural resistance to future infection. Most common infections can be effectively dealt with within 24 to 48 hours, as long as the body is left to call on its vital energies and healing powers. Obviously there are times when people require the powerful effects of conventional medicine, but most common problems are easily and effectively treated using simple natural methods.

Hydrotherapy — the use of water to maintain or restore health — has a long history and is currently regaining popularity.

HOLISTIC THERAPIES

The term therapeutic relates to the treatment of disease, the science and art of healing. A therapist is a person who is skilled in the treatment of physical, social, or mental disorders. This rather dry description of therapy may be true for many conventional treatments, but it fails to take into account the complexities of the interactions that occur in many complementary therapies. The term "health provider" has been coined to describe doctors and suggests that health is given out in the form of a prescription. Nothing can be further from the truth when we consider how therapeutic methods that follow the holistic concepts of health restore well-being. Maybe a new term, "health guiders," would better describe holistic health professionals, because most holistic treatment methods seek to actively involve the patient in attaining their health goals.

Holistic treatments may include hand-on therapies, such as massage as well as herbalism and homeopathy.

With holistic therapies, the responsibility for well-being falls in the lap of the patient, not the therapist. Holistic therapy aims to motivate the physical and emotional aspects of the patient using various methods, such as osteopathy, naturopathy, homeopathy, and diet to name just a few, to a level where the self-regulating and restorative powers of the body take over.

The following section outlines and explains the main therapies currently offered by complementary practitioners so you can make an informed decision about the therapeutic direction you wish to follow.

221

NUTRITIONAL THERAPY

Most people are familiar with the saying "you are what you eat." This is the basis of diet therapy. Food and nutrition form the key to long-lasting health. All the modern studies confirm the power of food in disease prevention. The World Cancer Research Fund recently published a 700-page book on the link between food and cancer, although the advice could fit easily on one sheet of paper—simply eat more fruit and vegetables, and eat less fat, sugar, and artificial chemical additives.

With the growing interest in diet therapy, a new health-care profession developed to fill the need. Nutritional therapy works on the idea that not only is a balanced diet necessary for health but in some situations food and nutrition can also be used to help stimulate healing and combat deficiencies.

VISITING A DIETARY THERAPIST

The nutritional therapist begins by very carefully documenting the patient's eating habits and dietary preferences. Using this basic information, he or she can then determine the patient's general nutritional health and areas of dietary weakness. The therapist then takes time to discuss the changes the patient will need to make. Together, therapist and patient work out a dietary plan that will set the healing process in motion. The plan may begin with a simple fast to detoxify the system. This is usually followed by a reintroduction of nutritious, healthy foods in a balanced combination tailored to meet the patient's specific needs.

Nutritional therapy is based on the premise that diet and health are interlinked. Following a prescribed diet will improve health and help you to overcome illness.

EXTRA HELP FROM VITAMINS AND MINERALS

Diet therapists appreciate that a good diet supplies all the nutrients needed for health, but they also understand that in the early phases of a nutritional program, specific vitamin and mineral supplements can help jump-start the healing process. In addition, the body does not store certain nutrients, and the person may by deficient in one or more of these. In these cases, too, supplements may be necessary.

However, for most people, taking supplements is not recommended over the long term, as long as the diet is kept balanced and varied (see p.164).

Nutritionists may use vitamin and mineral supplements as part of their treatments, particularly since these are not made by the the body.

LOOKING AFTER YOUR BOWELS

Another factor nutritional therapists concentrate on is elimination and bowel health. Proper, healthy elimination is necessary for the overall health of the digestive system, and to get rid of toxins. One way to maximize healthy elimination is to promote the health-providing bacteria that live naturally in the large bowel. Nutritional therapists may adjust the diet or prescribe supplements to ensure support for these "friendly" bacteria.

NATUROPATHY

*N*aturopathy refers to the treatment of disease using natural methods. Hippocrates *(c. 460–377 B.C.E.), the Greek physician known as the "father of medicine" was probably the first naturopath. Using all the healing elements available to him, he incorporated light, touch, temperature, water, food, and herbs in his treatment of disease. Today, this truly holistic approach is used by practitioners of naturopathic medicine.*

The central theme of naturopathy is the belief that disease results from an accumulation of waste matter (toxins) that congests the organs of elimination and assimilation. Modern naturopaths keep this belief close to their hearts but do not turn away from conventional treatments and modern knowledge in the appropriate situations.

TREATMENT

The fundamental principle of naturopathy is "do no harm": it endorses all forms of noninvasive therapy including regular exercise, massage, manipulation, hydrotherapy, diet therapy, and herbal prescriptions. When treating the whole person, certain disease states often require a therapeutic fast to help rid the body of the toxic overload. Fasting is not a treatment that should be carried out lightly. It can have very powerful actions, some of which may not be pleasant if you are unaware of them. Professional naturopathic guidance is necessary to avoid any complications.

VISITING A NATUROPATH

It is strongly advised that you look for a qualified and experienced practitioner before undergoing any form of naturopathic treatment program. The initial consultation is not unlike that of any medical practitioner. A detailed medical history and physical examination will be taken; it is essential for the naturopath to assess if your health problem would be suitable for the naturopathic approach. Treatment is normally discussed at the time of the consultation and nutritional and herbal prescriptions are given out to complement the program.

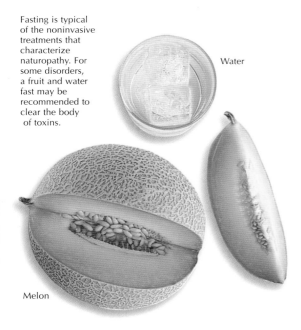

Fasting is typical of the noninvasive treatments that characterize naturopathy. For some disorders, a fruit and water fast may be recommended to clear the body of toxins.

Water

Melon

COMMON PROBLEMS PRESENTED TO NATUROPATHS

MENOPAUSAL PROBLEMS
•
IRRITABLE BOWEL SYNDROME
•
ARTHRITIS
•
ALLERGIES
•
SKIN CONDITIONS
•
HORMONE IMBALANCES
•
CHRONIC FATIGUE SYNDROME
•
CANDIDA ALBICANS
•
GUT AND BOWEL PROBLEMS

Naturopathy embraces a variety of therapies including nutritional therapy, massage, physiotherapy, and herbalism. Sage, for instance, is an antiseptic and astringent; yarrow can help lower blood pressure and aid digestion.

Yarrow

223

HERBAL MEDICINE

*H*erbal medicine may be considered the original medicine because many of the active agents found in modern drugs started life as a plant extract used in a traditional herbal remedy. Some of the best known herbal remedies that are still used today include White Willow (Salix album), now known as Aspirin, and Foxglove (Digitalis purpurea), used worldwide as the drug Digoxin to treat heart failure.

Plants do not give up their healing chemicals easily. Many of the active agents are contained within the tough cells found in the roots, stems, and leaves. In order to make use of the plants' drugs, special methods of extraction have been used over the centuries with great efficiency.

When the root's bark is used for medicines, a decoction is produced. Using this method of extraction, the roots are boiled in water until the required concentration of extract is achieved.

A tincture is produced by leaving plant material to "steep" (a process which draws out the active agents of the plant material) in alcohol or water. Once the process has been completed the tincture can be kept for many years, especially if it has been steeped in alcohol. A water-based extract can be mixed with an aqueous cream to produce an herbal cream that can be applied externally.

If the extracts are to be obtained from the softer parts of the plant (the leaves or flowers), a simple infusion is all that is required. Making an herbal infusion is just like making a cup of tea.

CONSULTATION

Like your general practitioner, the herbal practitioner will ask for a detailed medical history and carry out the appropriate physical examinations to assist in the diagnosis of a complaint. The difference is in the treatment offered. A complete treatment should include lifestyle advice, a recommended dietary adjustment, and the prescription of herbal extracts. Treatment normally follows a course of remedies and a follow-up consultation.

WARNING

Herbal medicine is normally very safe when used correctly, but some plants contain potentially poisonous chemicals. Just as you would ask a pharmacist to advise you about a drug, you should always take the advice of an experienced herbalist before using any plants, especially for internal use.

Digitalis, or foxglove, has been used for centuries and still forms the basis of some pharmaceutical drugs used to treat heart disorders.

All parts of a herb can be used to make remedies. Some remedies come in the form of cream, which can be easily absorbed by the skin. Tinctures are made by soaking the herb in alcohol.

Infusions are made in much the same way as a cup of tea. Herbs are steeped in hot water and drunk hot or cold.

Cream   Tincture bottles

Infusion

CHINESE MEDICINE

*T*he medical treatments offered in ancient China were complex and highly evolved, dating back almost 5,000 years. Treatments included acupuncture, acupressure, massage, moxibustion, cupping, and herbalism. The common aim of Chinese medicine, however, is to achieve balance in the body's internal energies, known as yin and yang (see p.230). The energy itself is referred to as chi or qi (pronounced "chee").

Traditional Chinese medicine works on a very different basis from Western medicine and follows entirely different principles. Anyone who seeks advice from a practitioner of Chinese medicine needs to disregard any preconceived Western notions about how the body works.

According to Chinese wisdom, herbs have five flavors, five chi characteristics, and four "directions" (see box below). A practitioner of Chinese medicine will take all these factors into account when determining which formula he or she needs to follow in making up a remedy to treat your particular complaint.

FORMULATING A REMEDY

The law of opposites applies to Chinese medicine. The process of formulating a herbal prescription is very complex, but it basically follows that when a condition of "cold" presented to the Chinese physician, herbs that bring about the opposite reaction in the body are given. In other words, herbs with "warm" or "hot" characteristics are prescribed. Osteoarthritis is a good example of a "cold" condition while rheumatoid arthritis is "hot" (see p.146–p.147).

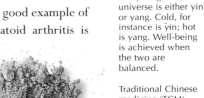

Chinese herbal preparations

According to Chinese philosophy, everything in the universe is either yin or yang. Cold, for instance is yin; hot is yang. Well-being is achieved when the two are balanced.

Traditional Chinese medicine (TCM) uses herbs to balance energy within the body. Herbs are classified according to taste: sweet, sour, bitter, pungent, and salty. They may also be hot or cold.

HAZARDS OF CHINESE HERBS

Just as with any form of medicine, Chinese herbs should only be taken under the guidance of a qualified Chinese herbalist or doctor of Traditional Chinese Medicine. Because many of the herbal prescriptions are boiled up at home, it's very important that the proportions are correct and the method of preparation is carefully followed. The only cases of poisoning have occurred when these two factors have not been carefully followed or when unqualified advice has been given.

ELEMENTS OF A CHINESE HERBAL FORMULA

THE FIVE FLAVORS	THE FIVE CHI CHARACTERISTICS	THE FOUR "DIRECTIONS"
• Sour	• Cold	• Sinking
• Pungent	• Hot	• Floating
• Sweet	• Warm	• Ascending
• Bitter	• Cool	• Descending
• Salty	• Neutral	

HOMEOPATHY

Homeopathy, *whose name comes from the Greek word* homios, *meaning like, and* pathos, *meaning suffering, is a complete system of treatment based on the Law of Similars which states that "like cures like," or that which makes sick shall heal. Homeopathy was founded by Dr. Samuel Hahnemann, a German physician practicing in the late 18th century.*

Hahnemann formulated three principles:

- A homeopathic substance can produce a set of symptoms in a healthy person and may be used in minute doses to treat a sick person who has the same symptoms.
- Potentizing substances (diluting them in water) increases their curative powers and prevents side effects.
- Homeopathy treats the whole person as an individual, not just a localized set of symptoms in them.

German physician Samuel Hahnemann (1755–1843), founder of homeopathy, encountered considerable opposition, not least from apothecaries angered by the minuscule doses of medicine that he recommended.

HOMEOPATHIC REMEDIES

The remedies come from a number of different sources, including plants, metals, minerals, and even some poisons. The remedies are made by potentizing (diluting) the substances in water and then vigorously shaking them (succussion) in a solution of alcohol and water. The resulting liquid is left for an extended period, usually a couple of weeks to a month, during which time it is shaken at regular intervals. It is then strained, to make a solution known as the mother tincture. This tincture is then diluted to make different potencies of the remedy. In homeopathic medicine, less is often more: the more the mother tincture is diluted, the stronger it becomes. Dilutions in various strengths are then added to tablets, granules, or powder to make a range of homeopathic medicines, which are stored in dark bottles.

Each homeopathic remedy is prescribed individually. In deciding on an appropriate remedy for a particular ailment, the homeopath will take into account not just your symptoms, but also such factors as your personality type and your overall state of well-being at the time. This explains the reason why two people suffering from headaches may not be prescribed the same remedy.

WARNING

Avoid strong-smelling or strong-tasting substances such as coffee, tobacco, mints, perfumes, and alcohol as they can render the remedy ineffective.

There are a wide variety of homeopathic remedies, which may come in the form of pills, tablets, granules, powder, or cream.

You should not eat, drink, or brush your teeth for at least 15 minutes before and after taking a homeopathic remedy. They must not be touched by hand, but tipped into the mouth from a spoon, bottle cap, or piece of paper.

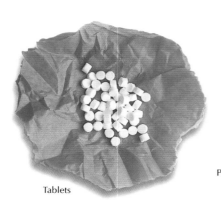

Tablets

Pills

Cream

Powder

BACH FLOWER REMEDIES

*T*he Bach™ *Flower Remedies are made from flowers and trees at the Bach Centre in England. They are used to help balance negative emotions, which allows the body to return to its natural state of health.*

Dr. Edward Bach (pronounced Batch), a physician specializing in pathology and bacteriology, noticed that many of his patients with physical ailments also seemed to be suffering from emotional problems. This led him to believe that many physical problems were caused by underlying emotional disturbances. He searched for a system that could help with the psychological aspect of illness and found that the answer lay in flowers and plants. He created 38 remedies in total, each having a specific effect dealing with common emotions such as fear, uncertainty, despondency, loneliness, oversensitivity, jealousy, and bitterness.

One of the best-known remedies, Rescue Remedy™, is recommended for use during times of stress or shock. It's a mixture of five other remedies, Cherry Plum for the fear of losing control, Clematis for absent-mindedness, Impatiens for impatience, Star of Bethlehem for comfort, and Rock Rose for use when feeling alarmed or scared.

HOW FLOWER REMEDIES ARE MADE

The heads of fresh blooms are picked and are placed in glass bowls of springwater. They are then left outside in the sunshine on a cloudless day for three hours, so that the water becomes potentized by the essence of the flower. The potentized water is then mixed with an equal quantity of brandy, which acts as a preservative, and stored in a dark glass bottle.
Alternatively, the flowering parts are boiled in water for half an hour. The water is filtered off when cooled, and brandy is added.

Edward Bach was an English doctor in the early 20th century. Certain that flowers could be used for healing, he was apparently able to detect their healing qualities by holding his hand over them.

Honeysuckle can be used to treat feelings of homesickness.

To produce Bach Flower Remedies, flowers may be soaked in springwater for three hours, or boiled in water for half an hour.

Honeysuckle

Vial and dropper

Water

Pure springwater forms the initial base of flower remedies. Once potentized by the flowers, the water is mixed with equal quantities of brandy. Bach Flower Remedies come in small vials, containing a dropper. They must be stored in a cool, dark place.

AROMATHERAPY

*A*romatherapy is an ancient art that uses essential oils to affect the body, mind, and spirit in order to aid relaxation or revitalization. Essential oils are extracted from flowers, herbs, resins, and spices, and can be used in a number of ways to restore the overall state of well-being in an individual.

Essential oils are used in many cultures to enhance or alter moods. Aromatherapy works through smell association and this occurs through a part of the brain known as the limbic system, which is responsible for emotion.

Different oils have different properties. While some oils are mainly relaxing, others will stimulate. In addition, scents are very personal—what is pleasant and induces a sense of well-being in one individual can be offensive to another. When choosing an oil or blend it is important to be aware of the oils' properties and make sure that the oil is right for you.

A few drops of rosemary added to a bath or an oil vaporizer relieves tension, tiredness, and sinusitis.

Rosemary

Aromatherapy oil

Lavender is a sedative and antiseptic. It encourages relaxation and can also be used for skin conditions.

Lavender

Aromatherapy oils can be added to baths, massaged, or inhaled. Mixed with water, they can be used in vaporizers or special oil burners to scent a room.

HOW TO USE ESSENTIAL OILS

As a general rule, you should never apply an oil directly onto the skin. Instead dilute the oil in a carrier oil such as almond or grapeseed.

•

Aromatherapy oils are powerful and can cause serious reactions is sensitive people, so they must be used with care. Precautions should be taken to rule out sensitivities. It's always wise to do a patch test on your skin first to make sure that you're not sensitive to the oil you plan to use. Simply apply the essential oil mixed with the carrier oil to the wrist and leave it for a few hours before use to ensure no irritations or redness occurs.

•

Some oils should not be used for conditions such as epilepsy, during pregnancy, or in direct sunlight. Always check the overall safety of the oil before using it.

MASSAGE

Add 4–6 drops of your chosen essential oil to 2 teaspoons of a carrier oil. For arthritis, try marjoram, lavender, or ginger; for fatigue try clover, peppermint, lemon, or eucalyptus; for insomnia try bergamot, chamomile, rose, or geranium.

BATH

Add 4–6 drops of essential oil to a warm bath.

STEAM INHALATIONS

Fill a large bowl with hot water and add 3–4 drops of essential oil. Place a towel over your head and inhale the vapors for a few minutes. This is ideal for sinusitis or congestion.

VAPOR

Place a few drops on a damp cotton ball and place on a radiator.

AYURVEDA

yurveda originated in India over 5,000 years ago and is one of the oldest forms of treatment in the world. It incorporates herbs, nutrition, rest, exercise, massage, yoga, meditation, and other lifestyle recommendations to restore balance and regain health of the mind, body, and spirit.

The word Ayurveda comes from two Sanskrit words, *Ayus* meaning life and *veda* meaning knowledge or science. Put together they mean knowledge of life.

The philosophy of Ayurvedic medicine is similar to Chinese medicine, which sees the body as part of the universe, sharing its energies. Good health is a balance of these energies.

According to Ayurvedic medicine, every body is composed of five basic elements: fire, water, earth, air, and ether. In addition, there are three basic constitutional types, and every body has the characteristics of one or more of these types. The character of an individual depends on which constitutional type is dominant in his or her makeup.

In the same way as other holistic therapies, Ayurvedic medicine sees the patient as a complete individual and not just a collection of symptoms. The Ayurvedic practitioner will find out as much as he or she can about your overall lifestyle as well as your health before making any recommendations.

 Air/Space

 Fire/Water

 Water/Earth

An ancient Indian therapy, Ayurveda makes use of yoga, meditation, massage, and herbal remedies to restore balance.

CONSTITUTIONAL TYPES

PITTA

Controls digestion and biochemical processes in the body. This individual is of average size, intellectual, with a large appetite. Anger is pitta's strongest emotion, and the individual is more vulnerable to illnesses such as infections, ulcers, jaundice, heartburn, acne, herpes, and Crohn's disease. Ayurvedic treatments recommended may include exercise, herbs, saunas, and avoiding the sun.

KAPHA

Governs fluid metabolism in the body. Kapha is robustly built with a generous temperament. These individuals may be prone to frequent colds, kidney stones, congestive heart failure, depression, benign tumors, swelling, obesity, sinus headaches, and cataracts. Ayurvedic treatments for this type may include deep massage with warming oils, aerobic exercise, and saunas.

VATA

Controls the functioning of the nervous system. These individuals are either very tall or very short and can eat large quantities of food without gaining weight. They sleep and eat irregularly and suffer from anxiety. Vatas are susceptible to insomnia, dry skin, heart palpitations, constipation, sciatica, depression, muscle weakness, and paralysis. Ayurvedic treatment may include a massage with warm oils, a stable sleep routine, light exercise, steam baths, and meditation.

ACUPUNCTURE AND ACUPRESSURE

Acupuncture and acupressure are ancient Chinese forms of medicine that go back 2,000 years or more. Both aim to balance the chi or flow of energy by working with points located along the body's energy channels known as meridians.

Yin and yang are complementary opposites. The interaction between them gives rise to the life energy, or chi, that flows through the body's meridians. Yang represents the fire element and yin represents the water element.

According to ancient Chinese wisdom, we're all part of the universe and share in its energy. Chi surrounds everything and acts as the driving force for life. A body with no circulating chi is dead. At death the body's chi is said to recirculate with the external (environmental) energy.

THE BALANCE OF YIN AND YANG

Yin and yang can be thought of as positive and negative; they need each other to exist and although they act in opposite ways they're interdependent with each other. The Chinese symbolized yin and yang with the physical elements they experienced in everyday life; yin represented water while yang was seen as a fire element. Our bodies contain both yin and yang in varying amounts and a balance is needed for health. Excessive yin damages yang, and cold symptoms are felt; too much yang will damage yin, and symptoms of heat are felt.

Acupuncture and acupressure seek to release any blockage of the life energy by applying needles or pressure to energy points around the body.

THE DIFFERENCE BETWEEN ACUPUNCTURE AND ACUPRESSURE

An acupuncturist uses fine needles that are inserted into acupuncture or energy points to balance energy flow and influence internal organs and disease states. An acupressure practitioner does not use needles, but will apply pressure to the same points to encourage the body to return to a healthy state.

SOME CONDITIONS THAT ACUPUNCTURE CAN TREAT	SOME CONDITIONS THAT ACUPRESSURE CAN TREAT	
MIGRAINES	NAUSEA	BABIES' COLIC
ARTHRITIS	SEASICKNESS	BACK PAIN
RESPIRATORY PROBLEMS	HEADACHES	FATIGUE
INSOMNIA	TOOTHACHES	
MENSTRUAL PROBLEMS		
DIGESTIVE PROBLEMS		
ANXIETY		
LABOR PAINS		

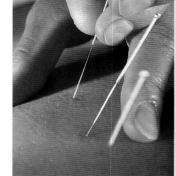

MASSAGE

There are many different kinds of massage therapy, ranging from Swedish massage to Shiatsu. They all have the same aim—to promote a feeling of physical and mental well-being—and all involve stroking, pressing, and kneading the soft tissues. However, each massage therapy works in different ways and on different areas of the body. Some work directly on muscles and soft tissues and others on acupressure points.

Massage was one of the earliest forms of therapeutic treatment. We know from references found in ancient documents that massage was practiced by the Egyptians and by the Chinese as far back as 3,000 years ago. Hippocrates, the early Greek physician, known as the "Father of Medicine," preached the benefits of massage.

One of the most popular forms of massage is Swedish massage which was developed by a gymnast named Per Henrik Ling in the early 19th century. This involves the four basic techniques of effleurage (stroking), petrissage (kneading), friction, and percussion (see box below).

OTHER FORMS OF MASSAGE

Shiatsu, meaning "finger pressure" is the Japanese form of massage. Pressure is applied to trigger points that are located along energy channels or meridians in the body and aim to balance chi or flow of energy.

SPORTS MASSAGE

This form of massage applies deep muscle techniques and mobilizations or movements of the joints, to treat injuries, ease stiff joints, and relax tense muscles. Many international sports teams have their own masseur to treat athletes before and after events.

BABY MASSAGE

Much research indicates the importance of touch for babies' physical, psychological, and cognitive development. One way of providing this much-needed physical contact is through massage. Baby massage enhances bonding with parents, along with promoting a healthy body and skin. Many clinics and health centers now offer classes in baby massage for expectant and new mothers.

Hippocrates (c.460–377), the Greek physician, was probably the first to lay the foundations of medical science. He advocated a daily massage.

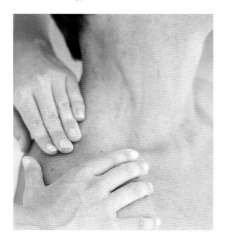

Many complementary therapies include massage. All forms involve applying pressure to different parts of the body to enhance well-being.

MOVEMENTS

STROKING OR EFFLEURAGE

These are long stroking movements used at the start of the massage, between other movements, and then at the end. The main purpose of this stroke is for relaxation of the patient and the tissues.

KNEADING OR PETRISSAGE

These are movements where the skin and surface muscle is rolled and squeezed to stretch and loosen tight areas of muscles.

FRICTION

The movements in this technique are warming, stimulating, and circular to increase the local circulation and break down areas of tightness.

PERCUSSION

The movements within this group involve short, brisk, tapping strokes with the edge of the hands to stimulate the circulation. They are also called *tapotement*, from the French word *tapot*, meaning "to drum."

CHIROPRACTIC

The word chiropractic is derived from two Greek words, cheir *meaning hands and* praktikos *meaning done by. Chiropractors use a number of examinations and manipulations to treat mechanical problems of joints with the aim of relieving pain, improving function, and increasing mobility.*

Chiropractic was founded toward the end of the last century by the Canadian Daniel David Palmer.

Chiropractic's main principle is that the functions of the body are controlled by the nervous system. Since the nervous system is integrated with the musculoskeletal system, any disruptions to either will affect the functioning of both. The aim of chiropractic treatment is to restore the balance and alignment of the whole structure.

Chiropractors place great importance on the spine. They believe that a minor spinal displacement affects the nervous system, so treatment will not only relieve mechanical problems such as back pain, but also other problems such as asthma and constipation.

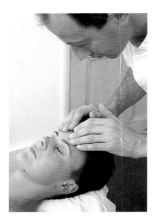

A McTimoney chiropractor palpates for tension on a patient's forehead. This form of chiropractic focuses on gentler manipulation of the joints and has also been successful in treating animals with musculoskeletal problems.

CHIROPRACTIC DIAGNOSIS

Along with observing, palpating (feeling) for areas of muscular tension and joint restrictions, and checking your normal range of movements, chiropractors often use X rays to assess the condition of their patients' spine and to rule out any underlying disease.

TREATMENT

Chiropractors concentrate on the area of pain using a number of manipulative techniques and mobilizations (moving a joint within its normal range of motion) with the aim of restoring movement and easing pain while easing nerve pressure and relaxing and stretching the muscles. As a general rule, chiropractors tend not

Here a chiropractor places her hands on the lower back of a patient while evaluating his posture. Any misalignment of the lumbar vertebrae can affect spinal nerves, causing a backache.

CONDITIONS WHERE CHIROPRACTIC MAY BENEFIT

BACK PAIN
•
MUSCULAR ACHES AND PAINS
•
SCIATICA
•
JOINT STIFFNESS

---

to perform massage techniques. Treatment often includes advice on bending and lifting and on exercises to prevent the condition from recurring. Chiropractic shares many aspects of treatment in common with osteopathy. The type of spinal manipulation, from the patients' point of view, is often identical, but chiropractic generally does not place much emphasis on therapy such as massage for the muscular component that may accompany mechanical back pain. In general, however, the differences between chiropractic and osteopathy are becoming less and less as time goes by.

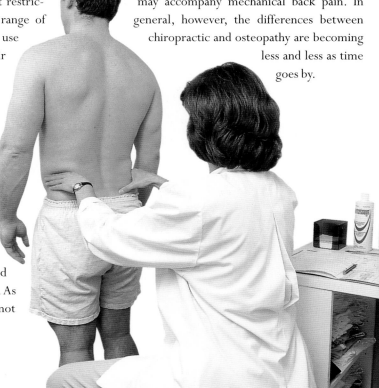

OSTEOPATHY

*O*steopathy is not a new form of medicine. The theory and practice of osteopathy dates back to the 1870s, when the physician Dr. Andrew Taylor Still discovered the healing benefits of manual therapy. The main underlying concept is that, given the best possible physical environment in which to work, the body can heal itself from illness and restore natural balance. Modern research has shown this to be the case in many disease states, and osteopathy continues to enjoy a unique place in holistic healthcare.

Osteopathy was founded by an American, Dr. Andrew Taylor Still, in the 1870s. Initially an engineer, Still came to believe that muscular and skeletal disorders could cause illness.

All the organs and tissues of your body receive a nerve supply from the spinal cord. It stands to reason that if the spinal column is not functioning correctly these nerves will be irritated and the tissues or organs they supply will suffer. Manipulation of the back at specific levels has been clinically shown to help improve cases of high blood pressure, hiatus hernia, and menstrual problems.

AT THE FIRST CONSULTATION

An osteopath will take a full medical history and perform the appropriate examination procedures before he or she starts looking at your body's framework. The specialist examination of the spine and joints forms the foundation for treatment. Osteopaths use many additional forms of diagnos-tic procedures when necessary, such as X ray, MRI scans, and blood tests, but these are only used to help confirm a diagnosis and exclude certain diseases that would make physical treatment unsafe.

SPECIALIST TREATMENTS

After graduation some osteopaths specialize in areas such as pediatric osteopathy, veterinary osteopathy, cranial osteopathy, or visceral (internal organ) osteopathy. This reflects the holistic roots of osteopathic medicine. By virtue of their training, osteopaths are skilled in the mechanistic approach to musculoskeletal problems that is commonly used by chiropractors. However, osteopaths also receive additional training in the more subtle aspects of healthcare required for their particular postgraduate specialization.

COMMON PROBLEMS THAT OSTEOPATHY CAN HELP

Many people only think of osteopathy when they have a bad back and it's safe to say that back pain forms the bulk of an osteopath's case load. Many other problems can be helped by this holistic approach:

IRRITABLE BOWEL SYNDROME
•
HYPERTENSION (HIGH BLOOD PRESSURE)
•
HEADACHE AND MIGRAINE
•
BACK PAIN ASSOCIATED WITH PREGNANCY
•
ASTHMA

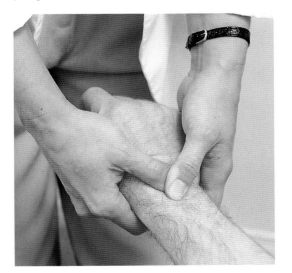

An osteopath first diagnoses the source of the problem, then uses massage and manipulation to improve the working of joints and muscles.

ALEXANDER TECHNIQUE

This technique teaches you how to use your body correctly and eliminate poor posture in everyday life. Following the Alexander technique will prevent excessive muscular tension, which often leads to aches, pains, and even illness.

The Alexander technique was founded by an Australian actor, Frederick Mathias Alexander, toward the end of the 19th century. During his acting career he began to experience problems with his voice and sought help from his doctor. However, despite thorough examinations carried out over many visits, the doctor could not discover why Alexander kept losing his voice, especially during performances.

Determined to find the cause of his problems, Alexander surrounded himself with mirrors and studied himself carefully as he spoke. He noticed that whenever he drew breath to speak, he would tense his neck muscles. This tensing drew his neck back and down, a movement that affected his vocal cords and also restricted his breathing.

Over the next several years, Alexander identified a number of other physical behavior patterns that were affecting his posture, such as gripping the floor with his feet. Slowly he began to change these habits. He learned to consciously give his body the correct instructions, which reduced the amount of effort and stress he was placing on his vocal cords.

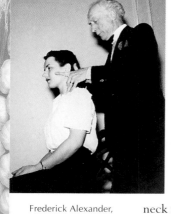

Frederick Alexander, founder of the Alexander technique, settled in London, where, during the 1930s, he set up the first training school for teachers of his technique.

AN ALEXANDER LESSON

During a lesson, your teacher will work with you on a range of everyday movements such as sitting, standing, and lying down, to teach you how to use your body with the least muscular effort. This will help you avoid future aches and pains.

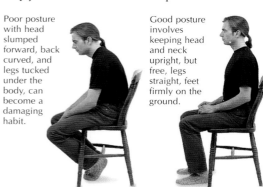

Poor posture with head slumped forward, back curved, and legs tucked under the body, can become a damaging habit.

Good posture involves keeping head and neck upright, but free, legs straight, feet firmly on the ground.

EXERCISE

This exercise will enable you to find your body's resting state.

Lie on the floor with your head resting on one or two books so it's just slightly raised and you're comfortable. Place your feet flat on the floor with your knees bent. This allows your muscles to relax, which changes the shape of your body, allowing the spine to lengthen, the ribs to widen, and the head to be in the correct position.

The Alexander technique has to be taught. In a first lesson, you will be asked to lie on the floor, while the practitioner moves your body into the correct position.

Your legs should be slightly raised, with knees bent.

Head rests on a book.

Feet should be placed flat on the floor.

234

KINESIOLOGY

The word kinesiology is derived from Greek—kinesi *meaning movement* and ology *meaning the study of. The science of kinesiology is relatively new. It originated in the mid-1960s, when George Goodheart, an American chiropractor, discovered that muscle strength reduced when the individual being tested was exposed to a substance they were allergic to. Since its introduction, kinesiology has been gaining acceptance as a noninvasive method to test for dietary allergies, nutritional deficiencies, emotional imbalances, and structural faults in the body's framework.*

The simple process of muscle testing has been used in conventional medicine to test for nerve damage. The muscle supplied by a damaged nerve is weak and easily detected by physical examination. However, the weak muscles that a kinesiologist is looking for are quite different. Kinesiology theory holds that muscles become weak because of a disruption in the body's energy flow and electrical system. Once the disruption is detected, the system can be "reset" and energy flow restored back to health with an increase in muscle strength. As the energy flow improves, so does the blood and lymph circulation, according to the theory.

Kinesiology is largely unproven and there are often conflicting findings when the same patient is tested by different kinesiologists.

TREATMENT

Kinesiology can be used as a treatment method as well as a diagnostic tool. When used as a treatment, the muscle balancing can help improve various conditions such as back pain, muscular tension, headaches, migraines, and other apparently unrelated problems like eczema, irritable bowel syndrome, anxiety, and depression.

VISITING A KINESIOLOGIST

Kinesiology does not hurt. When testing commences a limb is held out (normally the arm) and the potential allergy-provoking substance (e.g., some cheese) is held in the patient's mouth or may simply be placed in the patient's hand. As the substance is absorbed or sensed, and if the substance is the allergic culprit, the muscle strength reduces and the arm cannot resist the examiner's downward force. This would be recognized as a positive test. Muscle strength would not change if the patient was not allergic to cheese. After numerous tests have been carried out an elimination diet is discussed and a program of treatment planned.

Kinesiology is a diagnostic technique, often used to detect food allergies. Here a kinesiologist tests muscle response while the patient holds food in her mouth. If an allergy exists, the arm will easily move down.

WARNING
Even though kinesiology is safe and carries no risk to health, it's not recommended as the sole diagnostic method if you have an undiagnosed problem.

IRIDOLOGY

The science of "eye-gazing" dates back to the 1800s, when the Hungarian physician Ignatz von Peczley discovered that the changes in one eye of an owl with a broken leg disappeared when the owl recovered. Following his discovery, he set to work systematically examining eyes and noting a system of diagnostic methods that came to form modern-day iridology.

Von Peczley discovered that the iris could be divided into 12 areas, which he termed segments. These areas run from the central pupil out to the periphery and relate to specific areas of the body. Changes in a particular segment reflect the health or disease in that organ or tissue. In addition to the areas relating to different parts of the body the color of the iris indicates the patient's general level of health. His or her constitution can therefore be assessed by a careful examination of the iris, and specific health problems can be detected, often before external symptoms of disease can be felt or seen.

In iridology, the eye is a pointer to health. Here a healthy eye indicates that the body itself is healthy.

HOW CAN THE EYE INDICATE DISEASE IN THE BODY?

Iridology theory states that no part of the body functions in isolation. Every organ and tissue is in contact with every other part of the body. The eye is a convenient and easily visible indicator of health. With its ample nerve and blood supply, the eye can reflect very early signs of disease in distant body organs, making it a useful diagnostic tool,

especially for those not wanting to undergo conventional tests such as X rays and blood tests. Many iridologists have claimed to detect tendencies associated with genetic diseases that have inherited characteristics visible in the iris. Emotionally related problems may have subtle signs reflected in the iris that an experienced practitioner will notice.

In 1950 Dr. Bernard Jensen published his now commonly used iris diagnosis charts showing how the left eye corresponded to the left-hand side of the body while the right related to the right-hand side of the body. The use of iridology is purely diagnostic. For treatment, therefore, it is recommended to consult a practitioner who holds additional qualifications in a therapeutic modality.

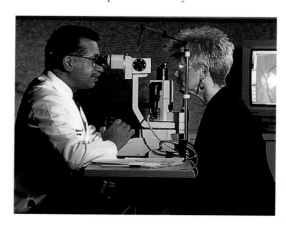

An iridologist examines a patient's eyes with a special camera. The resulting slides are enlarged and used for diagnosis.

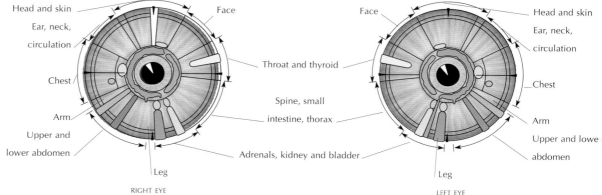

The iris of the eye is divided into sections, each corresponding to part of the body. Each iris also represents one side of the body. The right iris represents the right side, the left iris the body's left side.

Head and skin
Ear, neck, circulation
Chest
Arm
Upper and lower abdomen

Face
Throat and thyroid
Spine, small intestine, thorax
Adrenals, kidney and bladder
Leg

Face
Head and skin
Ear, neck, circulation
Chest
Arm
Upper and lowe abdomen
Leg

RIGHT EYE   LEFT EYE

REFLEXOLOGY

Reflexology, sometimes known as reflex zone therapy, originated in the Far East. Practitioners of the technique use compression on the feet and sometimes the hands along energy channels or zones. Each zone relates to a particular organ or area of the body, and the therapy aims to balance the energy flow through them, preventing disease and allowing the body to heal itself.

During treatment a reflexologist will feel all over the feet to locate tender points. This will indicate where the energy is blocked. This is sometimes felt as gritty, crunchy areas and reflexologists claim that these are crystals of accumulated toxins and waste products such as excess uric acid or calcium. The therapist will then proceed to use a variety of rubbing, rotating, caterpillarlike movements with the aim of breaking down these crystals. If there is an area of slight tenderness with a slight swelling, reflexologists claim that this signifies an area of weakness and will treat these to help the body heal itself of the weakness. Although the treatment should not be painful, these areas often feel tender as the therapist works to break down the crystals.

Treatments usually last between half an hour and one hour and in general sessions take place weekly. People feel different effects after a reflexology treatment: some people experience great relaxation and and enhanced sense of well-being while others suffer fatigue and exhaustion. A common reaction is increased urination, especially at night. This is said to be the body ridding itself of the accumulated toxins released by the treatment.

Applying pressure to particular points on the soles of the foot stimulates nerve impulses, breaking down "crystals" of waste matter and improving the flow of energy.

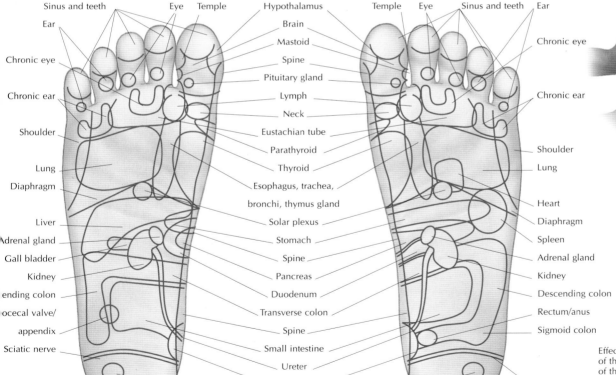

Sinus and teeth · Eye · Temple · Hypothalamus · Temple · Eye · Sinus and teeth · Ear

Ear · Brain · Chronic eye

Mastoid

Chronic eye · Spine

Pituitary gland

Chronic ear · Lymph · Chronic ear

Neck

Shoulder · Eustachian tube

Parathyroid · Shoulder

Lung · Thyroid · Lung

Diaphragm · Esophagus, trachea, bronchi, thymus gland · Heart

Solar plexus · Diaphragm

Liver · Stomach · Spleen

Adrenal gland · Spine · Adrenal gland

Gall bladder · Pancreas · Kidney

Kidney · Duodenum · Descending colon

ending colon · Transverse colon · Rectum/anus

ocecal valve/ · Spine · Sigmoid colon

appendix · Small intestine

Sciatic nerve · Ureter · Sciatic nerve

Bladder

Sciatic nerve and pelvis

Effectively the sole of the foot is a map of the body. Reflex points on the foot are linked to body parts and systems.

HYPNOTHERAPY

*T*he hypnotist induces deep relaxation in order to bring about an altered state of consciousness to treat both mental and physical problems. Hypnotherapy is often used to help people overcome addictions such as smoking, and dentists are increasingly using the technique for pain relief.

During hypnosis a young patient is asked to imagine he has a balloon tied to his right hand, and the arm raises accordingly. Similarly, the hypnotherapist hopes to access deeply buried traumas.

During hypnosis you remain aware of other people and in control but can become detached from your surroundings. Contrary to popular belief, you are not unconscious. The state is akin to when you daydream or when you become so absorbed in a book that your mental attention is fully focused and you're in a mental state resembling hypnosis.

A session usually takes no more than an hour. The hypnotist will initially aim to make you feel relaxed by asking you sit in a reclining chair and explaining what you may experience. He or she may then test whether hypnosis is suitable for you. Once you are in a relaxed state the hypnotist may ask you to focus on a single point and relax your limbs and will then make suggestions aimed to change the way you respond to things.

HISTORY OF HYPNOSIS

Ancient civilizations all around the world used a form of hypnosis to cure states of anxiety or hysteria. In the late 18th century an Austrian physician, Anton Mesmer, used a technique called mesmerism whereby he put people in trancelike states to effect cures. The term hypnotism was first used by a surgeon, Dr. James Braid, who saw a demonstration and developed his own theories and techniques.

By 1900 the French physician Dr. Pierre Janet made the important observation that the powers of hypnosis were due to its ability to link the conscious and unconscious mind. But not until the late 1950s did conventional medicine come to recognize that hypnosis could play an important part in the treatment of many common health problems.

The word mesmerism comes from Anton Mesmer (1734–1815), an Austrian physician who apparently cured patients by putting them into a trance.

The safety of hypnotherapy has always been questioned. In the hands of a qualified practitioner, however, hypnosis is a powerful but very safe treatment. Most modern therapists use light trances in their treatments, making the subject responsive to suggestion but not "out of control" or helpless. The risk of not coming around is highly unlikely.

CONDITIONS THAT HYPNOTHERAPY HELPS

WEIGHT LOSS
•
SMOKING
•
STRESS-RELATED CONDITIONS
•
ANXIETY
•
PAIN RELIEF
•
BEDWETTING

RELAXATION AND VISUALIZATION

*I*t is estimated that in the UK around 270,000 people each year take time off work due to work-related stress (see p.182). In the US, cardiovascular disease remains the leading killer. Stress can produce conditions such as heart disease, breathing difficulties, sleep disorders, hyperventilation, panic attacks, and digestive problems.

One of the first changes during stress is the rate of breathing. It becomes shallower and more rapid, coming mostly from the chest rather than the upper stomach or diaphragm. This alters the balance of oxygen and carbon dioxide in the blood which can lead to hyperventilation and panic attacks. Clearly, then, one way of overcoming and even preventing many stress-related problems is to learn to control and slow down your breathing during times of stress.

ESTABLISHING NORMAL BREATHING

The simplest method is to learn to overexaggerate the movements of the breath.

Lie in a quiet room where you are unlikely to be disturbed. Place one hand on your abdomen and the other on your upper chest. Take a slow, deep breath in through your mouth, making sure it bypasses the upper hand so that it reaches the lower hand on your upper abdomen. Hold the breath for a few seconds and slowly release the breath out through your mouth in a controlled way. Wait a couple of seconds before repeating the process. Initially only practice this for five breaths, as any more may leave you feeling lightheaded.

SLOWING YOUR BREATHING RATE

Visualization techniques use images you create in your mind to bring about physiological changes in your body. If you are in a stressful situation where you find your heart racing, a quick way of calming yourself is to "switch off" for a few seconds and imagine your heartbeat slowing.

SLEEPING DIFFICULTIES

There are many breathing and visualization techniques that can be used to overcome this problem.

Using the basic breathing technique, count one mentally as you inhale. Then count two as you exhale, continuing until you reach five. Every time you have an incoming thought, return to one. This may sound simple, but few people get beyond three before falling asleep. You can also try visualizing yourself in a place that you love, perhaps the beach or the mountains. This can be a very effective cure for insomnia.

ACHES AND PAINS

Using your natural breathing, concentrate on the specific areas of your body that are aching. Focus on these areas, for instance if you are suffering from a tense neck, see the knots and imagine them gradually becoming smaller. If they are painful imagine the heat as a red color that gradually changes to a cool blue.

PREPARING FOR A STRESSFUL EVENT

If you are worried about a forthcoming event such as an exam, picture the scene in your mind. Begin with the day of the exam, traveling to the exam, five minutes before it, sitting down, etc. If at any time your breathing increases, replay that time over until your breathing calms down. This method may also be used if you dealt badly with an event. Relive it in your mind and imagine how you would have liked to handle it. This may help you deal with a similar situation more positively in the future.

Visualizing a beautiful place in your mind and imagining that you are being transported there can help to overcome insomnia.

You can use visualization to help remove pain. Focus on the pain, imagining that the pain is red and hot. Gradually, visualize the color changing to a cool blue.

SPIRITUAL HEALING

Spiritual or psychic healing is believed to transfer or channel healing energy by laying on of hands. While some believe that this healing comes from God, others say it is energy passed through the healer to the patient.

A healer places her hands on or near the affected area, believing that a healing force flows through them. An ancient practice, it has had some surprising successes.

For centuries, spiritual healing has been practiced by many cultures and religions. Jesus Christ was said to have cured the sick by the "laying on of hands."

Over the past few years there have been great leaps forward in our understanding of how the immune system works. It has long been known that in a healthy person, the immune system can destroy everything from a bacteria through to masses of cancer cells. Many patients with severe and even life-threatening diseases have found that they have been helped by visualization (see p.239), and there appears to be a very strong connection between the mind and the immune system. Many people have also been helped by spiritual healing, and it's believed that its effectiveness may be based on a similar mechanism.

It has now been well established that there is a connection between the immune cells and the nervous system It may be that spiritual healing taps into this connection and stimulates the internal healing potential of the immune system.

VISITING A HEALER

Spiritual healing normally takes place on a one-to-one basis, but some practitioners perform their healing in group sessions. Most spiritual healers begin by talking to their patients in order to relax them and to allow them to open themselves to the idea of being healed. In most cases, this will be followed by a hands-on approach, with the healer and patient working closely together. The healer will often apply a very light touch (sometimes with the hands no more that just half an inch away from the head) to allow the healing energies to pass through and repair the patient's aura. During this time, the patient may sense a feeling of warmth emanating from the healer's hands, or tingling feelings at the site of the illness.

A healing session tends to last from about 30 minutes to an hour. Distant healing can be practiced on people living in remote places or those too ill to attend a healing center.

HEALING

RECIPIENTS SAY THEY EXPERIENCE HOT OR COLD SENSATIONS, WHICH LEAVE THEM WITH A SENSE OF WELL-BEING

•

HEALING IS NORMALLY DONE ON AN INDIVIDUAL BASIS, BUT GROUP HEALING IS BECOMING INCREASINGLY COMMON

•

HEALERS BELIEVE THAT THERE IS AN ENERGY FIELD OR AURA AROUND EVERYBODY, AND THEIR AIM IS TO REPAIR A DAMAGED AURA

•

HEALING IS OFTEN USED IN TERMINAL ILLNESS TO ENABLE THE PATIENT TO FEEL A PEACE OR ACCEPTANCE TOWARD THE END OF THEIR LIFE, BUT MOST USE IT TO REDUCE PAIN, AND IN TIMES OF STRESS.

REIKI HEALING

Pronounced **Raykee**, *this form of natural healing involves assisting the body and mind to effect a positive healing process. The process is started by the hand of the Reiki healer being placed in contact with the patient. This allows the energy to flow into the recipient. Reiki comes from the Japanese words* Rei, *meaning universal, and* Ki, *meaning life energy. Practitioners of the Reiki process channel this universal life energy to where it is required in the body.*

Reiki started in the late 1880s with Dr. Mikao Usui, a Christian minister working in Japan who had a lifelong interest in ancient healing arts. During his studies into healing, Dr. Usui discovered ancient texts that described a formula for healing that was written over 2,500 years ago. The text was incomplete, but he worked through the writings and revived the Reiki process. The same teachings are now practiced worldwide by many thousands of Reiki masters and practitioners.

TREATMENT

Reiki is a gentle yet powerful therapy. Treatments normally last about 90 minutes and the recipient lies fully clothed on the therapy table. The Reiki practitioner places hands on the recipient's body in a special sequence of positions that cover the whole body. Different people report a wide variety of reactions to Reiki healing—some feel a slight pleasant tingling and a sense of warmth, while others simply receive a profound feeling of relaxation.

VISITING A REIKI PRACTITIONER

Reiki practitioners do not diagnose, so a medical diagnosis is important. Many doctors and other health professionals now incorporate this type of healing into their clinics or refer patients to local healers.

Reiki can help with stress, anxiety, irritable bowel syndrome, migraines, menstrual pain, and some types of back pain. Its gentle, noninvasive nature makes it especially suitable treatment for the very young and the elderly.

Mikao Usui, a Japanese theologian, spent many years researching healing and claimed that the secrets of Reiki healing came to him in a dream. He also rediscovered ancient texts.

TYPES OF REIKI HEALER

According to the level of training (there are three levels), a Reiki healer may be referred to as:

LEVEL 1 PRACTITIONER
Connected to the world of universal energy

LEVEL 2 PRACTITIONER
Understands about positive energy and how to enhance the atmosphere at home or work

LEVEL 3 PRACTITIONER (REIKI MASTER)
Reiki Masters pass on skills to Reiki students and attune them to the energy of the universe.

The Reiki healer channels and directs life energy through the hands into the patient's body. It is a gentle and spiritual therapy.

AUTOGENIC TRAINING

Autogenic training is a system of self-help exercises for the body and mind designed to induce a state of deep relaxation. Once in this state, you can voluntarily regulate the autonomic nervous system. This system controls functions such as heart rate, blood pressure, breathing, and pulse rate, which are normally involuntary. The name comes from the Greek auto, *meaning self, and* genes, *meaning produced.*

Autogenic training was developed in the late 1920s by Dr. Johannes Schultz, a German neurophysiologist. It involves learning six standard exercises which include focusing on such sensations as heaviness in the arms and legs, warmth in the arms and legs, calm regular heartbeat, easy natural breathing, abdominal warmth, and coolness of the forehead. By learning these techniques you learn the art of passive concentration. This effectively improves the communication between the right and left hemispheres of the brain, which balances interactions between the brain and the body. More advanced techniques can be learned once these have been mastered. To be effective these techniques have to be practiced for 10–15 times two to three times a day.

Autogenic training is used to treat mostly psychological conditions such as insomnia, anxiety, tension, depression, and stress, although it can also be used to treat physical conditions such as irritable bowel syndrome, headaches, and peptic ulcers, which are often due to excessive stress.

BIOFEEDBACK

This technique is similar to autogenic training, except that the changes in the patient's heart rate, body temperature, muscle tension, skin conductivity, and brainwaves are monitored by a machine. The lie detector used in courts and by police departments is based on similar principles. A machine using electrodes attached to the patient's skin records subtle physical processes, such as pulse rate, heart beat, sweating, and muscular tension. These processes are registered on the biofeedback machine as electrical signals or sounds. By seeing their reactions registering on the biofeedback machine, patients become aware of where in their bodies they hold their responses to stress. They are then able to take steps to control and alter these responses before becoming overly anxious.

A biofeedback device, linked to your body via electrodes, monitors physical processes such as pulse rate, heart beat, and muscular tension. These are "fed back" as electrical signals or sounds. By recognizing your responses to stress, you can learn to control and alter these processes.

Relax the neck and shoulders

Rest your hands on your knees

Remove your shoes

So-called simple exercises relieve stress and physical tension and encourage deep relaxation. This slumped position can be used to relax tension in the shoulders and neck—and you can practice it anywhere.

COUNSELING AND THERAPY

*C*ounseling takes place on a one-to-one or group support basis. It can be a short-term or a long-term process. The counselor helps clients talk about and understand their problems, which enables them to cope more effectively.

Counseling is often offered to those facing problems such as bereavement, marriage difficulties, or specific illnesses. It can help people come to terms with their problems, or help them make a decision they feel comfortable with.

Psychotherapy is a more long-term approach used for people with more established problems such as depression, anxiety attacks, or relationship problems. It can last from months to years.

During short-term counseling a minor, temporary problem is often shown to be hiding myriad connected problems, and a more long-term approach may then be necessary.

A COUNSELING SESSION

Counselors don't provide the solution, but they will provide a secure, caring environment to enable you to talk and find out your real concerns. You will then be helped to reach your own solutions and the means of achieving these solutions. You will learn your strengths and will be encouraged to use them to reach satisfactory solutions to problems and also to recognize and achieve your goals.

Initially the counseling sessions will concentrate on immediate worries. However, it's important to work beyond them in order to progress and avoid repeating similar negative patterns that may be preventing a client from reaching positive solutions and goals. The counseling process will try to identify problem areas that the client may be unaware of and provide a course of action to help cope with recurring or forthcoming difficulties, leading to a more fulfilled life and a greater sense of security and well-being.

FORMS OF PSYCHOTHERAPY

PSYCHODRAMA
This form of psychotherapy involves a group of subjects who dramatize their individual conflicting situations of daily life. In the case of fears and phobias, this can offer a safe environment in which to act out and face the underlying problem.

PSYCHOANALYSIS
The method behind this form of psychotherapy involves diagnosing and treating mental and emotional disorders through ascertaining and analyzing the facts of the patient's mental life. Psychoanalysis tends to be a slower approach to the treatment of fears and phobias as patients come to understand their thought processes in detail.

GESTALT THERAPY
Gestalt therapists encourage their patients to focus on living for the present and create a whole or "gestalt" of their life experiences.

Find a fully qualified practitioner with whom you can establish a good rapport.

Swiss psychiatrist Carl Jung (1875–1961) worked with Sigmund Freud (1856–1939) for some years, before developing his own school of analytical psychology. He introduced the concept of introvert and extrovert personalities as well as the idea of a collective unconscious.

YOGA

There are many types of yoga, and they all aim to balance the mind, body, and spirit by using a combination of postures (asanas), breathing techniques (pranayamas), and spiritual and mental training. The spiritual, philosophical, and mental aspects of yoga are less widely practiced in the West. Here most people take up yoga as a form of relaxation and to regain suppleness.

One of the most important aspects of yoga is that it is noncompetitive. People of any size or age are able to learn and practice it, as long as they concentrate on their own capabilities.

The postures and breathing techniques are designed to improve the flow of prana, or life energy. Prana flows through energy channels called nadis, and ill health signifies a blockage somewhere along these channels. The body also has seven chakras, which are points of focused energy, and specific exercises in yoga concentrate on these areas, which are found in the crown of the head, the throat, the spine, the solar plexus, the center of the forehead, the heart, and the navel.

By improving fitness and suppleness, and helping people achieve and maintain a relaxed state of body and mind, yoga can be helpful in many physical and psychological conditions. These include stress-related disorders, circulatory problems, back and neck pain, respiratory difficulties, digestive disorders such as irritable bowel syndrome, fatigue, insomnia, arthritis, and depression.

Hatha yoga, which makes use of breathing techniques, called pranayamas, and different postures and movements known as asanas, is the most popular form of yoga in the West.

In India yoga is not just a gentle exercise, it is also a deeply spiritual experience and a fundamental path to self-realization and awareness.

FORMS OF YOGA

ASHTANGA
This energetic variety of yoga combines techniques from Hatha and Raja into flowing, continuous movements while concentrating on breath control.

KUNDALINI
A process whereby dormant energy in the spine is revitalized moving upward, and activating the major chakras. This also causes changes in consciousness.

HATHA
Concentrates on the postures (asanas) and breathing control techniques (pranayama).

RAJA
Concentrates on the mental aspect of yoga, focusing heavily on meditation.

T'AI CHI CH'UAN

T'ai chi literally means supreme unity. It is an ancient Chinese system using gentle, graceful, flowing, circular movements to enhance the chi or energy within the body, promoting health and a sense of well-being. T'ai chi is now a form of nonviolent martial art which aims to balance the positive and negative, or yin and yang (see p.230) within the body.

This technique is suitable for any size or age and attempts to balance and stimulate all the systems of the body such as the digestive, respiratory, and circulatory systems. It also teaches breathing control, focusing concentration, and relaxing the mind, and is often called the moving meditation technique.

T'AI CHI TECHNIQUES

There are two forms of t'ai chi movement sequences, short and long. The short version takes about five minutes to complete and contains 40–50 movements, while the long form takes around half an hour and contains over 100 movements. In both forms the movements are slow and focused with total breath control. There is a group of movements that can be used in self-defense which are faster but the movements still follow the t'ai chi philosophy and are carried out in a slow and highly co-ordinated fashion.

GETTING STARTED

In China space is limited and one of the great things about t'ai chi is the fact that all the actions and exercises were designed to be carried out in a small space. To practice t'ai chi at home all that's needed is the appropriate footwear (sneakers will do) and a flat area of about 54 sq.feet (5 sq.m). T'ai chi is best practiced in the open air, as is traditional in China. There it is a national activity, often incorporated into the working day, practiced before breakfast and sometimes before bed.

QI GONG

Closely linked to t'ai chi is qi gong, another ancient system of movements that combines exercise, breathing, and meditation. Its aim is to improve the flow of energy or chi around the body.

Movements are very slow, graceful, and measured. The exercises must be learned and are best practiced in the open air, wearing loose-fitting clothes.

The gentle flowing movements of t'ai chi are especially suited to the elderly. T'ai chi stimulates the body systems, retards aging, and coordinates mind and body. According to the Chinese, one must practice for 10 years before becoming a master.

USEFUL ADDRESSES

UNITED KINGDOM

**ACADEMY OF
ON-SITE MASSAGE**
New Street
Charfield
Wotton-under-Edge
Gloucestershire GL12 8ES

**AROMATHERAPY
ORGANISATION COUNCIL**
3 Latymer Close
Braybrook
Market Harborough
Leicester LE16 8LN

**ASSOCIATION FOR
THERAPEUTIC HEALERS**
6 Cleaver House
Adelaide Road
London NW3 3PT

**ASSOCIATION OF
MASSAGE PRACTITIONERS**
101 Barns Green Rd
London N22 4DF

**ASSOCIATION OF
MEDICAL
AROMATHERAPISTS**
11 Park Circus
Glasgow G3 6AX

**ASSOCIATION OF
REFLEXOLOGISTS**
27 Old Gloucester Street
London WC1N 3XX

**BRITISH ACUPUNCTURE
ASSOCIATION & REGISTER
(BAAR)**
34 Alderney Street
London SE1 4EU

**BRITISH ACUPUNCTURE
COUNCIL**
Park House
206-8 Latimer Rd
London WI0 6RE

**BRITISH ASSOCIATION
FOR AUTOGENIC
TRAINING AND THERAPY**
18 Holtsmere Close
Garston
Watford WD2 6NE

**BRITISH ASSOCIATION
FOR COUNSELLING**
37a Sheep Street
Rugby
Warwickshire CV21 3BX

**BRITISH HERBAL
MEDICINE ASSOCIATION**
Ray Hill
Sun House
Church Street
Stroud
Gloucestershire GL5 1JL

**BRITISH HOMEOPATHIC
ASSOCIATION**
27a Devonshire Street
London W1N 1RJ

**BRITISH HYPNOTHERAPY
ASSOCIATION**
67 Upper Berkeley Street
London W1H 7DH

**BRITISH MASSAGE
THERAPY COUNCIL**
Greenbank House
65 A Adelphi Street
Preston
Lancashire PR1 7BH

**BRITISH MEDICAL
ACUPUNCTURE SOCIETY**
Newton House
Newton Lane
Whitley
Warrington
Cheshire WA4 4JA

**BRITISH PSYCHOLOGICAL
SOCIETY**
St Andrew's House
48 Princess Road East
Leicester LE1 7DR

**BRITISH REFLEXOLOGY
ASSOCIATION**
Monks Orchard
Whitbourne
Worcester WR6 5RB

BRITISH SLEEP SOCIETY
PO Box 144
Wakefield
Yorkshire WF4 2XY

**BRITISH SOCIETY OF
EXPERIMENTAL AND
CLINICAL HYPNOSIS**
District General Hospital
Scathe Rd
Grimsby DN33 2BA

BRITISH WHEEL OF YOGA
1 Hamilton Place
Boston Road
Sleaford
Lincolnshire NG34 7ES

**CENTRAL REGISTER OF
ADVANCED
HYPNOTHERAPISTS**
PO Box 14526
London N4 2WG

COLLEGE OF HEALING
Runnings Park
Croft Bank
West Malvern
Worcestershire
WR14 4DU

**CONFEDERATION OF
HEALING
ORGANISATIONS**
113 High Street
Berkhamstead
Herts HP4 2DJ

**DR EDWARD BACH
CENTRE**
Mount Vernon
Bakers Lane
Sotwell
Oxon OX10 0PX

**FACULTY OF
HOMEOPATHY**
2 Powis Place
Great Ormond Street
London WC1N 3HT

**HOLISTIC
AROMATHERAPY
FOUNDATION**
90 Tudor Drive
Morden
Surrey SM4 4PF

**HOMEOPATHIC MEDICAL
RESEARCH COUNCIL**
Royal London Homeopathic
Hospital
Great Ormond Street
London WC1N 3HR

**INTERNATIONAL
FEDERATION OF
AROMATHERAPISTS**
Stamford House
2-4 Chiswick High Road
London W4 1TH

**INTERNATIONAL
INSTITUTE OF
REFLEXOLOGY**
32 Priory Rd
Portbury
Bristol BS20 9TH

**INTERNATIONAL SOCIETY
OF PROFESSIONAL
AROMATHERAPISTS**
ISPA House
82 Ashby Road
Hinckley
Leicestershire LE10 1SN

**LONDON SCHOOL OF
SPORTS MASSAGE**
Spilsted Oast
Stream Lane
Sedlescombe
East Sussex TN33 0PB

MANIC DEPRESSION FELLOWSHIP

8 High Street

Kingston-upon-Thames

Surrey KT1 1EY

MASSAGE THERAPY INSTITUTE OF GREAT BRITAIN

PO Box 2726

London NW2 4NR

MASSAGE TRAINING INSTITUTE

24 Highbury Grove

London N5 2EA

NATIONAL ASSOCIATION OF HOLISTIC HYPNOTHERAPISTS

19-20 St Georges Avenue

Northampton NN2 6JA

NATIONAL FEDERATION OF SPIRITUAL HEALERS

Old Manor Farm Studio

Church Street

Sunbury-on-Thames

Middlesex TW16 6RG

NATIONAL INSTITUTE OF MEDICAL HERBALISTS

56 Longbrook Street

Exeter EX4 6AH

REFLEXOLOGY SOCIETY

249 Fosse Road South

Leicester LE3 1AE

REGISTER OF QUALIFIED AROMATHERAPISTS

PO 3431

Danbury

Chelmsford

Essex CM3 4UA

RESPIRATORY SUPPORT AND SLEEP CENTRE

Papworth Hospital

Papworth Everard

Cambridge CB3 8RE

SANELINE

199 Old Marylebone Road

London NW1 5QP

SLEEP DISORDERS CENTRE

The Lane-Fox Unit

St Thomas' Hospital

Lambeth Place Road

London SE1 7EH

SLEEP DISORDERS CLINIC

Neurosciences Unit

King's Healthcare

Denmark Hill

London SE5

SLEEP MATTERS SELF-HELP GROUP (INSOMNIA)

PO Box 3087

London W4 4ZP

SOCIETY OF HOMEOPATHS

2 Artizan Road

Northampton NN1 4HU

TRADITIONAL ACUPUNCTURE SOCIETY

1 The Ridgeway

Stratford-upon-Avon

Warwickshire CV37 9JL

UK COLLEGE FOR COMPLEMENTARY HEALTHCARE STUDIES

Exmoor Street

London W10 6DZ

UK HOMEOPATHIC MEDICAL ASSOCIATION

2 Livingstone Road

Gravesend

Kent DA12 5DZ

YOGA BIOMEDICAL TRUST

Yoga Therapy Centre

Royal London Homeopathic

Hospital Trust

60 Great Ormond St

London WC1N 3HR

USA

ACADEMY FOR GUIDED IMAGERY

PO Box 2070

Mill Valley, CA 94942

ACUPRESSURE INSTITUTE

1533 Shattuck Avenue

Berkeley, CA 94709

ACUPUNCTURE INTERNATIONAL ASSOCIATION

2330 S Brentwood Blvd

St. Louis, MO 63144

AIDS ALTERNATIVE HEALTH PROJECT

3223 N. Sheffield Avenue

Chicago, IL 60657

AMERICAN ACADEMY OF MEDICAL ACUPUNCTURE

5820 Wilshire Blvd,

Suite 500

Los Angeles, CA 90036

AMERICAN ACUPUNCTURE ASSOCIATION

4262 Kissena Blvd

Suite 500

Flushing, NY 11355

AMERICAN ALLIANCE OF MASSAGE PROFESSIONALS

3108 Rte 10 West

Denville, NJ 07834

AMERICAN ASSOCIATION OF ACUPUNCTURE AND ORIENTAL MEDICINE

1400 16th St, NW, Ste 710

Washington, DC 20036

AMERICAN ASSOCIATION OF NATUROPATHIC PHYSICIANS

2366 Eastlake Avenue

Suite 322

Seattle, WA 98102

AMERICAN ASSOCIATION OF PROFESSIONAL HYPNOTHERAPISTS

PO Box 29

Boones Mill, VA 24065

AMERICAN COUNSELING ASSOCIATION

5999 Stevenson Avenue

Alexandria,

VA 22304-3300

AMERICAN HEALING ASSOCIATION

c/o Rev Brian Zink

811 Ridge Drive

Glendale, CA 91206

AMERICAN INSTITUTE OF HOMEOPATHY

23200 Edmonds Way

Suite A

Edmonds, WA 98026

AMERICAN INSTITUTE OF MASSAGE THERAPY

2156 Newport Blvd

Costa Mesa, CA 92627

AMERICAN MASSAGE THERAPY ASSOCIATION

820 Davis Street

Suite 100

Evanston, IL 60201

AMERICAN SLEEP DISORDERS ASSOCIATION

1610 14th Street, N.W., Suite 300

Rochester, MN 55901

AMERICAN SOCIETY OF CLINICAL HYPNOSIS

2200 East Devon Avenue

Suite 291

Des Plaines, IL 600118

AMERICAN YOGA ASSOCIATION

513 S Orange Avenue

Sarasota, FL 34236

AROMATHERAPY INSTITUTE OF RESEARCH
PO Box 2354
Fair Oaks, CA 95628

ASSOCIATED BODYWORK AND MASSAGE PROFESSIONALS
PO Box 489
Evergree, CO 80439

DESERT INSTITUTE OF HEALING ARTS
639 N 6th Ave
Tucson, AZ 85705

FOOT REFLEXOLOGY AWARENESS ASSOCIATION
PO Box 7622
Mission Hills, CA 9134

GUIDED IMAGERY AND MUSIC
Temple University
Presser Hall 0012-00
Philadelphia, PA 19122

HEAL
16 East 16th Street
New York, NY 10003

HEALING HANDS INSTITUTE FOR MASSAGE THERAPY
41 Bergline Avenue
Westwood, NJ 07675

HIMALAYAN INSTITUTE OF YOGA, SCIENCE, AND PHILOSOPHY
RRI Box 400
Honesdale, PA 18431

HOMEOPATHIC EDUCATIONAL SERVICES
2124 Kittredge Street
Berkeley, CA 94704

HUMANITIES CENTER INSTITUTE OF ALLIED HEALTH
School of Massage
4045 Park Blvd
Pinellas Park, FL 34665

INSTITUTE FOR MUSIC, HEALTH, AND EDUCATION
PO Box 4179
Boulder, CO 80306

INSTITUTE FOR THERAPEUTIC ARTS AND SCHOOL OF MASSAGE THERAPY
39 Main Street
Bridgton, ME 04009

INSTITUTE OF NATURAL HEALING SCIENCES
4100 Felps Rd
Suite E
Colleyville, TX 76034

INTEGRATIVE THERAPY SCHOOL
3000 T St
Suite 104
Sacramento, CA 95816

INTERNATIONAL ASSOCIATION FOR HOMEOPATHY
2366 Eastlake Avenue East
Suite 301
Seattle, WA 98102

INTERNATIONAL ASSOCIATION OF YOGA THERAPISTS
109 Hillside Avenue
Mill Valley, CA 94941

INTERNATIONAL FOUNDATION FOR HOMEOPATHY
2366 Eastlake Avenue
Suite 322
Seattle, WA 98102

INTERNATIONAL INSTITUTE OF REFLEXOLOGY
PO Box 12462
St. Petersburg, FL 33733

IYENGAR YOGA
2404 27th Avenue
San Francisco, CA 94116

MUSCULAR THERAPY INSTITUTE
122 Rindge Ave
Cambridge, MA 02140

NATIONAL ACUPUNCTURE DETOXIFICATION ASSOCIATION
3115 Broadway
Suite 51
New York, NY 10027

NATIONAL ASSOCIATION FOR HOLISTIC AROMATHERAPY
PO Box 17622
Boulder, CO 80308-0622

NATIONAL ASSOCIATION OF MUSIC THERAPY
8455 Colesville Road
Suite 930
Silver Springs, MD 20910

NATIONAL CENTER FOR HOMEOPATHY
1500 Massachusetts Avenue NW
Suite 42
Seattle, WA 20005

NATIONAL CENTER FOR HOMEOPATHY
801 North Fairfax Street
Suite 396
Alexandria, VA 22314

NATIONAL GUILD OF HYPNOTISTS
PO Box 308
Merrmick, NH 03054

NATIONAL HOLISTIC INSTITUTE
5900 Hollis St, Suite J
Emeryville, CA 94608-2008

NURSE HEALERS ASSOCIATION
234 Fifth Ave #3399
New York, NY 10001

CANADAPACIFIC INSTITUTE OF AROMATHERAPY
PO Box 6842
San Rafael, CA 94903

QIGONG INSTITUTE/EAST-WEST ACADEMY OF THE HEALING ARTS
450 Sutter Street
Suite 916
San Francisco, CA 94108

QIGONG UNIVERSAL
2828 Beverly Boulevard
Los Angeles, CA 90057

QUAN YIN HEALING ARTS CENTER
1748 Market Street
San Francisco, CA 94102

SCHERER INSTITUTE OF NATURAL HEALING
935 Alto-Street
Santa Fe, NM 87501

SOCIETY FOR ACUPUNCTURE RESEARCH
6900 Wisconsin Avenue
Suite 700
Bethesda, MD 20815

SWEDISH INSTITUTE, SCHOOL OF MASSAGE THERAPY AND ALLIED HEALTH SCIENCES
226 W 26 St
5th Floor
New York, NY 10001

WELLNESS AND MASSAGE TRAINING INSTITUTE
618 Executive Dr
Willowbrook, IL 60521

FURTHER READING

Ball, N., and Hough, N.
The Sleep Solution
(Vermilion, London, 1998)

Butler B., and Hope A.
Manage Your Mind. The Mental Health Fitness Guide (Oxford University Press, UK, 1995)

Cassileth, B.R.
The Alternative Medicine Handbook (Norton WW, US, 1998)

Corrigan, D.
Herbal Medicine for Sleep and Relaxation (Amberwood Publishing, UK, 1996)

Copeland, M.A.
Living Without Depression and Manic Depression (Amberwood Publishing, UK, 1996)

David, J. (ed.)
Cancer Care (Chapman & Hall, UK/USA, 1995)

Digeronimo, T.
Insomnia: 50 Essential Things to Do (Plume, 1997)

Ernst, E. (ed.)
The Book of Symptoms and Treatments (Element, UK, 1998)

Fontana, D.
Managing Stress (British Psychological Society 1989)

Fugh-Berman, A.
Alternative Medicine: What Works (Odonian Press, US, 1996)

Graham, J.
Multiple Sclerosis: The Self-Help Guide (Thorsons, UK, 1992)

Griggs, B.
The New Green Pharmacy (Vermillion, UK, 1997)

Guilleminault, C.
Sleep and its Disorders in Children (Raven Press, 1987)

Hartley, M.
The Good Stress Guide (Sheldon Press, UK, 1995)

Hay, L.
You Can Heal Your Life (Eden Grove, USA, 1988)

Hoffmann, D.
Herbs for a Good Night's Sleep: Herbal Approaches to Relieving Insomnia Safely and Effectively. Understand your Sleeplessness—and Banish it Forever! (Keats Publications, 1997)

Inlander, C.B., and Moran, C.K.
67 Ways to Good Sleep (Random House, 1998)

Jayson, M.I.V.
Back Pain, The Facts (Oxford University Press, UK, 1992)

Johnson, T.S., and Halberstadt, J.
Phantom of the Night, Overcome sleep Apnea Syndrome and Snoring—Win your Hidden Struggling to Breathe, Sleep, and Live (New Technology Publishing, 1992)

Keane C (ed.)
The Stress File (Blackwater Press, Dublin, 1997)

Kermani, K.
Autogenic Training: Effective Holistic Way to Better Health (Souvenir Press, London, 1996)

Lavery, S.
The Healing Power of Sleep: How to Achieve Restorative Sleep Naturally (Fireside, 1997)

Lipman, D.S.
Snoring from A to Zzz: Proven Cures for the Night's Worst Nuisance (Spencer Press, 1997)

Madders, J.
Stress and Relaxation (Macdonald Optima, UK, 1981)

Maxwell-Hudson, C.
The Complete Book of Massage (Dorling Kindersley, UK, 1998)

McCormick, E.W.
Coping, Healing and Rebuilding After Nervous Breakdown (Optima, UK, 1993)

Morgan, D.R.
Sleep Secrets for Shiftworkers & People with Off-Beat Schedules (Whole Person Associates, 1996)

Moyers, B.
Healing and the Mind (Doubleday, USA, 1993)

O'Hanlon, B.
Sleep. The Common Sense Approach (Newleaf, Dublin, 1998)

Payne, R.A.
Relaxation Techniques (Churchill Livingstone, UK, 1995)

Patel, C.
The Complete Guide to Stress Management (Optima, UK, 1989)

Pascualy, R.A., and Soest, S.W.
Snoring and Sleep Apnea. Personal and Family Guide to Diagnosis and Treatment (Demos Vermande, 1996)

Pauling, L.
How to Live Longer and Feel Better (W.H. Freeman, USA, 1986)

Price, S.
Aromatherapy for Common Ailments (Gaia Books, London, 1991)

Scott, E.
The Natural Way to Sound Sleep (Orion Books, London, 1996)

Thomas, H., and Sikora, K.
Cancer—A Positive Approach (Thorsons, UK/USA, 1995)

Tkac, D. (ed.)
The Doctor's Book of Home Remedies (Rodale Press, USA, 1994)

Tratler, R.
Better Health Through Natural Healing (McGraw Hill, USA, 1987)

Vickers, A.
Massage and Aromatherapy (Chapman Hall, UK, 1996)

Weekes, C.
Self Help for Your Nerves (Thorsons, London, 1995)

Wilson, V.N.
Sleep Thief, Restless Legs Syndrome (Galaxy Books, 1996)

INDEX

ACKNOWLEDGMENTS

Special thanks go to:

Herriotts Furnishings,
67 A/B Church Road,
Hove,
East Sussex;

Furnishing Touches,
94 Portland Road,
Hove,
East Sussex

for help with props.

Special thanks go to:

P Bennett (Kinesiology consultant)
Liz Cooke
Sonia Desvaux (Reiki consultant)
Caroline Eaves
Stephen Francis
Catherine Gellatly
Harriet Hart
Paul Lundberg (T'ai Chi and Qi Gong consultant)
Kay Macmullan
Clive Morris
Rosie Nobbs
Sonja Wirwohl

for help with photography.

PICTURE SOURCES

Key: a=above; c=center; b=below; l=left; r=right.

AKG London: 220bl, 238br, Eric Lessing 231cr, 240bl, 243br.
Dr. Edward Bach Centre: 227 tr.
Garden Picture Library: Densey Cline 63bl; Erika Craddock 215tr; John Glover 34br; Lamontagne 220tc; Mayle Le Scanff 224tl; Howard Ricell 6cla, 139br; Michel Viard 26bc; Juliette Wade 71bla.
Angela Hampton Family Life Picture Library: 84bl, 91br, 240tl.
Hulton Getty: 226tr.
Imagebank: 3cr, 3rc, 12, 14br, 16tr, 20tr, 22tr, 23br, 24tr, 24bl, 25tr, 25br, 30bl, 33tl, 34cla, 37cla, 37rca, 38br, 38tc, 39tr, 40tc, 42bl, 44br, 44cra, 45cr, 46bl, 46cla, 46tr, 47cla, 53cla, 53lca, 53rca, 53cra, 54tc, 54br, 55tr, 55br, 56bl, 57bc, 58br, 60b, 61br, 62cra, 62c, 64cla, 64tr, 66cr, 67tl, 70cl, 71bc, 71tr, 72bl, 73tr, 73br, 74br, 76tr, 78, 79lca, 79cla, 79rca, 79cra, 82bl, 82tr, 83br, 83cra, 84tr, 85br, 86cl, 87tr, 89cr, 90cl, 92tl, 92bl, 99tr, 100bl, 100tl, 102tr, 102c,103tr, 103br, 104, 105cra, 110tl, 110tc, 111bl, 113br, 115cra, 118cla, 120tr, 121tl, 124cla, 126tr, 127cra, 128tr, 129cra, 130bl, 132cb, 134bl, 136tr, 138tl, 140br, 145tl, 149lca, 149cla, 149cra, 150bl, 151tr, 154tc, 155tr, 166tr, 167tr, 174, 175cra, 176bl, 178bl, 178br, 179tr, 181br, 182cla, 183tr, 184bl, 184tr, 186clb, 187tr, 189tc, 189cr, 193lca, 195cl, 195br, 195tr, 196bl, 197br, 198br, 200bl, 200cra, 202bl, 202tr, 202crb, 203br, 204tr, 206bl, 207tr, 207br, 208cra, 211tl, 212bl, 213br, 221tr, 227bl, 230tr, 230cra, 235cla, 235crb.

Images Colour Library: cover tc, **cover** tcr, 10bl, 68tr, 94bl, 98tr, 101br, 107tr, 130br, 144cl, 146bl, 194bl, 204bl, 211br.
Osteopathic Information Service: 233tr.
PowerStock: cover bl.
The Society of Teachers of the Alexander Technique: 234tl.
Science Photo Library: Jonathon Ashton 140tr; Marc Clarke 87br; Sue Ford 147br; Dr. Gopalmurti 114cla; Damien Lovegrove 147br; Dr. P. Marazzi 33cra; Will & Deni McIntyre 242tl; Publiphoto Diffusion 232br; Francoise Sauze 219cra, 232tr, 238tl; Amy Trustrameye 77tr; BSIP VEM 87c; Hattie Young 105cla.
The Stockmarket: cover br, 3cla, 15tc, 16bl, 21br, 36, 41br, 52, 56tr, 57cr, 59bl, 69tr, 72tl, 77c, 156tr, 163br.
Tony Stone Images: 1c, 2, 3cl, 6tc, 11tc, 13cla, 13cra, 18tl, 29br, 35br, 37cla, 49tr, 50tr, 51tr, 59br, 69br, 74cla, 80br, 89tr, 93tr, 95br, 96bl, 98bl, 99br, 101tr, 106tc, 108bl, 109br, 109tr, 122tl, 123tr, 128cra, 130tr, 133tr, 134tr, 135cr, 144bl, 147tr, 148, 150tc, 155cl, 160br, 162tr, 164bl, 165br, 170crb, 171cr, 173tr, 175cra, 175cla, 175ca, 176tc, 177r, 178br, 180tl, 180br, 185tr, 187cb, 188cl, 192, 193rca, 196tr, 197tr, 198tl, 199clb, 201cra, 203tr, 206tr, 208tr, 209tr, 212tr, 217bl, 219cla, 225br, 230bl, 231bl, 239tr, 244tl, 245bl, 245br.